Writing Docudrama

Writing Docudrama

Dramatizing Reality for Film and TV

Alan Rosenthal

Focal Press

Boston   Oxford   Melbourne   Singapore   Toronto   Munich   New Delhi   Tokyo

Focal Press is an imprint of Butterworth–Heinemann.

ℛ   A member of the Reed Elsevier group.

Copyright © 1995 by Alan Rosenthal.

Library of Congress Cataloging-in-Publication Data

Rosenthal, Alan, 1936–
    Writing docudrama : dramatizing reality for film and TV / Alan Rosenthal.
      p.   cm.
    Includes index.
    ISBN 0-240-80195-4
    1. Motion picture authorship.   2. Television authorship.   3. Historical drama.   I. Title.
  PN1996.R69   1994
  808.2′3—dc20   94-37070
                                                                                  CIP

British Library Cataloguing-in-Publication Data
A catalogue record for this book is available from the British Library.

Butterworth–Heinemann
313 Washington Street
Newton, MA 02158

10 9 8 7 6 5 4 3 2 1

Printed in the United States of America

For
Tal, Tzofnat, Gil,
and
Tomi

the bringers of joy

Contents

APPENDIXES

Acknowledgments

First, my thanks to all those people and organizations who let me look at their films and burrow through their scripts. In particular I would like to thank Ruth Caleb of the BBC, Ian McBride of Granada TV, and Brian Siberell of HBO; they all gave me immense help and made this book possible. I would also like to thank Henry Breitrose, David Elstein, Gail Evans, Seth Feldman, Peter Goodchild, John Katz, and George Stoney, who helped me tie up some loose ends.

I also have an immense debt of gratitude to scriptwriters Michael Apted, Michael Baker, Stephen Davis, Michael Eaton, Gerald Green, Ernest Kinoy, Roberto Loiederman, Peter Prince, Antony Thomas and Fletcher Watkins. All of them took time out to talk to me, show me their work, discuss the intricacies of docudrama, and allow me to quote from their scripts. They showed me how it could be done.

I am also very grateful to the following stations, producers, organizations and authors, who provided me with different materials and allowed me to produce extracts from their documents or scripts: the BBC; CBS; Joe Cacaci; Bob Cooper; Granada TV; Home Box Office (HBO), a division of Time-Warner Entertainment Co.; David Hodgson; Andrew Morton; NBC; the National Film Board of Canada; Patchett-Kaufman Entertainment; Thames TV; Martin Poll; Prime Time; University of California Press; the Writers Guild of America; and Stephen Zito. Along with thanks I would also like to acknowledge that all the script or document extracts used retain the copyright of the original owners.

Many friends assisted me with this book over and above the call of duty. Ben and Melinda Levin, together with Don Staples, showed me Texas hospitality, found films for me, and pointed me in the right direction.

Harrison Engle toiled tirelessly in Los Angeles, tracking down writers and getting me script permissions. Later Ken Dancyger and Stuart Schoffman went over different sections of the book and gave me very constructive criticism. My debt to them is enormous.

Two very strong influences on me while writing the book were Leslie Woodhead and Robert Freedman. As head of docudrama at Granada TV, Leslie was the person really responsible for introducing me to the subject. Since then we have had many talks, worth their weight in gold. Robert Freedman, another old friend, is a New York lawyer, and possibly the top American authority on film finance and distribution contracts. With infinite patience Robert guided me through the complex world of film legalities. In Chapter Thirteen the wisdom is Bob's, the mistakes mine. My thanks to both Leslie and Bob for everything.

Unbounded thanks also to George Custen and Julie Ziegler. Professor Custen's book *Biopics* was a treasure chest of information constantly by my side. Julie was my research assistant, and made excellent contributions to every single aspect of this book. Without her this book would not have been possible.

Finally, thanks to four women. My wife Miki and friend Bobby Cramer helped me in Jerusalem and New York, and offered suggestions, coffee, and cake when these things were most needed. Next I have to thank Karen Speerstra, who first saw the possibilities of this book and waited patiently for it to get off the ground. My last guiding light was my editor, Valerie Cimino, who provided excellent advice and tremendous enthusiasm along every inch of the way. Together, the four made up a wonderful support network.

Preface

When I first took up film, all I heard about was the "auteur theory." It was the decade of the director, who was both God and King. Very reluctantly the producer had moved aside to admit that other talents were necessary in filmmaking besides finance and organization. Today, however, we've entered the age of the writer. Finally, the writer is getting not just the proper financial rewards that are his or her due, but also the recognition that without a good script there is no film.

There is also the recognition that script writing is a demanding occupation. Unlike many other film professionals, you cannot bluff your way through. While many a director has been saved by his director of photography, or by a creative editor, the writer stands—or should I say sits—alone. It is a daunting prospect, but also an exhilarating one.

How can a textbook like this best help you to get going as a writer? By offering you two things . . . maps and tools. The maps show the terrain, the difficulties, the obstacles, and the problems you face. The tools, consisting of techniques, hints, and suggestions, show you how to overcome the problems. Whether you get to the end of your journey successfully obviously also depends on your talent, luck, drive, and energy . . . but with this book as your guide you should have a great send-off.

However, the fact-fiction or docudrama path is like no other. You are entering strange terrain, half trodden and yet still waiting to be explored.

If normal drama is represented by the familiar lowlands and valleys, docudrama can be seen as the slightly more interesting and challenging mountains and peaks. A brief map of the area is given in Chapter Three, but a lot is still unknown territory.

Do you need specialized skills for this kind of venture? Well, there's the beauty. Provided you have some essential basic talent you can write good docudrama; that is, if you are also willing to put in the training, look at the maps, observe the techniques, and listen to others who have gone before. Though writing fact-fiction parallels in many respects the writing of other forms of drama, it is also, as suggested above, tremendously different, and how you cope with the difference is one of the major concerns of this book. Beyond techniques, attitudes to truth, and responsibilities to audience, one other thing seems to me to differentiate docudrama from normative drama . . . the mindset of many of the writers.

While some of them see reality-fiction as just a specialized branch of drama, whose purpose is to entertain using fact-based material, many other writers working in the genre see their work as more socially challenging. While they too want to entertain and provide pleasure to the viewer, they also want to provoke their audience, to present hard questions, and occasionally to change the current scene. I like to consider myself part of this second stream, which accounts for a lot of the subtext of this book.

However, the journey is yours. If your technique and craftsmanship are good, and those are what this book will give you, and you've got drive and energy, then there is nothing that can match scriptwriting. So good luck on the trip.

Clearing the Decks

1

□ □ □
□ □ □
□ □ □

Introduction

In February 1993 one item, above all others, dominated the American news media. This was the story of David Koresh and his Branch Davidian cult followers, who were being besieged at Waco, Texas, by the FBI. What intrigued me, following the events, was that Koresh was said to have joked with one reporter as to who would play him in the film. Maybe Tommy Lee Jones or Bruce Willis.

The end was no joke. Koresh died in a blazing inferno along with ninety others. Yet he was right. They did film his life as *Ambush in Waco*, though he didn't stay around long enough to say whether they did a good job.

It was an amazing story. It had sex, charismatic personalities, weirdos, religion, battles, the lot. No writer could have invented a juicier story. It was made for the screen. Once more, fact was better than fiction. That got me thinking about the films and TV programs that had most intrigued and fascinated me over time. I was amazed at how many of them were based on real-life stories. Among the features I clearly had to include *JFK*, *Malcolm X*, *Schindler's List*, and *My Left Foot*. Among TV movies, it was hard to forget *And the Band Played On*, about the AIDS epidemic, or *Death of a Princess*, about an execution in Saudi Arabia.

Fact-based films are not just intriguing, they are also increasingly popular. For a jaded audience they offer something different from the run-of-the-mill comic-book heroes; characters larger than life, from Hitler and Stalin to Gandhi or Lawrence of Arabia; intriguing stories and situations that would be rejected as impossible fictions if one couldn't point to their undeniable base in reality.

For the producers, hunting for a killing, there is the knowledge that if they find the right real-life story, they can really hit the jackpot. Thus *Diana: Her True Story*, about the problems of Diana and Charles, was seen on almost every television screen throughout the world.

A popular form. An increasing demand. These are intoxicating words for a writer, particularly as this is a relatively easy way in for the newcomer. So you say to yourself, "How do I do it? How do I master this genre?" There's the rub. Despite the rise of university and film school courses in scriptwriting, hardly any of these courses deal with the creation of fact-based scenarios. The same is true of film books.

Enter any decent bookstore and you can find script texts by the dozen, with the most intriguing titles and advice under the sun: how to write a script while in the bath, while making love, while giving birth. Write a script in a week, a day, an hour, while having a cup of coffee, while recovering from your operation. There is no end to the advice. All seems fine until you suddenly realize there is an enormous omission. There isn't a single book—not one—that attempts to assist you in writing fact-fiction. Could it be that writing fact-fiction presents different challenges than standard scriptwriting and that authors are slightly wary of giving advice? Certainly fact-fiction is a complex form that eludes simple rules. It certainly can't be written in five minutes while recovering from a post-coital depression. Whatever the reasons, there tends to be little advice to be had on writing fact-fiction.

The object of this book is to fill that gap: to provide you with a thorough, down-to-earth understanding of all the ins and outs of writing fact-based fiction, from finding the initial idea to signing off on the finished script.

This is a book about techniques, dramatic conflict, story agendas, pace, structure, and dialogue writing. It is also a book about ideas and concepts. Its goal is to help you think about the film as a totality before you put a single word on paper.

In essence, this work is about all the problems you face from concept to completion. It deals with ideas—finding them, researching them in detail, and turning them into viable stories; it deals with all the stages of script development and fine-tuning; it covers experimental forms and touches on the problems of truth and accuracy; and it touches on agents, rights, and legal problems in writing docudrama.

Some topics I explore in depth, and other matters are touched on only briefly. You will see, for example, that the concentration is on writing for features and prime-time television drama, and that other programs that use fact-fiction techniques, like *Hard Copy*, *NYPD Blue*, *Top Cops*, and other true-crime series, hardly get mentioned because of space pressure. I also spend little time telling you how to sell your screenplay, because there are books galore on the subject. Instead, the concentration is on writing: how to develop your skills and how to realize your potential. In short, the goal is to help you become the terrific writer you always knew you could be.

Origins

This book arose out of a series of course discussions I had with students at the Australian National Film School. The subject was how to go beyond documentary technique and bring some of its ideas into feature filming. Before we knew it, we were deeply immersed in all the problems and possibilities of writing dramas based on fact.

First we started exploring the sheer range of fact-based fiction movies and TV dramas, and then we started hunting for a definition of the subject. Ultimately these discussions provided the basis for Chapters Two and Three of this book. One of the most interesting discussions arose out of the question, "How would the same subject be treated as a documentary and as a feature?" Here we screened two recent films of Michael Apted, *Incident at Oglala* and *Thunderheart*. Both films dealt with the same murder incident on an Indian reservation, but one used documentary technique while the other used fiction.

After analyzing Apted's films, we looked at three films based on the search for Hitler's diaries. *Shtonk*, a 1992 German feature, merely used the Hitler diaries as a starting point for creating a very broad farce, which only now and then touched reality and real people. By contrast, *Selling Hitler*, an English TV drama-documentary series, stayed very close to the facts, though it also emerged as a broad comedy. The third film was a straight documentary on the case.

As the course progressed, we started looking at some of the problems of drama-doc, such as creating an interesting script around a dull personality. Here we looked at a few of the letters to Warner Brothers penned by the scriptwriters of *Yankee Doodle Dandy*. The film, which featured James Cagney, tells the story of the rise and success of George M. Cohan, one of America's great songwriters. The problem for the scriptwriters was that Cohan's life was excruciatingly dull, yet the studio contract with Cohan bound the writers to stay close to the truth. So letter after letter pleads for the right to invent, to create a romance, and to add humor. Luckily, the writers were finally allowed some "creativity," saving what otherwise might have been a very dull picture apart from the songs. As the course continued, my own interest in drama-doc grew stronger and stronger. I'd written a few drama-docs, but my main work in the past was as a writer-director of documentaries. More and more I was being pulled in the direction of fiction, and the writing of fact-based dramas began to appeal to me in a very strong way. I'd always liked the form, and having grown up in England, was very familiar with it.

Much of the best British output of the war years, like *Target for Tonight*, was expressed in drama-doc form. Then, after a few years' hiatus, Peter Watkins once more shook the form into life with *Culloden*, and frightened the wits out of the BBC with his banned nuclear drama *The War Game*. Later on, while I was still a film novice, Leslie Woodhead started putting together a tremendous specialist drama-doc department at Granada TV. Meanwhile, Peter Goodchild was doing the same thing in London, using BBC Science features as his base for series such as *Marie Curie*.

Gradually everything started coming together . . . personal preference, students' needs, and teaching obligations. Before long I was involved in a mutual exploration with my students regarding the whole question of writing docudrama.

It was clear that there were one or two absolutely fundamental issues. Did normal writing principles apply to this form? How relevant was the standard three-act structure? Did the usual method of hunting for dramatic turning points still work? What liberties could you take with character presentation and truth? These were just a few of the questions, but among the most important.

The sessions were challenging, the debates endless, and the working sessions and experiments great. And somewhere along the line, the idea for this book was born.

Observations

This book is laid out in what is for me the natural progression for writing the fact-based script. First there is a preliminary clearing of the decks, which looks at the popularity of the form and the width of the subject, and tries to define the boundaries of docudrama or fact-fiction.

Second, the book addresses the real problem at hand: that is, how to write. It starts by discussing ideas, proposals, research, and story definition. It then deals in depth with writing the drama script and the complications ensuing from the need to adhere to reality. This section represents the core of the book.

Learning the specialized craft of writing drama-doc is very similar to learning painting. In painting you can, from the start, ignore all rules and paint in the wildest, most experimental forms. However, it is probably advisable to get grounding in naturalistic art before proceeding to the wilder shores of creation. In the same way I think it is necessary to understand how basic drama scripts are constructed before embarking on all the problems involved in the more complex form of docudrama.

From the core script the book moves on to discuss experimental forms, writing dialogue, adaptations, and the slippery problem of truth. The final chapter deals with options, legalities, agents, and lawyers, and lastly offers a perspective on the entire process. In addition there are seven appendixes, which examine certain subjects, like script approach or network requirements, in a little more depth.

This book is designed to help you at whatever stage you're in. You can read it from start to finish, but you don't have to. You may want to skip general discussions and plunge straight into the chapter on selecting a subject. Conversely, you may opt to go straight to the chapter on adaptations, as that is the problem that concerns you at the moment. You may want to know more about experimental form, or your problem may have to do with purchasing an option.

In the end this is your book and you have to use it in the way that helps you most. I hope it will assist you at every stage in the scripting process. Its aim is to make you a competent writer, and also to let you know you can have an enjoyable time along the way.

Attitude

Everyone believes he or she can write.

According to legend, a Hollywood producer is strolling through a mall and suddenly he says, "My God, where's the script?" whereupon half the people in the mall dig into their bags and produce their bound masterpieces. There is a school of thought that says scriptwriting is the easiest thing under the sun, that everyone has a story in him or her, that no technique is needed and no discipline required. Just give me the paper and I'll give you the masterpiece. Rubbish! Very few people can write, and very few people can write good scripts. Anyone who tells you otherwise is talking nonsense.

Scriptwriting requires resilience, patience, determination, inventiveness, and creativity. Many people have the first three. It's the last two qualities that provide the main stumbling blocks. That's just for starters, without talking about the need for "chutspa," intelligence, and even sometimes a conscience.

Beyond all this there is another problem. Beyond understanding the needs of dramatic construction and how to bring people and situations alive, the writer of docudramas needs a keen sense of journalism. A simple sense of invention is not enough. Very frequently the story has to be ferreted out, dug up, wrenched from reams of newspaper reports and months of research.

And lurking around everything is the word "passion." Writing drama-doc is an exciting and very interesting way of earning a living. Add passion, belief in your subject, and belief that what you're doing matters, and the whole task takes on a different and possibly more rewarding dimension.

Gandhi was a script like that. It came out of passion, as did *Born on the Fourth of July*, *JFK*, *Malcolm X*, *Schindler's List*, and *The Killing Fields*. These were films born out of dreams, born out of fury, anger, involvement. All these scripts reflect the desire to make a statement, to make a movie with meaning, to change the world. Whether they did or didn't is irrelevant. What remains is their passion, and that was fantastic.

We can also see this element of passion in the best of TV docudramas. Peter Watkins' film *The War Game*, about a nuclear holocaust, certainly has it. This was the film that critic Kenneth Tynan called "possibly the most important film ever made." Antony Thomas's film *Death of a Princess* has it. Britain's *Cathy Come Home* has it. HBO's *And the Band Played On* has it.

Passion is not always necessary. You can write happily without it, but when you find a film that excites you, that involves you, that requires passion, only then will you understand what this writing drug is all about.

Method

In many ways books on scriptwriting are like books on diets. They too offer neatly packaged formulae for success, except they replace inventive menus with shortcut gimmicks and hygienically wrapped rules. Thus the *Scarsdale Diet* and the *Manhattan Weight Watcher's Guide* turn into *Zarkofski's Guaranteed Script Selling Course*. Ten easy rules and your money back if you don't sell a script within three months.

Maybe it all works, but not for me.

My own method in approaching this book has been relatively simple. I didn't climb any mountains to consult the oracles, but I did try to talk to the best professionals around before getting down to work. My questions were always, "How do you work?" and "Why do you do things this way?"

I asked them about beginnings, structure, and dialogue writing, and also, "What do you enjoy most about writing?" and "What is the most important thing you have learned over the years?"

I asked them to tell me about their research problems, to show me their drafts, to let me see their first proposals, and I asked them for permission to use excerpts from their work. This book is a distillation of their advice and represents how experienced professionals tackle the writing of fact-based dramas.

As I've mentioned above, I have to tried to include a lot of script extracts in the book, as I believe example and analysis to be very useful teaching tools in this field. Though most of the illustrations are taken from docudramas, I have also occasionally cited well-known fiction films that seemed to illustrate the point I wanted to make more clearly than a lesser-known docudrama.

Finally, I have to say that the book also comes out of my own experience as a writer, filmmaker, and teacher, and is affected by my quirks, background, experience, and preferences. I have been writing and making films for about twenty years and have developed various techniques and approaches that make sense to me. They represent an attempt to put logic into that peculiarly attractive but elusive thing we call scriptwriting.

However, a warning: first, all writers are different. The way A approaches a subject and a script may be totally different from the way B approaches the same problem. My method of writing may not work for you. Our temperaments and approaches may be light-years apart, and that's fine, so long as you know clearly why your methods work best.

What follows from there is that this book is not sacrosanct. There are no rules in scriptwriting, though there are many hints and suggestions. What is accepted as gospel today may be rejected tomorrow. Monday's beloved three-act structure may get thrown out of the window on Tuesday.

What I hope you will do is read the book, accept what is useful, and then turn out a superb script that will show everyone you are for real, and have to be taken seriously as a professional writer.

2

□ □ □
□ □ □
□ □ □

The Popular Genre

Docudrama and Television

Whether you call them docudramas, drama-docs, fact-fiction dramas, or something even more exotic, one thing is clear . . . reality-based stories are the most popular drama genre on television today. In fact, it would be a most unusual week in which we didn't see at least two or three stories based on real incidents featured on TV. And it's been that way for a long time.

If we were watching a few years ago, the week's films might have centered on *victims* of appalling crimes, such as the woman in *The Longest Night*. This ABC film made for TV told the story of Karen Chambers, a young woman who was kidnapped and buried alive in a wooden box. Alternatively, we might have wanted to watch NBC's *Death of a Centerfold*, which told the story of a Playboy magazine model who was murdered by her husband-manager.

But fashions change. A few years later the rage was for showing women who had courageously overcome illnesses and physical handicaps to take up or resume careers as actresses or sportswomen. So we were treated to the stories of Patricia Neal (CBS), Babe Zaharias Didrikson (CBS), and Maureen Connolly, or Little Mo, on NBC.

Today we seem to be back to blood and gore, with television revelling in the real-life stories of women murderers or would-be murderers. In the month before writing this chapter I saw a film about a woman who had killed her lover's wife, another about a woman who took out a murder contract on the mother of her daughter's rival, and a third on an ex-prostitute who had become a serial killer. When I looked up coming attractions one thing was very clear. The torrents of terror would be increasing rather than abating.

The public is fickle. Tastes change. Tomorrow murder may be out and the private lives of generals back in. In some senses it's all a guessing game. Yet underneath all this, and regardless of changing fashions and subjects, two highly provocative and encouraging facts stare the writer in the face.

First, the public loves docudrama, which for the sake of simplicity is the term I'm mostly going to use throughout this book. Second, there is a bustling, thriv-

9

ing market out there for good scripts. Never has there been a better time than now for the writer to plunge in and master the genre.

Let's consider the following.

- Of the 115 movies shown on TV in the first broadcast season of 1992, 43 were docudramas.
- Later in the year, both the Frank Sinatra and Jackson family series drew the top audiences of the week, which meant audiences in excess of 25 million viewers.
- In the overall 1991 TV season, seven out of the top ten highest-rated movies made for TV were based on real-life happenings.
- In 1991 the *highest* rated TV film of the year was CBS's *A Woman Scorned: The Betty Broderick Story*, about a woman who killed her ex-husband and his new wife.
- In 1989, the top-rated film was *Baby M*, based on the famous child-custody case, while a series on the Kennedy family outdrew first network broadcasts of *Robocop* and *Indiana Jones and the Temple of Doom*.

Popularity and high ratings . . . these are the goals producers dream about, and for which network executives are willing to kill. No wonder the hunt for the best-selling docudrama formula figures high on their list of priorities.

Sometimes the hunt reaches the heights of the absurd when we see different networks issuing films on the same subject within weeks, if not days, of each other. For example:

- Liberace died from AIDS in February 1987. In October of the same year ABC presented *Liberace*, while in the same week CBS played *Liberace: Behind the Music*.
- On May 27, 1992, Carolyn Warmus, a 28-year-old former Westchester County teacher, was convicted of the murder of her lover's wife. Early in September 1992, ABC screened *A Murderous Affair: The Carolyn Warmus Story*. Three weeks later, in October, CBS screened *Danger of Love*, exactly the same story from a slightly different point of view.
- The ultimate absurdity took place in 1993 when all three networks featured dramas about Amy Fisher. But more on that later.

This race for the best-selling formula doesn't just embrace aging music stars, nubile murderesses, Marilyn Monroe, and the Kennedy clan. It hunts around the world's disasters, politics, the gossip columns, and even has the audacity to pry into palace bedrooms. In 1992, the British royal family, working through the travails of what Queen Elizabeth II called her "Annus horribilis," also became prey to the hunters of ratings. This time all three networks had a go. What we eventually saw, in order of screenings played out over a few months, were

- *Fergie and Andy: Behind the Palace Doors* (NBC), a massive assault on the Duke and Duchess of York that needed last-minute updating when the Duchess was photographed topless with her financial adviser, John Bryan
- *The Women of Windsor* (CBS), a three hour-drama that originally focused on Fergie and Andrew but shifted its gaze to Charles and Diana as their troubles came into the world spotlight
- *Charles and Diana: Unhappily Ever After?* (ABC), a two-hour special examining the breakdown of the fairy-tale marriage
- *Diana: Her True Story* (NBC), a four-hour special on the breakdown, but with more inside information

Though the competitive stab at the same subject seems at the moment to be dominated by murder biographies, or observing the sad unwinding of a royal family, occasionally competition will jump at more enduring news subjects. The classic example was the opportunity provided by the Israeli raid on Entebbe.

In late June 1976, Arab and German terrorists took over an Air France plane flying from Athens to Paris, and subsequently had the plane diverted to Entebbe in Uganda.

While a few people were freed, over 100 others were held as hostages by the terrorists with the complicity of Ugandan ruler Idi Amin. On July 4th the Israelis, flying over 1,000 miles in Hercules transport planes, staged a spectacular secret raid on Entebbe. After a few minutes' battle, the hostages were freed with the loss of one Israeli soldier, who was in fact the commander of the rescue team.

This was marvelous stuff, better than anything that could have been dreamed up as fiction. This time not only the networks dived in but feature film producers as well. Once again ABC got there first, with the end result being

- *Victory at Entebbe* (ABC) aired December 13, 1976
- *Raid on Entebbe* (NBC) aired January 9, 1977
- *Operation Yonatan*, feature film produced by Menachem Golan and Yoram Globus, released in the spring of 1977

Like their feature counterparts, TV producers tend to repeat successes, hence the past search for "victim" films or the current vogue for women killers. In practice, however, the subject range of successful docudrama is enormous. Thus the 1989 TV season included not only a highly popular Kennedy series, but also films on George Bush's flying career, Leona Helmsley's court battles, the career of Oliver North, the final days of Richard Nixon's presidential career, the death of Rock Hudson, and the problems of implementing interracial bussing in Boston.

More recent seasons have also featured films on AIDS like *And the Band Played On*, dramas about corporate scandals, such as *Barbarians at the Gate*, and even the British series on the forging of Hitler's diaries.

In any survey, however brief, one thing emerges very clearly. The U.S. networks, in general, tend to stay away from all but the most sensational hard news and political stories, and go for more personal human conflicts. The Entebbe-type film, and the films about Waco or the New York Trade Center bombing, are the exception, not the rule. This simple home truth has to be borne in mind when you start considering where to devote your efforts.

Yet the dramatic journalistic news story has, in its own small way, found an honored niche in docudrama, with British television in the vanguard. On the American side, HBO is the only company that can be considered as being deeply involved in this more serious fare.

I deliberately said "honored niche" because it seems to me that the political drama-doc is in many ways much more fascinating, challenging, and ultimately rewarding for a writer than the standard movie of the week. It's certainly fascinating to write, though as you'll see, it tends to present many more problems than the standard biopic. I also believe it is more highly regarded by the public, though this doesn't necessarily translate into higher ratings.

What are some good examples of this genre? I would definitely cite in any list of favorites *The Tragedy of Flight 103: The Inside Story*, about the downing of a Pan Am plane over Scotland by Arab terrorists; *Invasion*, about the '68 invasion of Czechoslovakia; *Skokie*, about the neo-Nazi march through a suburb of Chicago; *Citizen Cohn*, not so much a biopic as a study in political corruption, and *Yuri Nosenko, KGB*, the story of a Russian defector.

Docudrama and the Feature Film

If television is a great marketplace for docudrama, what about the feature film? Are there the same possibilities? Are there the same opportunities for writers? What about the scope, and whatever the current situation, will it change in the future?

Now the feature industry is even worse than TV at predicting the future, but my brief answer to the above questions would be as follows.

1: Marketplace

Far fewer features are made than TV films, and of those made a much smaller percentage is devoted to stories based on real happenings. Quite clearly, there are fewer opportunities for the writer of this genre in main-line filmmaking. However, as you can see in Appendix A, Hollywood is still turning out at least five or six docudramas a year.

2: Scope

The corollary of the above is that though the marketplace is smaller, the scope and rewards of the feature film writer are greater than those of the TV writer.

And having said all that, I would be prepared at any time to swallow my words because, to quote screenwriter William Goldman's famous adage, "Nobody knows anything."

Till TV came along, the reality-based film, or to put it more correctly, dramas suggested by history or biography, formed probably less than five percent of the Hollywood output. Since 1971, when TV got into its stride with docudramas, the percentage has fallen even lower. However, when the biopic was a hit or the historical drama connected to something in the public mind, then the sky was the limit. And to repeat, no one knew anything.

Take the case of *The Jolson Story*. In the early twenties, singer Al Jolson was the greatest star of American vaudeville. In 1927, he helped revolutionize movie history when he appeared in *The Jazz Singer*. Yet by the mid-thirties, after a dazzling film start in the early Warner talkies, his career was virtually dead.

When World War II ended, Jolson was a washed-up has-been, almost totally forgotten by an American public raving over Crosby and Sinatra. So the idea of a film dealing with Jolson's life was not a suggestion that met with much Hollywood enthusiasm. One man, Harry Cohn, the boss of Columbia studios, disagreed with the general assessment that such a film was doomed to failure. His hunch was correct. As it turned out, *The Jolson Story* became one of the three top-grossing films of 1946.

Though Hollywood makes relatively few fact-based dramas, when it does make them, the films can sometimes offer the writer a scope beyond anything available on TV.

David Lean's *Lawrence of Arabia*, with a script by Robert Bolt, works fantastically on film. The wide screen adds a breathtaking sweep to the astounding views of the Jordanian desert that make for half the film's attraction. A similar magic is to be found in the panoramic vision of India in Richard Attenborough's *Gandhi*. However, it would be hard to imagine either of them being done as television originals.

The same is true of *Mutiny on the Bounty*. Like Lean's desert epic, *Mutiny* allowed for wide-scale action, panorama, landscapes, and photographic vision, all more suitable for film than television.

Sometimes Hollywood will remake an old fact-fiction story with a slightly different twist, allowing for changes in fashion, in audiences, and in sexual mores. *Compulsion* (1959) is the account of the trial of two wealthy American boys accused of the "thrill" murder of a friend. Though the names are changed, the film is obviously based on the notorious Leopold-Loeb case of the twenties. Just over 30 years later, Hollywood released *Swoon*. Again it was obvious that the film was based on the Leopold-Loeb case, but this time the possibility of a homosexual relationship between the accused boys was raised, which was absent from the first film.

Historical romances and adventures have of course been a steady source of inspiration for Hollywood, particularly in the area of the western and the gangster movie. The Jesse James gang is forever riding into the sunset. Billy the Kid is being shot down for the fifteenth time by Pat Garrett. Capone is once again snarling and Legs Diamond romancing another moll. All good clean or dirty fun, but not much of it based on fact.

William Goldman writes that he spent years researching the story of *Butch Cassidy and the Sundance Kid*. But he also writes that in the end almost everything in the script is invented incident. The same is true for *Bonnie and Clyde*.

Both *Butch Cassidy* and *Bonnie and Clyde* were great movies, but like the films of Billy the Kid and Jesse James, they don't have much to do with dramatizing reality, or with this book. Where fiction and invention account for ninety-five percent of the script, we are into standard scriptwriting, and that's something for another time and another place.

If we put the historical romances aside, what are we left with? Well, actually quite an impressive list. Admittedly, during the eighties relatively few reality-based features were made either in Hollywood or in Europe, but in spite of their paucity they often made a strong impression.

Black Hunter, White Heart was a thinly veiled account of director John Huston working in Africa. *Cry Freedom*, by Richard Attenborough, told the moving story of South African freedom fighter Stephen Biko. *Reds*, Warren Beatty's film about revolutionary reporter John Reed, was a strong contender for an Academy award. *Gandhi*, *Chariots of Fire*, and *Out of Africa* actually pulled off that achievement. *Mississippi Burning* and *Scandal*, while receiving few awards, succeeded in piling up controversy.

So far the last decade of the century has augured well for drama-docs, with the pace being set by *Bugsy*, a hyped gangster biography, and the controversial *JFK*. And if 1991 was a good year for the making of fact-based features, 1992 and 1993 turned out to be even more remarkable.

Starting with the release of yet another film about Babe Ruth in February '92 (the third biopic on the baseball player), the two seasons eventually listed two Columbus films, *Swoon*, *Lorenzo's Oil*, *Chaplin*, *Hoffa*, *Schindler's List*, and probably the most hyped film of the year . . . *Malcolm X*.

What does all this mean? Is there some movement of an audience which is growing tired of comic-book fantasies and wants its films to grow out of authentic, documented, real-life situations? Given the success of films like *Jurassic Park* and *Cliffhanger*, I doubt that, but I do think change is in the air.

So, with no claims to real prophecy, I would say one thing is clear. If you do have a good real-life story to relate, and you can write a good screenplay from such a story, then the market in the 1990's is probably the best and most receptive it's been in years.

3

□ □ □
□ □ □
□ □ □

What is Fact-Fiction?

You want to write fact-fiction, or reality-based dramas, but wait a minute. What are we talking about? What is this hybrid form which floats uneasily between documentary and fiction? What *is* docudrama?

When I was a kid and growing up in England, I would occasionally visit the British Museum. In the Ancient Middle East section one granite carving fascinated me above all others. This was the huge sculpture of a most amazing animal. Its body was that of a bull. Its head was that of a bearded man. It had wings, and to complete the picture it was adorned with the tail of a lion. Altogether it was a very strange beast.

What I didn't know then but realized only later was that I was looking at the concrete representation of the fact-fiction film. Like my British Museum sculpture, the fact-fiction film is a most peculiar animal.

Firstly there is the difficulty of the name, and the bewildering labeling. *Docudrama. Dramatic reconstructions. Faction. Reality-based films. Murdofact. Murdotainment. Fact-based dramas. Biopics.* Where will it all end? Maybe we should announce a competition for something definitive, but that might bring worse horrors, like "factovies" or "factoramas." For the sake of simplicity, and as there is no one accepted name for the genre, I am mostly going to use the term "docudrama" throughout this book.

Of course the problem is not really in the name, but in defining what we are talking about. A fairly prosaic but workman-like definition of TV docudrama is that given by Tom Hoffer and Richard Alan Nelson, two American academics. They call it

> A unique blend of fact and fiction which dramatizes events and historic personages from our recent memory . . . It is a TV recreation based on fact even though it relies on actors, dialogue, sets and costumes to recreate an earlier event. The accuracy and comprehensiveness of such a recreation . . . can vary widely and is conditioned not only by intent but also by factors such as budget and production time.[1]

Leslie Woodhead, a very distinguished maker of English docudramas, presents the problem a little differently:

> We filmmakers swap labels like baseball cards but the resultant sets are hopelessly ill matched. One of my colleagues has identified three major strands to the form while another has isolated six varieties. For my money there are about as many valid definitions as there are drama documentaries . . . At the end of last year I found myself on a platform for yet another drama-doc tussle with no fewer than seven distinguished program makers, all of whom could be considered employers of the form. You won't be surprised to hear that no two of us could agree on what it is.

However, after describing the confusion, Woodhead presents us with a handy way of looking at the problem.

> [Instead of hunting for definitions] I find it much more useful to think of the form as a spectrum that runs from journalistic reconstruction to relevant drama with infinite graduations along the way. In its various mutations it's employed by investigative journalists, documentary feature makers, and imaginative dramatists. So we shouldn't be surprised when programs as various as *Culloden* and *Oppenheimer* or *Suez*, or Cabinet reconstructions refuse tidy and comprehensive definitions.
>
> (Leslie Woodhead, "The Guardian Lecture," 1980.)

Woodhead's presentation is excellent, though many would dispute the word *relevant*. Are all the dramas about the royal family relevant? Not really. And can this word be applied to the hullabaloo around Amy Fisher? Probably not, but were these programs fun and mildly amusing? Yes, I think so.

The real operative word is *spectrum*. If you wanted, you could claim that fact-fiction goes back beyond Shakespeare. In other words, docudrama covers an amazing variety of dramatic forms, bound together by two things. They are all *based on* or *inspired* by reality, by the lives of real people, or by events that have happened in the recent or not too distant past. Furthermore, they have a higher responsibility to accuracy and truth than fiction. In Chapter Seven, however, we discuss certain films, like *The War Game*, which have been called docudramas but which are not based on factual happenings.

For the writer, the sheer width of the spectrum makes reality-based dramas both highly attractive and also immensely problematic. The trouble with a form that runs the gamut from biopics like *Yankee Doodle Dandy* to political analyses like *JFK*, and from imaginative reconstructions such as *The Thin Blue Line* to historic ballyhoo such as *1492: The Conquest of Paradise*, is that sometimes you can't see the forest for the trees. In the face of these difficulties it helps, as a rough starting point, to go beyond Hoffer and Nelson and see docudrama as being divided into two strands, or two totally separate areas.

Biography and Entertainment

This category probably makes up ninety percent of the docudramas we see in the cinema and on TV. It runs from *Sergeant York* to *The Babe*, from *The Josephine Baker Story* and *Mae West* to the Frank Sinatra and Jackson family TV mini-series. It also includes all the current titillating murders of the week.

What generally categorizes these films and scripts are a desire for the highest audience ratings, an emphasis on entertainment values, and a rather loose regard for the truth. When they are made for U.S. television networks, they tend to come under the supervision of the drama departments rather than news and documentary.

Reconstructive Investigations

Though highly honored, this is a much smaller category and includes pieces such as *Death of a Princess, Friendly Fire, The Tragedy of Flight 103: The Inside Story, Tailspin: Behind the Korean Airliner Tragedy, Hostages, The Atlanta Child Murders, Afterburn, And the Band Played On,* and miniseries such as *Murderers Among Us: The Simon Wiesenthal Story* and *Oppenheimer.*

What we are looking at here is a very serious form, much closer to journalism and news than conventional drama. Though it uses dramatic forms, characters, and dialogue, its motivating force is that of the restless inquirer and the investigative reporter. It wants to uncover and reveal for the public good, and not just in the name of higher ratings. Its highest goal is to present a powerful, enthralling drama that nevertheless also gets as close to the truth as possible. I would venture that this is the most socially important side of docudrama. It's what gives the genre its moral imperative, and separates it at its best so clearly from normative fiction drama.

Leslie Woodhead, who has done some of the best films in this category, such as *Invasion*, about the 1968 Russian invasion of Czechoslovakia, calls it the form of last resort. "It is a way of doing things where ordinary documentary can't cope . . . a way of telling a story that would be impossible by conventional documentary methods."

Obviously there is a tremendous amount of overlap in the categories, as one can see merely by looking at *Jim Jones* and *Stalin. The Guyana Tragedy: The Story of Jim Jones* was about a gruesome mass suicide that held the headlines of the nation for days. Here was tragedy of mass proportions that raised a multitude of questions. Who was James Jones? Who were his followers? What was the special charisma of a man who could induce hundreds of individuals and families to drink poison and end their lives in the jungles of South America, thousands of miles away from home? (Many of the same questions, incidentally, were to be asked after the death of David Koresh in Waco, Texas in 1993.)

Quite clearly here was a case for a strong, serious reconstructive investigation. What emerged, however, was a film that played to the most spectacular extremes possible.

In 1992 HBO made a three hour film about Stalin with Robert Duvall. The reviews varied. Some critics were put off by the emphasis on Stalin's private life. Personally I felt that the domestic scenes were necessary to reveal the inner man, and acted as an interesting counterpoint to the overtly political portions of the film. What one got in the end was a fascinating combination of news and private-life drama.

Does it all matter? So what if edges blur? Does one have to think in categories? Cannot one have a highly entertaining and compelling docudrama that both captures the ratings and also deals seriously with a subject of general concern? Well, as I've already said, the blend of riveting drama with seriousness and concern is maybe the highest goal, wonderfully exemplified by HBO's *And the Band Played On*.

Yet while admitting all that, I think there is still a strong case for making lists and thinking in categories. Such actions help you define where you want to go as a writer, and what your task is on a particular subject. Thinking briefly about your choices, journalism, entertainment bio, or anything else, helps you to clarify your approach.

Writing drama-doc is not easy. The form is seductive, entrancing, fascinating. To my mind it is much more appealing than writing comic-book action adventures, but you have to watch out. There are so many traps along the way, that the clearer you are as to where you want to go, what your objectives are, and how you want to get there, the easier the whole task becomes.

Once you've answered these questions, the way ahead is much easier. You've done what needs to be done, and can turn to the typewriter or word processor with a clear mind, knowing that now you're finally ready for the fun to begin.

Notes

1. Tom Hoffer and Richard Nelson, "Docudrama on American Television," Journal of the UFA, XXX, Spring 1978, p. 21.

4 □ □ □
□ □ □
□ □ □

Choosing
the Subject

On Sunday, November 22, 1992, the front page of the Arts and Leisure section of *The New York Times* bore the legend "MURDER, MAYHEM STALK TV. Television in frenzy over real-life sagas." Although the article discussed TV docudrama in general, its main story dealt with the strange and lurid case of Amy Fisher.

This young lady, then seventeen years old, had fallen in love with a garage mechanic called Joey Buttafuoco. The fact that Joey was married was seen by Amy as only a minor hindrance to true love. Using a loaded pistol, she had taken a pop at Joey's wife, Mary-Jo, wounding her but not killing her, an act for which Amy later got 5 to 15 years imprisonment.

This time not one, not two, but all three networks saw in this story the seeds of a best-selling docudrama. They were right; NBC's film got one of the highest film ratings of the season.

If Amy's act showed little imagination, neither did the names of the movies. ABC called its film *The Amy Fisher Story*. NBC added a twist to this, calling its film *Amy Fisher: My Story*. Only CBS aimed higher, calling its epic *Casualties of Love: The Long Island Lolita Story*. For their part, the critics were a little more inventive, Richard Corliss, for example, of *Newsweek*, calling the whole combined effort "Trashomon."

The most interesting aspect of the whole affair is not the Fisher story itself, rather a dull, tawdry tale as tales go, but the rush for the rights. Was it a great story? . . . no! Was it an unusual story? . . . no! Yet all three networks were correct in sensing that this story would fire the jaded palettes of millions of Americans needing rest and titillation after a hard day's work. As John O'Connor wrote later in *The New York Times*, "No network has yet gone broke overestimating its audience's appetite for sleaze."

The choice of the Amy Fisher story was actually made by three independent producers working together with the networks. They all guessed correctly that the story would appeal to a mass audience and work well on U.S. TV.

In this case the producers did the work of finding the story, and this may be the way things are moving. But for a writer to be worth anything, he or she has to be able to pick out the story, the situation, or the idea that can be transformed into the successful screenplay.

The main question appears to be

1: What story should I choose?

That in turn prompts two other questions:

2: Does the story have appeal?
3: Can I sell it?

In practice, the questions of appeal and marketability are with you a great deal of the time. They are the background constants that are always in your mind and against which any subject is tested. However, as this book is about writing rather than selling, I've left my comments on the marketplace to Appendix E. Appeal is a different matter entirely. It is the one subject that can't really wait, and is worth considering before we even begin thinking about specific ideas.

The Appeal

All this may seem a bit strange. You may say that logically the story should come first. You get this blinding idea, the film that just has to be done, the movie for which the world has been waiting, and only afterwards should you begin to examine all the other factors: whether it has a broad or limited appeal, and whether it looks sufficiently commercial to interest a producer.

However, a writer has to establish a basic sensibility out of which he or she works. He or she needs to understand audience demand, audience satisfaction, what works and what doesn't, what makes a best-seller and what makes for a boring evening, what makes for irresistible viewing and what will send the audience out to baseball.

He or she needs to know . . . what appeals.

Of course, if you knew that answer, and you were right even eighty percent of the time, you'd be a millionaire. Clearly we are talking of the almost impossible ideal. Yet we have to believe it's achievable, or that at least we understand the concept . . . because if your story has no appeal, it's doomed. That's why you need to understand the elements of appeal before you even begin to consider the story. Your stories will change, but your understanding of what makes them work with an audience is your launching pad for everything.

Truth Is Stranger than Fiction

In terms of appeal you have, of course, a terrific initial advantage without doing anything. The very act of choosing to write a reality-based drama already puts you ahead of the game.

Why should that be?

It seems to me almost axiomatic that where you have two similar stories, one true, one invented, the former has greater appeal. The sense that this strange event actually happened holds a psychological fascination for us that is missing in invention. The reality is telling us something peculiarly hypnotizing about the ultimately subtle, incomprehensible, and often unexpected nature of our world. Ultimately it is closer to us, and often affects us in strange and deep ways that are inaccessible to fiction.

In 1993 Disney studios made *Alive,* based on the true story of a Uruguayan rugby team whose plane crashed in the Andes in 1972. Sixteen members of the team, many under the age of twenty, survived over two months in the mountains by eating those who had died. The book by Piers Paul Read had been a best seller in 1974 and had been in development at various studios for 18 years till Disney finally picked it up.

Resorting to cannibalism for survival is an extremely strong theme and not new to literature and history. Thus the story of the survival of some of the Donner party through cannibalism is one of the most heart-rending events in U.S. history. But both the story of the Donner party and the epic of the rugby team and their feats of heroism get their strength from being true. Imagine both stories as fiction and one can see immediately what is lost.

In 1977 Menachem Golan made a film called *Operation Yonatan,* based on the amazing rescue of Israeli hostages at Entebbe airport already mentioned. A few years later he made *Delta Force,* about a fictional U.S. commando rescue in Lebanon. Both use similar gimmicks and a similar crash-happy style of directing. But whereas *Delta Force* is considered by many to be throwaway third-rate movie making, *Operation Yonatan* holds you spellbound chiefly because you know this really happened.

One of the more moving TV docudramas made in 1992 was *Fatal Memories.* This told the story of a young woman in her late twenties who suddenly started remembering episodes from her past. Gradually her memories revealed that as a little girl she had seen her father kill her nine-year-old friend. Eventually the police were told and the woman testified against her father in court. As reality it was fascinating. Had it been fiction we might have said, "Who are you kidding?!" and not given it the time of day.

A similar brush-off might have occurred had not *Schindler's List* and *In the Name of the Father* been based on reality. The story of Oskar Schindler and his saving of nearly a thousand Jews from the Nazi death camps is one of the most bizarre stories to come out of the Second World War. As fiction it would have been forgettable melodrama. As truth it takes its place as one of the most emotional and moving films ever made.

For its part, *In the Name of the Father* presents us with a classic miscarriage-of-justice story, not exactly a new theme in the annals of cinema. Here again reality, plus the power of the directing, lifts a film from banality to create a tremendously memorable screen experience.

The Dramatic Elements

For your story to appeal it has to have drama, conflict, strong characters caught up in interesting situations, and a satisfying resolution.

Well, that was an easy one!

Not really, because the elements mentioned above are going to be discussed over and over again in this book. The point here is that a writer has to recognize when he or she has hit on the right context to play around with all the above elements. Not all conflicts are worth our attention. The L.A. *Times* doesn't pay much attention to what's happening in Botswana because it knows its readers couldn't care less. In contrast, it pays a lot of attention to what is happening in Russia and even more to signs of clashes in the White House.

Again, not all situations are interesting, nor is every average player worth our glance. Write a drama about John Major, the English Prime Minister, and his governmental problems, and you'd probably have the audience asleep in five minutes. Give them a bloodthirsty tyrant like Stalin and they'll come back clamoring for more.

The Passionate Elements

What we need to train ourselves to do is to look at the forces underlying the conflicts . . . the passion, the fury, the emotional hunger, the need for sex or fame at all cost, and then we can decide whether the story is worth telling. In other words, we have to start looking at the emotional turn-ons that fascinate us.

Now no one knows this better than *The National Enquirer*, one of the best-selling papers in the U.S. I look at it every time I go to the supermarket and am always amazed by its headlines. A typical story might read as follows:

Flash. Elvis Presley is alive on Mars. He has had a sex change, practices satanism, and says he killed Marilyn Monroe for the love of President Kennedy.

Of course no one would believe it, but that's not the issue. It's a stupid story, but people would love it, because it embraces so many of the elements our psyches openly or secretly crave or are passionately interested in:

Sex . . .
Sensation . . .
Action . . .
Violence . . .

The inside dope on the great . . .
A normal world turned upside down . . .
Fanaticism . . .

Analyze any top-rated TV movie of the week and you'll probably find it contains at least four or five of the above elements. There's a lesson here. Whereas a moralist might agonize over the debased delights of the average viewer, the writer has to note what interests the TV audience and act accordingly.

Following this line of thought, journalist Robin Abcarian related the story of Richard Worthington in the L.A.*Times* of May, 1992.

In September '91 Worthington, a devout Mormon and father of eight, had stormed into a maternity ward in Utah, killed a nurse and held seven people hostage for 8 hours. Worthington believed a baby girl was waiting in heaven to be born to him and that the doctor had sterilized his wife against her will.

Commenting on the story, Abcarian wrote, "This tale has all the elements of a (TV) hit: birth, death, religion, terror, insanity, remorse . . . The story was, to be perfectly cynical, a made-for-TV movie before it ever became one."

What also seems to appeal are pictures about human actions pushed to the edge, behavior that runs against all our norms, behavior that we cannot understand but which nevertheless fascinates us.

On the positive side, this behavior is captured in the heroic drive, as seen in the stories of Captain Scott heading for the South Pole, or Burke and Wills crossing nineteenth-century Australia. On the negative side there are the stories of Koresh and his band, Jim Jones and his suicidal followers, and the grim story of the footballers who turned to cannibalism in *Alive*.

The Psychological Appeal

Not everyone is willing to see appeal purely in terms of satisfying voyeuristic interests relating to sex and violence. Critic Mary Hardesty, for instance, sees the appeal of drama-docs as serving the public's insatiable appetite for information while providing it with an opportunity to debate historical, social, and political issues.

Writing in an edition of the *Journal of the Director's Guild* discussing trends on television, producer Tony Eltz put the matter this way:

> There's value for the viewer in seeing that a very scary thing has an explanation. For example, we recently produced *Deadly Medicine*, which helped viewers to understand why a nurse might be driven to murder 32 babies.

John Matoian, CBS's Vice President for movies and mini-series, has his own comments on the appeal of the murder drama-docs. "People are looking for windows into behavior. Hopefully they'll gain insight from these kinds of movies."

Maybe, but I doubt it! My feeling is that raw voyeurism comes first in appeal, and all social explanations are secondary.

The Appeal of the Genre

Another way of looking at appeal is to leave out psychological speculation entirely, and merely look at the genres that seem to have had continuing attraction over time. Obviously the genres intertwine, and many times subjects can be said to straddle different categories. A simplified run-down on the groupings would clearly include the following.

Secrets Behind Closed Doors

This area would include exposes of the rich and the famous. It touches on their dark hidden lives, and quite often reveals sexual scandals. Examples would include *Scandal*, *Diana: Her True Story*, *Citizen Cohn*, and all the stories of the Kennedy clan, including *J.F.K: Reckless Youth*.

The Lives of Entertainers

This genre is staple fare for both TV and film. With luck, not only do we see the entertainers dance, sing, or play, but we also get a story replete with sex and drugs. So everyone is satisfied.

The Private Lives of Heroes

Here the attempt is made to understand the movers of history, to get behind the public mask and understand the real, private person. Examples range from Gandhi and Malcolm X to Churchill, Stalin, Lindbergh, Oppenheimer, Freud, and Pasteur.

Understanding History

This genre often overlaps with the previous one, but the emphasis is on the events and historic process, rather than on the individual. Here I would cite *Washington: Behind Closed Doors*, *The Final Days*, *Bomber Harris*, *Invasion*, and *Strike*.

Investigating Contemporary Events

The urge in this category is to make a dramatic and penetrating analysis of national or world events that have captured the public imagination.

The stories behind the Beirut hostages, the Chernobyl nuclear disaster, or the terrorist attack on the World Trade Center in New York are good examples of the genre. Other noted stories in this genre would include *Friendly Fire*, *Death of a Princess*, *Tailspin: The Korean Airliner Tragedy*, and even comedies like *Selling Hitler*.

Lurid Scandals

This area seems, at the moment, the most prolific genre for TV. The genre covers all the small-town titillating crimes of sex and violence and aberrant human behavior that provide the staple diet of *People* magazine. This is *Peyton Place*, but for real.

These are the stories that acquainted us with such alleged murderesses or would-be murderesses as Amy Fisher, Wanda Holloway, Elizabeth Ann Broderick, Jean Harris, and Carolyn Warmus.

Weird Human Behavior

This is really a sub-category of contemporary events and lurid scandals. It is very much a minor genre (one is tempted to say "Thank God") and includes the exploits of David Koresh and Jim Jones. But because I believe the public appetite is growing for the bizarre, for stories about Satanism and the like, I have a horrible feeling this genre is ready to become a growth industry.

Stories that Touch the Heart

Certain stories have a way of touching the soul, of bonding people together. These are often stories that show human nature at its best, stories of community endeavor, of family sacrifice for a common good, of battling against illness and winning, and so on.

And if they contain kids or animals, even better. When eighteen-month-old Jessica McClure fell down a well in Texas, she became an instant celebrity. When she was safely rescued, it's no wonder that *Everybody's Baby: The Rescue of Jessica McClure* became one of the most widely seen films on TV.

Finding the Idea

You know all about appeal. Now all you have to do is go out and find the idea. At this point it's not uncommon to feel like the guy who has read all the books on sex and romance but still balks at the hunt and the chase.

Courage is the solution to both. In other words, the time has come to abandon theory and get down to action. Here I have to say I think it's easier to find a good story than a good date.

The stories are all around you. In books, articles, on television, and on the radio. They arise from the anecdotes of friends, from a story in a diary, from the memory of a relative.

Your sources are fairly obvious and it is interesting to look at a few scripts and where they have come from.

1: Books

Goodfellas, Diana: Her True Story, Papillon, Barbarians at the Gate, And the Band Played On, JFK: Reckless Youth, Selling Hitler

2: Newspaper and Magazine Articles

The Killing Fields, Fatal Memories, The Betty Broderick Story, Andy and Fergie

3: Radio and TV

Chernobyl, Skokie, all the Entebbe films, *The Tragedy of Flight 103, Exxon Valdez,* and the films on Koresh and the World Trade Center

Obviously a great number of sources overlap. While the Chernobyl disaster was happening, it was being covered by every branch of the media, and no single branch can lay claim to being the film source. That's also true of almost all the well-known news stories that transfer to film.

Some stories hit the headlines, fade from the public eye, and then seem to get a second wind as times change. Thus the story of Malcolm X was written years before Spike Lee made the film. The notorious Attica prison riot occurred in 1971, but *Against the Wall* was only filmed by HBO in 1994. The story of John Reed was also an "oldie" before Warren Beatty decided to go ahead with *Reds.*

What you should be looking for is either the "hot story" or the unknown. The first is very appealing, but very difficult to bring off. Today most of the networks and major producers of docudramas not only employ scouts to search for the hot stories, but also spend vast amounts of money in purchasing the story rights. Hence the feeding frenzy of producers around Amy Fisher and the royal family.

In this context, the most dramatic illustration was the 1994 media pursuit of the Nancy Kerrigan and Tonya Harding story. What was understood very fast was that nothing could be more Hollywood, as critic Bronwen Huska put it, than the story of a beautiful skater whose Olympic dreams were nearly shattered by the henchmen of her fiercest rival. The story had greed, a beautiful heroine, and proper villains. Over 40 companies vied for the rights, with producer Steve Tisch finally making an alleged million-dollar deal with Nancy Kerrigan.

A few years ago, a local newspaper reporter might pick up on a small town scandal that would eventually be spotted by a writer. Today that all seems ancient history. In its place are specialized services, such as L.A. based Industry R&D (IRD), which was established in 1992 to search for sensational tabloid news.

Discussing this phenomenon in *Entertainment Weekly,* Dana Kennedy wrote:

IRD has a network of 500 sources who tip off the agency to local stories and make what IRD executive Tom Colbert blithely calls "victim referrals." The good stories are then funneled to IRD's 17 clients—an eclectic bunch including five movie-of-the-week companies, one police show, one hard-news client, and three ABC newsmagazines.

This situation does not seem to leave much room or leverage for the average writer. That is not to say that it is impossible to find the dynamic story before anyone else—in fact the authors of *Silkwood* did just that—just that usually it's very difficult getting control of all the elements.

Nevertheless, there are still a tremendous number of stories out there waiting for you. In the end, forging scripts out of these overlooked treasures can often be more rewarding than reworking the flashy news story.

Take the case of *Chariots of Fire*. According to David Puttnam's biographer, Andrew Yule, David found the story by chance on a dreary afternoon in L.A. While searching in a bookcase, Puttnam came across a history of the Olympic Games.

> In the chapter on 1924 it became clear, just by reading down the lists of medals and times, that the British runners had done extremely well. The dark horse was Scot Eric Liddell. Having refused to run in the finals of the 100 meters, he had amazed everyone by breaking the world record on his way to a Gold in the 400 meters.

Intrigued, Puttnam then put a researcher on to the story, and finally got Colin Welland to write the script. As always, there were the doubters, like director Alan Parker. His advice to Puttnam was to abandon the whole thing. "I thought it was a terrible idea about a load of pompous English twits. I told David to forget it. That's how much I knew."

It's also worth considering the origins of *Death of a Princess*. In 1978, a small item appeared in most western newspapers: "Saudi Arabian princess shot to death while her lover is beheaded." For a few days the item grabbed the headlines, then was quickly forgotten. Except by one man: Antony Thomas.

Thomas, a noted British documentary filmmaker born in South Africa, had become intrigued by everything that *wasn't* mentioned in the story. Who was the Princess? Why was she killed? Under what circumstances?

In the end Thomas got ATV to back his research, which took him through Lebanon, Saudi Arabia, and Egypt. The resulting film, *Death of a Princess*, finally made in 1980, was shown widely in Europe and the U.S., and is generally regarded as one of the classics of docudrama.

This ability to ferret out a story, or see possibilities that no one else has thought of, is essential for a writer. Often the glimmerings of an idea may come to you through the telling of an anecdote, or the recollection of an odd moment in history, such as that which formed the basis of *The Dunerra Boys*.

The inspiration for that series came from a few forgotten moments of the Second World War.

In 1939 and 1940 thousands of German refugees, mostly Jews and intellectuals, flooded into England. Fearing that a few of them might be spies, England bizarrely decided to transport part of this flotsam of humanity to Australia. So suddenly hundreds of German Jewish scientists, doctors, writers and businessmen, the most harmless of the harmless, were shipped around the world and interned in a remote part of rural New South Wales.

The transport boat was called "The S.S. Dunerra" and many of the guards on the boat were viciously anti-Semitic. And if conditions on the boat were bad, those in the Australian camps at first were even worse.

Was it material for a good script? Writer Ben Lewin and producer Bob Weiss evidently thought so, and together produced one of the most moving and yet funny series ever seen on Australian TV.

Looking for the Winner

When I was putting this chapter together I thought I'd set myself an exercise. I'd become the student. I'd start looking for ideas, the same as you. I would file them away, produce them later, tell you where I found them, and try and justify my interest in them.

The elements I would look for would include everything we've discussed so far. Stories with conflict, passion, sex, jealousy, murder. Stories with strong personalities, opposing interests, weird situations. Stories that caught national or world interest. Stories that could be done as comedies. The only things I demanded from all of them was that they should have clear "heroes" and strong dramatic potential.

Unfortunately two of the stories I tracked got away early. I watched the David Koresh story unfold, and collected reams of material on him, only to see a TV movie appear while I was still preparing the chapter. The same fate affected my research and recording of the bombing of the World Trade Center. But here are the rest of the stories.

1: The Case of Judge Wachtler

This story originally caught my eye in *The New York Times*. Sol Wachtler was a former Chief Justice of New York State who had hopes of being Governor. On September 9th, 1993, he was sentenced to 15 months in prison for threatening to kidnap the daughter of his former lover, Joy Silverman.

Among other things, the story involved the sending of obscene letters, and the hiring by Wachtler of a private eye to stalk his lover and threaten her with compromising photographs of her new lover.

What attracted me was the bizarreness of the drama and the unbelievability of these actions by a senior judge. The story had sex. It had cops. It had the mighty brought low. It was a sad human story, but a great one for TV.

2: The Ern Malley Affair

This was a story I discovered in *The Australian Magazine* while flying from Sydney to New Zealand. It was very funny, obviously one of the great hoaxes of the century, and it struck me that done well, it could be another spoof drama like *Selling Hitler*.

In 1943 a sheaf of poems arrived at an Australian literary magazine, sent in by a woman named Ethel Malley. The poems were those of her dead brother, Ernest Malley. Within a few months the poems were hailed as the works of one of Australia's greatest geniuses, whose death was clearly a tragedy.

Then it became clear that behind the tragedy was a comedy. Ernest Malley had never existed. He and his entire works had been made up one afternoon in a barracks in Melbourne by two young poets who wanted to make fun of the literary establishment.

There was more to the story. The action inspired an obscenity trial, and haunted Australian social and literary history for years. The story was dotted with wonderful characters, and altogether I thought it was worth a spin.

3: The Tragedy of Salman Rushdie
I had followed the Rushdie affair for years, from the publication of *The Satanic Verses* to the insane death *fatwa* pronounced on Rushdie by Ayatollah Khomeini. However, I didn't start thinking about the possibility of a film on him till I saw an article called *Out of the Shadows* in an English magazine.

What shook me was that years had passed since Khomeini had died but Rushdie was still under threat. Here was one of the world's greatest writers forced to live in hiding. Bounties were still being offered for his murder. Here and there a few of his publishers and supporters had been stalked or killed, and no one seemed to care.

It seemed to me that all the elements were there for a great story. Religious fanaticism. Secret murders. Indifferent governments. A frightened wife who gets a divorce. A righteous fugitive always on the move.

Yet it was also a story that would make a writer hesitate before going ahead. As I write this chapter, Rushdie is still in jeopardy and there is no way of knowing how a film might affect his fate. Second, the story, at least today, is incomplete. It's a story with a first and second act, with a third act yet to be written.

4: The Codebreakers
This time it was a minor headline in the London *Times* which caught my eye. The headline ran, "Codebreakers' reunion sheds light on Enigma." The article itself was about a reunion in London of English wartime codebreakers.

During the Second World War, they had all lived in a large house in Bletchley Park, London. Many were mathematicians. A few were chess players and crossword solvers. In general, they looked like a group of out-of-work university professors. Appearances were deceptive. Among them they cracked the vital German, Italian, and Japanese secret codes that together revealed so many of the enemy's plans, movements, and strategy.

My thinking here was that the story could go in all directions. We had crazy, strong personalities who in their own secret way were doing as much to win the war as Patton or Montgomery. In fact, they were "The Quiet Heroes," and definitely story material.

5: The Rise and Fall of William McBride

This was a medical story I heard about over New Zealand radio. The facts are simple, and tragic in their own way.

In 1961, Dr. McBride was considered a world hero after being the first scientist to link the drug thalidomide with birth defects. Honors were piled on him and he became a Commander of the British Empire as well as being called Australia's father of the year.

In order to maintain his celebrity status, he started looking for another drug that was doing more harm than good, i.e., the next thalidomide. He found it in debendox, which he claimed could cause limb deformities in the fetus. The only trouble was that the results were based on massive alteration and manipulation of research results.

In August 1993, the name of William McBride was struck from the New South Wales medical register. To me this was another Wachtler story, whose essence was the hero struck down by a fatal flaw in his character. It lacked the sexiness of the Judge's story, but this was made up for by the way all the world had been gripped by the original thalidomide story.

6: Hollow Heroes

One of my favorite docudrama series is *Bodyline*. This is an Australian series about the national passions and controversies aroused when Britain played Australia in a number of cricket matches in the thirties. Cricket sounds like the dullest of games and yet the fury aroused by the games almost led Australia to sever its ties with England.

I thought the events surrounding the French football team Olympique Marseille in the summer of 1993 might well be the basis for another *Bodyline*. The essential facts of the story I picked up in *Le Monde* newspaper. As the story grew, it eventually hit the world press, with the best coverage coming to me from *The Sydney Morning Herald*.

In May 1993, Olympique Marseille, one of France's prestige football clubs, beat AC Milan 1-0 to win the European soccer championship. All France celebrated. As *The Herald* put it, "The national psyche seemed to receive a spiritual facelift. Bankers, businessmen and grandes dames whooped like teenagers, honking horns and waving banners along the capital's main boulevards."

Later all hell broke loose. On investigation it turned out that the club's owner, Bernard Tapie, and its manager might have bribed the members of another team to throw an earlier match so that Marseilles could save its energy for the championship game. As the inquiry proceeded, it turned out that other national and European games might have been rigged.

But the story is not just a soccer one. As the proceedings progressed, police started investigating the whole financial empire of Tapie, the flamboyant rags-to-riches owner of the team. All this came less than a year after Tapie was forced to resign as Minister of Towns after being accused of swindling a business associate.

In the end Marseilles were stripped of their title, but at the moment of writing there are a number of court actions in progress and the affair is far from being at an end.

Again the story seemed to me to have all the elements of a winner: individuals reaching the peak of national adulation suddenly brought low by corruption and scandal. Sad, yes. But dramatic and compelling? Absolutely!

Most of these stories hit me as I was going about my daily chores. I didn't go looking for them. They were there, staring me in the face. In short, the stories are all around you.

Naturally, there were lots of other stories I thought about that I haven't mentioned above. There was the story of Jack Kevorkian, the doctor who aided the chronically ill to commit suicide and was put on trial. There was the horrific report of the two ten-year-old English boys who battered a two-year-old to death. There was the shoot-out between the FBI and some gun-wielding American Nazis. There was no end to the possibilities.

That's what it's all about. The stories are out there. They are waiting for you, begging for you. Where do you begin? By looking and listening. By making lists and filing odd ideas of what strikes you as immediately compelling or a possibility for the future. But don't wait too long. The collection process isn't an end in itself. Finally you have to make a decision, and that's when you choose your best idea, turn on the computer, and get going.

Proposals

One of the greatest scenes in recent films takes place in the opening moments of Robert Altman's *The Player*. What we see is two writers feverishly trying to persuade a jaded Hollywood producer to back their script. To make their point they act out the story in 40 seconds, trying to give it pathos, humor, drama, and tragedy.

This is what we call *the pitch*. You may be involved in this experience, in which case, God help you, but more likely you will have first done a *proposal*.

A proposal is a short description of the film you want to do, and its objective is to fire the interest of a producer to back the project. It's a prospectus, a sales document, a device to sell a film. It's not nearly as elaborate or worked out as a treatment (which we'll discuss later), but should show clearly what the film is about and where it's going.

Generally the proposal is used by the independent writer when the story is a little off the beaten track, and he or she has to persuade the producer that the story is interesting and has potentially strong audience appeal. Where the story is well known, such as the life of Roy Cohn or the forging of the Hitler diaries, the writer would probably just pitch the idea and not bother with a formal proposal. However, many networks and producers still like to see a formal proposal just so that verbal discussions can be a little more concrete.

There is no standard form for a proposal. Try to keep it short rather than long, as few producers have much patience or time for reading anything of great length. In any case, all you are trying to do is inspire initial interest. The real work will come later.

In your proposal you set out the most attractive aspects of your idea. You explain its topicality, its relevance, and its potential audience. If the film is for television, you may want to suggest a particular slot for your idea, such as *Most Wanted* or *FBI True Stories*. All these things help the proposal, but in the end only one thing matters . . . is your story any good? You therefore set out a short synopsis of the story, making it as colorful, dramatic, and powerful as you can.

Roberto Loiederman is a young L.A. writer who among other things has done scripts for *Knots Landing* and *Dynasty*. When Loiederman heard that Turner Broadcasting was thinking of doing thirteen Indian stories, he sat down and wrote a proposal for a reality-based film describing the discovery of the Grand Canyon. The proposal is very attractively written, and the beginning of it is produced below:

BEYOND THE HUNDREDTH MERIDIAN.   Roberto Loiederman.

The bodies of three men lay baked and bleeding on a plateau high above the inner gorge of the Grand Canyon, arrows sticking from their backs. Far below, and much farther downstream, the six companions they had deserted some days before plunged almost helplessly through enormous, boulder-choked rapids . . . their rowboats battered to the point of worthlessness.

A small, tough, bristly man—a self-made, down-to-earth American folk hero—clung to the gunwales of one of the boats; his stump of a right arm waved with determination at his remaining men, exhorting them on.

John Wesley Powell's expedition through the Grand Canyon is perhaps the last great American adventure of territorial discovery. A true story of the West, Powell's expedition has all the elements of the classic Western: Indians, gunfights, famous historical characters . . . and a successful struggle against impossible odds.

The then-unknown river wreaked havoc on their little boats—and on their lives—at every turn. This expedition had the same effect on the American spirit that Sir Richard Burton's exploration of the Nile had on the English (as seen in *Mountains of the Moon*): it galvanized the country and gave it an authentic hero.

The trip down the river—for all its incredible hardships—was also for Powell a voyage of discovery. Not only did the river challenge his personal courage at every turn, but at the same time the Western landscape constantly broadened his scientific understanding. Partly through his contacts with Indians and Mormons, partly through his own scientific explorations and observations, he came to understand the ecological nature of the land beyond the hundredth meridian.

Soon after the Civil War, in the late 1860s, there remained one last unexplored part of the United States: the Colorado River and the fabled canyon that had been rumored by Indian and white man for more than 200 years.

Major John Wesley Powell had his right arm shot off in the battle of Shiloh, but that didn't stop him for a moment. He was determined to be the person who would fill in the last unknown gaps in the U.S. map.

A journalist published articles in eastern papers about Powell's proposed expedition. Soon the country became fascinated with the romantic image of the one-armed Civil War officer bravely leading his band down the unknown stretch of river.

But there were others who, rather than support Powell, were actively trying to stop him. One of these was a shadowy figure named Sam Adams, who himself wanted to be the first down the river.

Adams presented himself to Powell, but when Powell rejected him, Adams made contact with Jack Sumner—a treacherous Indian-hating trapper—and arranged for Sumner to go with Powell and sabotage the expedition.

Powell gathered his band of men. And what a group it was. Besides Sumner there were other wild men of the west: *O. G. Howland*—a skilled trapper and mountain man...the illiterate *Seenca Howland*, O.G's brother, a wild trapper...*Andy Hall*, a rambunctious teenager, already a skilled trapper/mountain man, who was invited on the trip when Howell saw a home-made boat Hall had made. Then there was a man called *Bill Hawkins*, an expert marksman and joker who worked as cook for the expedition. What Hawkins kept hidden was that he was wanted for murder back in Missouri.

Powell's wife—Emma Dean, for whom he named one of the boats—helped in the preparations, then waved a fearful farewell as the four boats pushed off at Green River, Wyoming, on May 24th, 1869.

Running the river was forever dangerous. The sun baked the party into submission, then violent rainstorms broke their will to go on. The heavy oak boats at times had to be carried over rocks and around impassable, boulder-choked water passageways. And the constant accidents: at one rapid the men were thrown out. At another the bobbing heads of two men disappeared in the foam. At another they lost one of their boats, with rations, clothing and scientific instruments.

The constant accidents, the dangers, the hardships, all gave rise to internal dissension among the men. But even more dangerous to the expedition was Jack Sumner, who was constantly trying to sabotage the trip...

Loiederman's writing is a model of everything one looks for in a good proposal. It fires the imagination, draws you into the story, provides you with the vital background, intrigues you, and clearly shows you how everything will develop.

When you present a proposal, the producer is going to consider three or four very important questions:

Is it a good, exciting story?
Is it a story which is likely to appeal to the public?
Does it have strong and interesting characters?
Does it have plenty of physical and personal conflicts?

If your proposal can answer these questions as affirmatively as this one does, you know you've passed the first hurdle.

Starting to Work

5

□ □ □
□ □ □
□ □ □

Research

Research is the master key to fact-fiction films, and you undertake it with two objectives in mind. You are looking for facts, and you are trying to get to the heart of the drama. In order to proceed with your script, you must know your subject in depth, inside out, and upside down. Only when you really know the subject will you be able to see where to go: how to shape the film, structure it, select the dominant characters, create an interesting story line, and so on. Research provides you with your lexicon of options.

As a writer, the odds are you are going to be heavily involved in this process. In some cases the total burden of the research will fall on your shoulders. In other cases you will be directing the principal lines of the research, probably with the aid of the producer.

As a researcher, you need to combine the penetrating brazenness of the good journalist with the painstaking attention to detail of the Ph.D. candidate. You must be observer, analyst, student, and notetaker. Over a period that can be as short as a few weeks or as long as six months or a year you must become an expert on the subject of the film, a subject you may never even have known existed before; not easy but always fascinating.

Research can be broken down into four sections: (1) print research, (2) photograph and archive research, (3) direct interviews, and (4) on-the-spot involvement with the subject, or location research. In practice, you are likely to be involved in all four forms of research at the same time.

Printed Material

Within the limits, you try to read as much as possible about the subject. This is particularly true of historically based drama-docs. Your aim is simple: within a short time you want to become, if not an expert in the field, at least a person with a superior knowledge of the subject. Print research can involve scanning the major bibliographies and subject biographies, and reading papers, magazines, trade and technical journals, articles, diaries, letters, and even congressional records and court trials.

If the material is highly technical, complex, or jargonized, you should get someone to help you, so that the material becomes comprehensible to you as a mere mortal. If you don't understand the material, you will never be able to see its relevance to the subject or say anything sensible about it in a film.

The BBC series on the life of nuclear physicist J. Robert Oppenheimer dealt, at least on a superficial level, with fission theory. Not an easy task for a researcher, but it had to be tackled and made comprehensible. Michael Baker's script on the Exxon Valdez oil disaster involved lengthy research on the development of the Alaskan oil industry and the complex measures for pollution control. Again, we saw a case of an immense amount of material that had to be assimilated and understood before the script could be started.

There are problems all along the way. You will often read too much and in too much depth, making it difficult to isolate the valuable or relevant material. After a while, however, you learn to scan and to distinguish the important fact from the obscuring detail.

Another problem is that much of the material may be out of date or presented from a biased or self-serving point of view. When I think that the material comes from a highly interested and partisan source (particularly in films of a political or controversial nature), I try to check the biases of the informant as well. I also double-check statistics, remembering the old adage, "There are lies, more lies, and statistics."

There is one point which I think is terribly important, certainly in investigative docudramas. Go back to the original sources for your information. Don't be content with second- or third-hand reports. If you are doing a film about a character or an incident in World War One, don't just read a few history books. Instead, start digging out documents, wills, diaries, and contemporary newspaper accounts. If you are doing a film on government policy, you have to start digging into official records, state papers, memoranda, and the like. This is not easy, but it is necessary.

Newspapers

Besides suggesting stories as subjects for docudramas, newspapers and magazines can very often provide a lot of the basic research and background detail for the subsequent film. In the notorious Amy Fisher case, NBC and CBS both used participants in the original dramas as their principal sources of information. Excluded from that process, ABC based its account very largely on newspaper reports and court records.

One of the most interesting journalistic stories of the eighties was the "hijacking" and trial in Israel of Mordecai Vanunu. Vanunu had worked in Israel's secret nuclear center for a number of years, moved to Australia, converted to Christianity and then sold his revelations about Israel's atomic program to the British *Sunday Times*. Later, he was kidnapped by the Israeli Secret Service and brought back to Tel Aviv. After his closed trial, Vanunu was imprisoned in solitary confinement.

In such a situation it might seem that research is limited. The principal himself was not available for questioning, nor were any Israeli official sources, nor was Cindy, the Israeli secret agent and girlfriend. Nevertheless, TBS television turned out a reasonably interesting drama-doc.

In this case, ninety percent of the research came from in-depth articles by the English *Sunday Times* "insight" team. The other ten percent came from interviews in Australia and England, and with Vanunu's family.

Although the newspaper accounts can be very useful, they often have to be taken with a pinch of salt. Are they accurate? Are they sensationalist? Can they be believed? How thorough are they? Obviously, there is a world of difference between the reporting of Woodward and Bernstein regarding the Watergate cover-ups and *The National Enquirer* reporting on Elvis Presley having risen from the grave and performing in Nashville.

After a while you learn to discriminate. You might suspect a yellow journalism crime story, but if it appeared in *New York* magazine, then the odds are that it has been meticulously researched and is quite accurate. The same is true of *People* or *US* magazine. The story may be lurid, but the probability is that the basic facts are relatively reliable.

What one also looks for in a newspaper, besides facts, is the feel and atmosphere of a time and a place, or the way a particular community reacted to a particular story or incident. This can also be very helpful where there has been no original TV coverage.

A good example here is *Fatal Memories*, the story of Eileen Franklin-Lipsker, the girl who witnessed the murder of her best friend by her father. Both the *Los Angeles Times* and *The San Francisco Chronicle* gave full coverage and comment when the story broke in December 1989.

In May 1990, both papers also ran engrossing accounts of the subsequent court case. Though the articles were very useful for research, what may have helped the writer just as much were the newspaper reports of the nine-year-old girl's disappearance around September 1969 and the community reaction when the battered girl's body was discovered a little while later.

Freedom of Information Papers

A problem facing many researchers is that they suspect that the information is there but they can't get their hands on it. In the private sphere, there is often little that can be done. If someone doesn't want to release an intimate diary or letters, that's it. Or if a company doesn't want to release its memoranda, again one may just have to accept the situation. However, things are slightly different in the realm of information held by the government on individuals. Such a case may well be covered by the 1977 Freedom of Information Act.

As a result of this act, interested parties can gain access to previous secret information collected about themselves or well-known individuals by the government. This ability to open previously closed and jealously guarded doors proved vital in the research of films as various as *JFK*, *Chaplin*, and *Citizen Cohn*.

The Freedom of Information Act also proved extremely useful in preparing the series on J. Robert Oppenheimer for the BBC. When I talked to Peter Goodchild, the producer of the series, he told me the following:

> Initially the problem seemed to be how to breathe life into Oppenheimer and make him less of a totem. We needed to find out more about his personal life and relationships. And here we were among the first to benefit from the new Act. The reports we uncovered showed how continuous the surveillance of him was. It showed pretty clearly that he had been propositioned by Haakon Chevalier and others, and that the prosecution counsel at the hearings had tried to get the FBI to intervene when he thought the panel was swinging in favor of Oppie. In a nutshell we really felt we had got something of an inside track.

Books

Books also provide you with enormous research potential, but have to be absorbed with caution. Where a sole book is the principal source for your film, like Tom Wolfe's *The Right Stuff*, about the U.S. astronauts and space program, you may have to be careful of its accuracy. Less wariness may be needed, of course, if your brief is merely to adapt the book "as is" and forget anything else. This was the course followed in adapting *The Longest Day*, which describes the D-Day invasion of Normandy, and in doing *Young Winston*, about the Boer War adventures of Winston Churchill.

Sometimes the book is so famous, and other information so scarce, you may have no other option than to do a straight adaptation without much further research. This was true about the book *God's Banker*, an investigation of the Mafia connections with Papal banking and business. Sources were limited, and like the Vanunu case, mouths were sealed. However, whereas a film was made about Vanunu, *God's Banker* hasn't yet been produced, rumor attributing this to fear of Mafia reaction.

One of the staple offerings of docudramas is the biopic, and in many cases the biography or autobiography becomes almost the chief source. Often, as in the case of Hemingway, Van Gogh, Churchill, and countless others, there are as many as two or three good biographies and the researcher picks his or her way through all of them, or at least the best of them. Usually there is no problem. You pick up the story, you get slightly different viewpoints from book to book, and one supplements another.

The problem comes when the books are in dispute, and the viewpoints radically differ. Then you pays your money and you takes your choice. For example, one of the most provocative books out on Frank Sinatra is *His Way* by Kitty Kelly. The book is fascinating and deadly, and a very unpleasant picture of Sinatra emerges from it. Quite clearly it could have been a fascinating basis for a docudrama. However, the series that was eventually made by Sinatra's daughter presented a basically positive view of Frank, with Kitty Kelly's views being almost totally ignored.

Diaries, Etc.

When Hitler's diaries were "discovered" a few years ago, the journalistic world went mad for a few months. What revelations would come out? What workings of the mind would be revealed? What insights would be discovered about the dictator's mind? Alas, it was all fake and merely provided material for a British docudrama on the hoax itself.

We hunger for revelations and inner secrets, and often the juicier and the more lurid, the better. And in searching for the concealed, we turn to the diary. We do this because we know that if the writer can't bury his or her hidden passions, fears, and hopes in the confiding secrecy of the diary, then there is probably nothing worth burying at all.

At least we might have said this a few years ago. Today I'm not so sure. In an age of tape cassettes and videotape recorders, the diary can take many forms.

In the end we turn to diaries for research, not only out of a lurid thirst for scandal or a whiff of sexual impropriety, but also in a quest for something much more serious. We know that if the diary or the journal is honest and reasonably accurate, we can get a glimpse into the inner life, thoughts, hopes, frustrations, and dreams of our subject.

The diaries can be ancient as well as modern. Columbus's navigational journals helped in the scripting of *1492: The Conquest of Paradise*, while Darwin's journals helped form the basis of the British series on the explorer. Freud's notes, diaries, and letters helped enormously in the writing of the series on his life, while similar help was provided by Oppenheimer's journal in the BBC films. When Leslie Woodhead did a film on Soviet dissident General Grigorenko, the very basis of the film was provided by Grigorenko's detailed diaries, which he had managed to smuggle out of prison.

Diaries can be a wonderful tool . . . up to a point. One has to remember, however, that they are often written with an eye on posterity, and with a view to historical self-justification. This is particularly true of political, military, and literary journals. They may be fascinating, but are they truthful? . . . well, that may be something else again.

Court Transcripts

Sometimes, in one of my more cynical moods, I find myself wondering whether drama-docs could exist without what now seems the inevitable court scene. In 1992 over ten drama-docs, ranging from *Willing to Kill: the Texas Cheerleader Story*, through *Her Final Fury: Betty Broderick, the Last Chapter*, to *A Murderous Affair: The Carolyn Warmus Story*, and all the Amy Fisher films, featured or climaxed with court scenes.

Clearly the writing is on the wall. Like it or not, digging into court transcripts is going to be one of those research jobs you are going to have to face sooner or later. It may be tiresome work, involving a great deal of reading, but it is also quite fascinating and in most cases absolutely necessary. This is not just because of the search for truth and accuracy, but comes from the fact that in most cases the trial record is more dramatically fascinating than anything you could invent.

Today what we see most often are trial scenes in murder recreations, but trials or trial-like confrontations are also quite often used to provide discussion of much wider issues in docudramas.

In *Stanley and Livingstone*, the Society of British Geographers meets to judge the maps that prove that Stanley could actually have found Livingstone. In *The Mountains of the Moon*, the same society sits in judgment on the rival claims of Burton and Speke to have found the sources of the Nile. In the Canadian Film Board's *Democracy on Trial: The Morgentaler Affair*, the whole basis of the film rests on Dr. Morgentaler's three trials for running an abortion clinic in Montreal.

Richard Attenborough's film *Cry Freedom* is a look at the way the life of journalist Donald Woods is changed by his relationship to Steven Biko. In contrast, Thames TV's *A Miserable and Lonely Death* is a much more modest affair.

This latter film is a simple reconstruction of the inquest into the death of Biko and is based almost entirely on the transcripts of the inquest. Nevertheless, the film has an immense power, derived from the simplicity and directness of the transcripts, which I think was lost in Attenborough's more wide-ranging film and script.

The power of trial transcripts can also be seen in Leslie Woodhead's *A Subject of Struggle*. Woodhead's film was about an elderly Chinese lady put on trial by the Red Guards at the height of the Cultural Revolution. In 1972, when the film was made, the nature of the revolution was a tremendous puzzle, and no film of any duration had come out of China about it. Woodhead obtained the trial transcript, talked to Sinologists about it, and then used the transcripts as the basis of his film.

Photo and Archive Research

The need for photo and archive research arises most frequently in history-based docudramas. This kind of search can give you three things:

1: The feel and look of a period, whether it be the sixties or the thirties
2: An understanding of your main characters, their habits, their appearance, and their actions
3: An understanding and insight into certain key events that are necessary for your film

Often you will be looking at the archives as both a source of inspiration and as actual visual material that can be incorporated into the final film. The assassination of Kennedy in *JFK* is possibly the most simple example. A more involved use of archive can be seen in *Citizen Cohn*, the film about Senator McCarthy's chief lawyer and henchman, Roy Cohn.

In *Citizen Cohn*, the writer uses archive film as an element of the picture, making the Senate committee hearings on communism and communist affiliation an integral part of the script. Beyond this, he has quite clearly used archival information as the basis of a good number of actual incidents in the film.

Your sources for photographs and stock footage are fairly obvious. In the usual family/incident/injury/murder docudramas, such as *Friendly Fire*, *Afterburn*, *Fatal Memories*, *Little Mo*, or the Amy Fisher or Texas cheerleader cases, your materials will probably be obtained from family or friends, and from their private albums, attics, and old super-eight and videocassettes.

In regard to historical and political films, your sources may be more complex. Depending on your film, you may be searching government archives (such as the British Imperial War Museum in London or the National Archives in Washington, D.C.), local and press archives, or television archives. The latter, for example, were used very widely in *Citizen Cohn*.

Once you have a general source for your material, you may still find it difficult to locate what you want. Archives are often arranged haphazardly, and although you know there is gold somewhere around, it may be terribly difficult to find. To some extent, the difficulties have been alleviated by computers and the possibility of a database and name search, but many archives still go by the index card system.

Most archives list their collections by film title, by subject and occasionally by reporter or cinematographer. If the archive is good, a film's title card should list the subjects of the principal scenes; for example, "Hitler reviewing his guards in Nuremberg. Peasants in costume. Hitler's hotel at night. Torchlight parade." Obviously, the better the archives are indexed, the easier it is to find material.

Occasionally a problem can arise through the sheer age of the archive. Some films may be indexed incompletely because the original archivist failed to recognize the importance of certain materials. Thus, the material you want may exist, but may not be indexed. For example, you may be looking for war criminal X in German archives indexed in 1947. But if Captain X only came into prominence in much later investigations, he may appear on much of the stock footage but be unidentified in the files. This means that archive research often depends as much on intuition, on asking and probing, as it does on hunting through files.

Interviews

Your objective in direct interviews is to talk to as many "experts" on the subject as possible. Again, as in print research, you have to make some shrewd guesses. Since time is limited, you try to assess which people are the best, the most important, and the most open, and you allocate your time accordingly.

Today a very high percentage of TV docudramas revolve around the sudden bizarre incident happening to an ordinary family or the next-door neighbor. What complicates the situation is that the main persona will now often only talk after the payment of huge sums of money.

In the Amy Fisher case, the Fishers allegedly collected $80,000 from KLM productions for film rights, which meant exclusive interview rights. Against this, the Buttafuocos got between $200,000 and $300,000 from Tri-Star for their version of the same story.

When HBO wanted to make a film about Wanda Holloway, the scheming mother in the Texas cheerleader case, they eventually paid Mrs. Holloway's former husband and her daughter $130,000 for joining in the deal. They also paid Verna Heath, the intended victim, $50,000 for her participation.

What is also clear from the above cases is that money pays for a specific point of view. You manage to interview the husband and the daughter of the murdered woman; then your story will probably go one way. Interview the murderess and her lover, and the story will probably be biased in another direction.

Outside these domestic dramas, what kind of interviewees are you looking for? Usually those most seriously involved in the subject. They can range from technical experts and authorities to the ordinary people who have undergone the experience documented in the film, such as local fishermen in the HBO Exxon Valdez drama, or security officials in the Lockerbie air disaster. In brief, your perspective and the breadth of your subject will dictate to whom you talk, and your questions will obviously range from the general to the specific, depending on the topic.

Sometimes even the shortest interview can add perceptions that are valuable for the script. For example, Peter Goodchild, the producer of the Oppenheimer series, happened to meet a British writer, Evan Jones, who knew Oppenheimer. One of the incidents that Jones described was how he was invited to dinner at the Oppenheimers' house and saw how fast Oppie's wife succumbed to drink. Evidently the physicist himself also hit the bottle very hard. What was clear was that the two were at each other's throats and were a very unhappy couple. It was a small revelation, but invaluable for the script.

Peter Prince, who wrote the scripts for the seven-part series, also had this to say about the interview and research process.

Goodchild and I went on a month-long visit to the U.S. in order to talk to as many survivors of the Oppenheimer era as possible. This was very helpful to me not just, or primarily, for the information it provided, but because it gave me a chance to sample the actual characters of those who were going to fill my story. Although they were now forty years older than when the real events had taken place, in a number of cases I still got a very strong and, I think, accurate impression of how they must once have been. E.g., I was particularly struck by something competitive and rather menacing in the air when I met Edward Teller, the "father of the hydrogen-bomb." I'm sure that helped me portray his younger self in *Oppenheimer*.

Occasionally the interviews can alter your first perception of the story, and lead you in a totally different direction. This happened to Antony Thomas, writer and director of *Death of a Princess*. The story concerns the events leading up to the public execution of a Saudi Arabian princess for adultery, and actually caused a rift in British and Saudi Arabian diplomatic relations when it was first broadcast.

Thomas told me the story of the research as follows:

I presented the idea to ATV. They were interested in it and off I went, only to discover that the research was utterly baffling. I discovered very early on that many elements of the story I had been told were simply not true.

The most solid lead was that the Princess was supposed to have met her lover at the University of Beirut. So I felt I should begin in Lebanon, and find people who had known her, who had taught her, who were her class-mates . . . Then came the shock. After two days in Lebanon I discovered part of this wonderful dramatic story was nonsense. The girl had *never been* to the Arab University of Beirut.

But I soon discovered something else very interesting, that the girl had become some sort of mythological figure in the Arab world. She had become both a personal symbol and a political symbol, and everyone was adopting her to their cause. Thus for a Palestinian family that talked about her she had become a freedom fighter. So this ability in the Arab world to deal in myth, hearsay and legend took off in regard to the Princess. I was slow, but gradually I began to see the importance of these elements.

Approached correctly and sympathetically, most people will be willing to talk to you for your research. Occasionally, however, you will run into difficulties if the subject is professionally wounding or controversial. Thus it was no surprise to the researchers in the Lockerbie disaster film that both Pan Am officials and the Germans were reluctant to talk. In this case a former policeman, with no fear for job security, and ex-employees of Pan Am helped break the logjam.

What if the subject is personally painful or the events bordering on the crim-inal? . . . do you go ahead, or back off? Everyone has to sort that dilemma out personally. Several years ago I interviewed Sue McConnochy about a film she was doing on war criminals. I was interested in her difficulties in talking to Germans for the film, because she was investigating not just memory and experiences, but also possible participation in war crimes and atrocities. Her comments were very interesting.

> Initially it was quite difficult to get people to open up. However, once the Germans agreed to see you and talk it was all much fresher than the English people's reminiscences because it hadn't been told before.
>
> The problem was getting to the shadow figures and the possible criminals. This was often done through a series of contacts. One was in the position of being given confidential information which one was not supposed to broadcast or pass on. You were only allowed to go and see these people on the understanding that you gave nothing away.
>
> Now once you'd got into a position of trust, once you'd got onto the "circuit," you were handed on from one to the next. And it was an almost impossible situation as a researcher (and as a human being) because I was dealing with people who, in the period of their lives that we were talking about, had not operated with the same code of behavior, morals, whatever you call it, that I by nature and upbringing operate on.
>
> (Alan Rosenthal, *The Documentary Conscience*
> [Berkeley and Los Angeles: University of California Press, 1980])

About the same time I met McConnochy, I also spoke to Peter Watkins about the making of his famous anti-nuclear war film *The War Game*. Watkins commented:

> As far as research went and talking to people you have to differentiate between people in general and government bodies. The experts, professors and so on were extremely cooperative and very interested. A few were a little skeptical of an amateur blundering into their domain, but they freely supplied what little information they had. The government bodies were different. In general they said no.
>
> (Alan Rosenthal, *The New Documentary in Action*
> [Berkeley and Los Angeles: University of California Press, 1971])

The Home Office, responsible for internal affairs and security in England, refused to help Watkins in the making of the film. In fact, not only did it refuse information, but it also withdrew all official help and tried to hinder the research by preventing the Fire Service and the police from giving Watkins details of their plans in the event of a nuclear holocaust. Officially there was a complete clampdown.

Reliance on only a few interviewees on anything controversial has its dangers. In such a case, as in the Exxon Valdez film, it's best to interview or try to interview a broad range of people. This way you can contrast opinions and estimate how much of what you are being told is biased or partisan.

Obviously you have to rely on common sense. You are not aiming for balance; you are trying to get at the truth, and it could be that the one-sided view just happens to be the truth.

During the interviews you will ask both the easy and the awkward questions. Sometimes you may have to play the probing investigator, but more often you are asking common-sense questions that any interested person would bring up.

In a technical film, and again HBO's *Dead Ahead: The Exxon Valdez Disaster* and *Afterburn* are good examples, you may want to accumulate facts and find out about problems, systems of work, difficulties, successes, side effects, and results. In a human or portrait film, you will probably want to find out about human experiences, memories, changes, thoughts, and the consequences that certain actions have wrought on peoples' lives.

Often the interviewing will be difficult or painful, as you touch on emotions and sensitivities. You are not just collecting facts but trying to gain a perspective that goes beyond the facts. An adjunct to this is that you always have to keep in mind whether you want the emphasis to fall on facts or on emotions, because each may pull you a different way.

As usual, a warning. There is a tremendous difference between interviewing someone about the current scene and about the past. In both cases you have to be aware of bias, but in talking about the past you also have to be aware of the pitfalls of memory and romanticism.

Sometimes, of course, the events of the past are etched more strongly on the mind than are the events of yesterday, but not always. Whether impelled by love or hate, or just age, the memory can be a strange distorting mirror. So beware.

Location Research

Much of your research will be done on location. While one of your objectives is to get to know your characters, an equally important goal is to get a feel for the background and the atmosphere of your story.

In order to write *Dead Ahead: The Exxon Valdez Disaster*, Michael Baker had to spend months in Valdez, Alaska, observing all the details of the town, the way the oil industry worked, and not least in importance, getting a feeling for the beauty of the locale.

Similarly, the atmosphere of the schools, the church meetings, the beginning-of-the-season football game, are all the small-town details which became vital to the Texas cheerleader story and had to be researched *in situ*.

Before writing *Shoot to Kill*, the true story of the deliberate killings of IRA members by special police units, author Michael Eaton spent weeks soaking up the atmosphere of Belfast and other northern Irish towns.

The list is endless. The point clear. If you have the chance to see where everything happened, then go there. The experience will make all the difference to your writing.

The Dark Exploration

Research is vital to most drama-docs, and yet it is a difficult subject psychologically. This is because you know that only a fraction of the material you are accumulating will ever be used in the final film. As a colleague of mine, Jim Beveridge, once put it: "Research is like an iceberg. Seven-eighths of it is below the surface and can't be seen."

It's also, when you think about it, a rather strange quest, a little like Columbus's voyages. Columbus thought he was looking for India and yet in reality knew he didn't have a clue where his trip would take him.

Much film research is like that. You know vaguely you are doing a film about the death of a princess, or an ecological disaster in Alaska, but you are not sure what story will emerge on the other side of the research. So often the voyage is not just backup for your writing, but a crucial search for the basic dramatic elements themselves.

Research in Practice: An Example

In 1988, both the BBC and HBO screened *Yuri Nosenko, KGB*, which was written by British playwright Stephen Davis.

In this major docudrama Davis tells the story of Nosenko, a Russian KGB officer who defected to the CIA in 1964 and was held in close confinement in a windowless secure facility for a number of years. During this time there was round-the-clock observation of Nosenko and continuous hostile interrogation in an attempt to see whether he was a true defector or a KGB plant.

While writing this book, I interviewed Davis at length on the preparation of the script. I was especially interested in the research process, particularly as the script dealt with such a "hush-hush" story. The original story got into the public record by accident, and then became the center of a book written by Edward Jay Epstein.

I was curious. How did Davis proceed after reading the book?

My first move was to go to Epstein, who became the story consultant, and get a little more background. That's not to say he did more than consult and encourage, but he was very intelligent and had very strong CIA connections which I wanted to get reopened.

It was very difficult to approach the CIA people, who are under a legal obligation not to reveal their sources and who are very inhibited indeed in talking to people like me. And I was prodding a very sensitive spot . . . the secret community of the intelligence world.

I knew the key to my story was to get hold of primary sources. And I thought my advantage in being able to do this was to be able to say to those sources that I *wasn't* a journalist. That I wasn't going to write about them in the first person. That I wasn't going to quote them and expose them in the normal way journalists are expected to do. That I wanted to tell the story from a coherent point of view and that they ought to trust me.

Now in retrospect that was a pretty stupid assertion to make, especially to the CIA, but I stuck to that line for a long time. That I could go places as a dramatist where a journalist couldn't have gone.

But it had one particular advantage, which was that I was able to meet sources in the story who might not give me much information but who nevertheless were helpful to me as a dramatist. I would be getting a picture of who these people were and the atmosphere of the worlds they lived in.

And what followed was leg work. Tramping around North America and western Europe trying to track down and elicit interviews with some of the retired and not retired people who were connected with the Nosenko case. All the time I was building up a detailed picture of what happened. And I was constantly comparing it with other accounts and cross checking it against the backgrounds of other espionage cases.

.I got mixed reactions from the people I contacted. About half of them were willing to see me, and half put the phone down. And of the half that put the phone down some have since gone on record with other writers. Maybe they were prepared to debrief to a journalist but not to mess around with a dramatist. They may have thought it was frivolous.

. . . One of the vital things I was trying to get in the interviews was a time sequence of events. And this is still a method I find crucial in this kind of work. The timetable of the sequence of events is the key to everything. It's no use using anecdotes out of sequence.

My working method was to write the most detailed account of the interviews, and then build up a log of the Nosenko defection from the first time he made contact with the CIA through the next seven years of the case. At the same time I tried to map the Nosenko developments against every known public event of the cold war years.

This would lead me to certain assumptions and I would then go back to my sources and get them to confirm or deny these assumptions.

. . . My estimate is I must have spent a year on the writing and research. All the time I was trying to understand the nature of the story, trying to understand the real bona fides of the defector.

And what excited me from a professional point of view, *and I knew would animate the drama*, was that I knew my journey of research was a journey into the dark and silent world of intelligence. And what is important in writing drama is that you can identify with the characters, and you can go on the journey they go on. And that's what research helps you do.

Some Practical Hints

Although research itself is largely a matter of patience, application, and common sense, there are a few practical tips that may help you along the way.

1: Identification

People you visit, see, or write to, want to know who you are. Get yourself a business card that identifies you and also gives your address and profession, such as "Larry Price, scriptwriter and film producer." Also, get yourself some well-printed stationery that says the same thing, because you are going to be writing a lot of letters. And if you are working for a producer or production company, make sure you've got their stationery as well.

2: Reference Library

It's also not a bad idea to start building your own reference library and index card system. It needn't be elaborate but should be immediately practical. For myself I keep to hand the names and addresses of U.S. and European archive libraries, key U.S. television stations, newspaper libraries, and main district and state courts. I also have a few general film and television yearbooks hanging around, a couple of beat-up general political histories of Europe and the United States, and a ten-year-old copy of the *Encyclopedia Britannica*. For what it's worth, I also keep the current copies of *Newsweek* and *The Economist* for quick contemporary reference.

3: Payments

Many libraries and archives are free, but there are a good number of others that demand payment by the day or by the week. Specialized services in free libraries may also demand payment, and most definitely will for all photocopying. A few take checks. Most prefer cash.

4: Interviewing

When you want to get a foot in the door, you use whatever method fits the situation. If you are interviewing a public figure, then a phone call to his or her secretary mentioning your interest, followed by a letter, will probably do the trick.

When you are dealing with a private person in the public eye, things may be more tricky. Here you try and find out as much about the person as you can before making contact. If the person is gun-shy of reporters, then you try the low-key approach. If he or she is hungry for publicity, then you drag out your NBC or BBC credentials and jump in there.

When you want to meet a private person for research but he or she is not in the news, your best bet may be a letter followed by a phone call. Again, I would play things fairly softly in the letter. You say who you are, how you've heard about his or her relationship to the story, and that you'd very much like to hear some more if he or she can spare the time. Follow this up with a phone call, and nine times out of ten the person will agree to talk.

5: The Sequence List

The most important suggestion for you to follow is that offered by Stephen Davis. As you proceed with the research, make yourself a sequence chart which shows when events occurred, and who was involved in the events. You'll find this list helps you enormously when you come to write the film, and keeps you on track as to who did what to whom, and when.

6

□ □ □
□ □ □
□ □ □

The Dramatic Elements

You've found your subject. It looks commercial. It has audience appeal. You've done your research and you think you are onto a winner.

You've got a good story. It's about an attractive person with whom the audience can identify, caught in a threatening life crisis. You've got villains. You've got complications. You've got twists in it and surprises, and even a certain amount of humor. You've also got a lot of physical action. The hero goes through various reverses but eventually comes out fine.

You know you have all the essentials of a good script. So how do you proceed? By planning. Before you start writing the script you need to know exactly where you're going, with whom, at what speed, and roughly what's going to happen along the way.

The procedure is a little like building a house. Before a single brick is placed, the architect has had to think about overall structure, form, design, materials, colors, plumbing, electricity, relationship of rooms, heating, and a dozen other factors. He's thought about them, and integrated his conclusions into his final master plans. You are the film architect, and you have to do the same kind of thinking before you come out with your plan, which in this case we call the script, or scenario.

Now unless the architect gets the overall form and structure right, the building will be a mess, and no amount of interior planning or use of wondrous materials will save it. Exactly the same is true of scriptwriting. In your case, the whole framework and success of your script depends on the fusion and cohesion of four vital dramatic elements:

1: Story
2: Conflict
3: Structure
4: Character

There are, of course, many other factors in the script which are going to be important, and they include dialogue, atmosphere, tension, surprise, humor, pacing, beginnings, and endings. Most of these topics relate to broader considerations of form and approach, and are dealt with in the next chapter. However, important as they are, these subjects can only be discussed when you've got the main elements settled in your mind.

The Problem of Reality

You're ready to jump in . . . but hold it. Aren't there a few problems here? Discussion of all these elements is fine, but this book is about fact-based dramas, tales drawn from life, movies based on reality. It's about situations that are already given to us, conflicts that are already to hand, characters who have an independent existence aside from our typewriters, stories that don't yield easily to ideal theories of structure. Do the same dramatic criteria apply to this genre? And even if they do, how do you impose these elements on a *found* or given situation?

The answer to the first question is a simple "yes." The elements of drama are universal and exist as much, if not more, in real life than in fiction. The real question is the second one, which can also be expressed this way. How do you create an interesting form and a compelling dramatic structure out of fascinating but often muddled, shapeless, and complex real-life events? And how do you do it when your creative stretch is shackled by truth?

The solution is to gain a broad understanding of the main elements of drama, and then focus this knowledge on your real-life situation. Your work then becomes a sifting process. First you have to find and identify all the elements that have a potential for use in your script; interesting characters, fascinating situations, major and minor conflicts; you have to recognize themes that will involve the audience, possibilities for sub-plots, potential action scenes, and incidents that reveal passions at their most extreme.

What you find become your raw materials. Then the juggling and arranging process starts. Slowly you try to work out the interaction of your characters, story development, evolution of the conflict, and the appropriate structure to carry the weight of the movie. Get the relationship of these elements correctly balanced and you are more than halfway home.

Story, conflict, characters, structure . . . it doesn't matter in what order you place them. The important thing is that these are the elements that give direction to your script, drive it forward, and give it the possibility of coming to a successful conclusion. These elements provide the framework and backbone for everything you do and you must get them right. So your first job is to review your research, and see how the material you've gathered relates to the above four subjects.

At this point you may be wishing you'd stuck to fiction. Damn it, you may be saying, I wanted to be a writer and instead I've become a fisherman. Instead of happily dreaming up characters, I'm casting my net into the sea of life, drawing up a mixed catch, throwing three-quarters of what I've caught away, and then I have to sort and weigh and box what's left. Who needs it? You do! Because you may not know it yet, but there are treasures in that deep you've never considered even in your wildest dreams.

Story

In this and the following three sections, we're going to examine the basic dramatic elements a little more closely, and see how they work in helping us construct a good script. To make things a little more interesting, I've occasionally chosen fiction films as illustrations when I think they provide very clear examples of the problem under discussion.

What's the first problem? . . . finding a good story, and in Chapter Four we already discussed many of its essential elements and the basis of its appeal. We take an interesting character, and usually present him with a goal or a mission. We present him with a series of problems on the way, and the manner in which he overcomes the problems, or succumbs to them, gives us the body of the story.

We call the action or unfolding of the story the plot. Some films, like *JFK*, will have elaborate plots, densely packed with surprises, twists, and reversals. Other stories, like *Citizen Cohn*, may have simpler plots and depend more on our interest in complex characters.

Your first task is to decide *what kind* of a story you are dealing with. Your research has shown you a story with many possibilities that could go in all directions. Now you must find its main premise, its strongest underlying element. You must find and commit yourself to one basic idea that propels the story forward.

Most stories resolve themselves into one of three types:

1: Goal oriented
2: Issue oriented
3: Journey transformation

Goal Oriented

Two good examples of goal-oriented stories are *The Treasure of the Sierra Madre* and *The African Queen*, both directed by John Huston. In the first story, the goal is to find a fortune in gold. In the second, the goal is the blowing up of a German ship in the First World War. Both are relatively simple stories, full of marvelous characters and replete with action and plot twists.

Most of today's feature films are goal oriented. In *The Fugitive*, it is Harrison Ford's need and quest to find his wife's murderer that drives the film forward. In *Under Siege*, Steven Seagal's goal is to frustrate the hijackers and return the boat to the authority of the American navy.

This goal-oriented story line also pervades many docudramas. In *Willing to Kill*, the goal of Wanda Holloway is to make her daughter the leading school cheerleader. As that general goal gets more and more frustrated, her goal narrows into the killing of the mother of her daughter's rival. In *Death of a Princess*, the goal of the journalist Paul is to discover the true story behind the killing of the young Saudi Arabian girl. In *Barbarians at the Gate*, the goal of the hero, Ross Johnson, is to take over one of the largest companies in the U.S.

Issue Oriented

A large number of stories take their inspiration from issues of public or general concern. The film sets up the issue, and the unfolding of the plot shows you how the issue was solved, or affects people's lives.

In *Gentleman's Agreement*, journalist Gregory Peck poses as a Jew in order to write a series of articles about the Jew in modern American society. The action threatens his future marriage and his relationship with his friends. As is clear, the center of the film is a general inquiry into the nature of prejudice and anti-Semitism.

Issue-oriented films are particularly attractive for docudrama, and public problems and concerns have provided the basis for some of the best films in the genre, such as *And the Band Played On* and *Skokie*. Ernest Kinoy's script of *Skokie* dealt with a threatened neo-Nazi march on a suburb of Chicago that stirred up immense public controversy. Here the issues in conflict were freedom of speech and the wounded sensitivities of a large group of the public.

Across the Atlantic, Granada TV's 1989 *Who Bombed Birmingham?* dealt with the imprisonment of six men falsely accused of blowing up a Birmingham public house. Here the film actually helped to bring about the release of the men. In Canada, the NFB film *Democracy on Trial* stirred up controversy by highlighting the trials of a crusading abortion doctor, and helped produce a climate for liberalizing Canada's abortion laws. In 1965, Peter Watkins decided to deal with the issue of nuclear warfare, public indifference, and the devastating results of an atomic attack. As we mentioned earlier, his resulting film, *The War Game*, became the most widely discussed BBC production of the year.

Journey Transformation

Many films find their main interest in character transformation as their heroes journey through life. This is the key element that underpins *Coal Miner's Daughter* and *Malcolm X*. The story then resolves itself into a depiction of the character at the beginning of the script, and the influences, events, and people who bring about the transformation.

We are also interested to see what the character does once he has gone through the transformation, or while he is in the process of change. It is this process of transformation that provides the key interest in Peckinpah's *Straw Dogs*. In the film, Dustin Hoffman plays a mild American mathematician living in a small English village. He is at first presented as a cautious, mild man who cannot act even when his wife is raped. Later on he gives a mentally retarded man refuge in his house when the latter is being hunted by a local gang.

When the house is subsequently attacked, Hoffman goes wild and in a number of brutal sequences succeeds in killing or maiming most of the gang. This possibility of transformation from weakness to strength is hinted at throughout the picture. When it happens in the final sequences, the effect is devastating.

Now, looking at stories in terms of goals, issues, or journeys is obviously extremely simplistic. On the one hand, many of the elements can often be found in the same story, and on the other, such a listing can in no way cover the multiplicity of story elements. Nevertheless, simple or complex, the essence of the matter is that you must very quickly find the underlying premise of your story. It may be one of the above. It may be something else, but you've got to find it. Once you've found it, you can begin to think about the direction of your story, and all the incidents and events and twists that are going to make it exciting and dramatic.

It helps if you make yourself a simple list of some of these essential points. Ask yourself, "What is the issue that underlies my film? What are the goals of my main character? If he or she changes, how does he or she change?" What you have on your list may never appear openly in your film, but your answers are going to be the subtext that drives your film, or the pillar of fire that lights your way.

Conflict

Without conflict there is no drama. Conflict means confrontation, and is the key element of your film. Without it you are lost. Without it you have no story, or no story that will interest an audience.

Conflict is that element which stands between you and your goal. It's the barrier, the opposition, the hurdle that prevents you realizing your aspirations. It's frustration. It's denial of your needs, your dreams, your hopes.

Sometimes the conflict is external: John Wayne against the Mexican troops in *The Alamo*, or David Koresh and his followers against the FBI in *Ambush in Waco*. Sometimes it's internal, as in *Oppenheimer*, where the physicist struggles with his doubts about unleashing nuclear warfare. Sometimes it's cosmic: the Children of Israel versus God in *Moses the Lawgiver*.

Conflict requires an opponent. It may be nature itself, as in *Nanook*, *Scott of the Antarctic*, or *Alive*. More often it may be a simple villain. It may be the other suitor of the woman you love. It may be the forces of society. It may be big business. And the opponent or opposing force comes in many forms, not always evil. In *Diana: Her True Story*, Diana's opponents are not just the royal family, but tradition and societal norms. In *Baby M*, the battle is over custody of a child, with both sides having a certain moral justification.

Occasionally, the opponent is time itself. In Pabst's classic *Kammaradschaft*, French and German miners battle to free their trapped comrades before they suffocate. It was this same battle against time which underpinned the race to rescue baby Jessica in *Everybody's Baby*, and in *Lorenzo's Oil* the parents' battle is also against time, as they seek a cure for their son's illness.

The element of conflict is also never considered alone. Once you start thinking about conflict, you also have to consider its relationship to *needs, goals,* and *action,* and their revolving interplay within the script.

Your hero *needs* to sing. His goal is to become the best singer in America. His parents reject the idea. Here already are two opposing forces at work. *Action* is needed to resolve the conflict and satisfy his needs. Your hero leaves home. He rises in the music world, and then wants a particular job. Someone opposes him. Once more, conflict. Action is now needed to overcome this drawback as well. He bypasses the opponent, goes for a secret audition, and wins the job. Such is the basic scenario for a dozen films, ranging from *The Jolson Story* to *Sinatra*.

What one sees on further analysis is that there is often one long-term goal, and then a series of intermediate minor goals . . . getting the job, winning the girl, getting into television, etc. Barriers are set before each goal, requiring a response or action from the hero. And so the film proceeds through challenge and response to the final reel. Conflict is the key, and it is your character's response to the conflict, challenges, or barriers before his goal that gives you the substance of your film.

In the same way that you made a list of your underlying story issues, it is also worth listing your conflict points, both major and minor. You can set this down in various ways. I find the simplest way is to list things as follows:

Conflict or dilemma	*Action taken*	*Consequences*
(1) Jolson wants to sing. Parents oppose.	Leaves home.	Break with parents but enters professional world.
(2) Sinatra wants more opportunity. Tommy Dorsey opposes.	Leaves Dorsey.	Breaks friendship but enters big-time music world.
(3) Diana furious with Prince Charles. Can't get his love and attention.	Throws herself down the stairs.	a: Charles furious b: Royal family becomes more antagonistic. c: Marriage worsens.

Besides noting the action taken, you must also note the consequences. These can be minute or immense, and often they are totally unexpected. Sinatra's act in leaving Tommy Dorsey's band *does* improve his career, but Princess Diana's act of throwing herself down the stairs, contrary to expectations, *worsens* her relationship with Prince Charles.

Your film is going to be full of conflicts, full of major and minor barriers which confront the hero at each stage of his or her plans. As each barrier is crossed, we are suddenly going to see another barrier ahead. What *you* have to do when you are preparing your script is select the best or most interesting of the conflicts from the real-life situation, and gradually work them into your script in the most effective logical and emotional way.

Conflict comes in many forms, some of which I've discussed above, and it's worth looking at a few of them more closely.

Hero-Villain

This is the standard conflict in most action films. Characters are simplistically presented, with clearly clashing goals. The villain wants to find the money dropped from the plane. Stallone will do everything to frustrate him. The conflict between the two is worked out in a series of hair-raising sequences until the villain plunges to his death. So much for the basic conflict in *Cliffhanger*. In *The Raid on Entebbe*, the hijackers holding the hostages are the bad guys, and the Israeli soldiers who try to effect a rescue are the heroes.

Inner Conflict

Here the elements begin to get more interesting and more subtle. Often the hero or heroine is faced with a moral dilemma. The path of action and resolution is far from clear and the audience becomes fascinated following the hero's decisions and indecision.

In *Citizen Cohn*, Roy Cohn's father begs him to give up helping Senator McCarthy and support the cause of liberalism. The conflict here is between the father's path of decency and the allure of fame and self-aggrandizement. To his father's fury, Cohn chooses the latter.

In *Fatal Memories*, Eileen Franklin-Lipsker discovers that her father is a murderer. Her morality impels her to inform the police. Her sense of family ties and obligations impels her to keep quiet. This conflict between the two impulses then forms the basis of the whole first act of the TV drama.

Though *The Firm* eventually turns into an action drama, its first third is really about the moral conflict being suffered by Tom Cruise. He has discovered that his boss is crooked, but he has a young wife from a rich background, and if he keeps quiet he will soon be earning millions.

That straight moral dilemma is then complicated by another twist. Cruise indulges in a one-night stand, and is threatened with exposure to his wife if he pursues the problems of his firm. Again there is conflict. Silence will buy a quiet home life, but is it worth his peace of mind, and can he live with that guilt in the future?

Relational Conflicts

These types of conflicts form the basis of most screen romances and love stories. The usual goals of the couple are romance, sex, love, and possibly marriage. But the clash of personalities, and the different minor needs, goals, and aspirations of the couple make for a series of conflicts that bar the way to happiness.

Excellent examples of this kind of conflict can be seen in all the films about the British royal family, from *Fergie and Andy: Behind the Palace Doors* to *Charles and Diana: Unhappily Ever After*. If one prefers an American perspective on relational conflict, then there are the numerous films on the Kennedy family, including *A Woman Named Jackie*.

The problems arising from moral and relational conflict are also very clearly seen in *Indecent Proposal*. The film is about the dilemmas created for a young couple when Robert Redford offers to buy Demi Moore's services for a night from her husband. The immediate conflict is whether to say yes or no to the offer. But that is just the fuse that lights many other conflicts in their relationship.

Societal Conflict

This conflict usually pits one man or woman, or a group, against a larger group or organization. The opponents can be family, the tribe, big business, bureaucracy, the government, even the country. For once, the issues at stake are usually not money but status, tradition, justice, corruption, and progress. Two film examples which show this conflict very clearly are *Friendly Fire* and *Afterburn*. Both films were very highly rated, and tell similar stories of families battling the government to expose the truth about their son's or husband's death while serving in the military. This kind of conflict appears very often in TV reality-based dramas, and seems to have become particularly popular in the early nineties.

A third example, *Diana: Her True Story*, appears on the surface to be a Cinderella story gone sour, or a story about falling in and out of love. In reality, it is a study of a major societal conflict, with a young girl totally opposing tradition as embodied by the most powerful family in the land. Ironically, *Edward and Mrs. Simpson* shows the other side of the coin, with its story of King Edward VIII and his forced abdication of the English throne because of his love for a divorced woman.

Lorenzo's Oil is also about societal conflict. Superficially, it appears to be mainly concerned with the search for a cure for a terrible disease. Look more closely and one sees that there is a deep conflict underlying the film, between the accepted practices of medicine and the risky path of experiment.

A chapter back I suggested that the Rushdie story would make a great movie. Again we can see why: because the story so clearly embodies the struggle of one man against society, in this case Salman Rushdie versus the mullahs and their edicts.

The Complications of Conflict

While we appreciate that conflict is usually needed in a good script, problems can arise in putting theory into practice. One mistake is to present too many conflicts. So many hurdles are placed in front of the hero that we lose interest. We know (at least in fiction) that he's going to prevail in the end, so after a while we cease caring when he faces another villain. This was almost the problem of Harrison Ford in *The Fugitive*. As it happens, the film was saved by the intricacy of the plot twists and some excellent directing . . . but it was a narrow escape.

There's also another lesson here. *The Fugitive* was actually based on an old TV series that went on for years. Like *The Perils of Pauline*, each episode ended with the hero at risk, only for him to escape or be saved in the next installment. But that was weekly TV, where I think we tend to tolerate, and maybe even need, a much greater number of conflicts, crises, battles, and confrontations than we do in film.

The conflict also needs to be made clear and as far as possible personified in interesting characters. It's all very well to argue that the conflict in *Nanook* is man versus nature but it gets more interesting when the villain is personified. We like and need films where the villain can be seen, identified, and more than likely destroyed.

A good example can be seen in the film *Jaws*. What after all is *Jaws*, if not man against nature? This time nature comes not in the form of howling winds and pack ice, but in the form of ravenous jaws and razor-sharp teeth. *Jurassic Park* was also a man-against-nature film, and I think Spielberg is still counting the dollars.

I mentioned before that the conflict in *Lorenzo's Oil* was clearly medical tradition versus experiment. However, to leave it as such would not have been sufficient for the film. The conflict is therefore quite correctly brought down to earth by presenting it as a struggle between Lorenzo's parents and the doctors and doubting heads of the parents' support group.

Your script is also at risk if you present unequal protagonists and antagonists. When one of your main characters is always stronger, brighter, and swifter than the other, then much of your conflict goes down the drain. That's why the Superman story was neglected for years as film material. It just wasn't interesting until the development of special effects placed the focus elsewhere, off the man and onto the gimmicks.

Sometimes you may need to change the nature of conflicts and confrontations within your film. What starts out as a societal conflict may change into a relational conflict. There's no harm in that, but just be aware of what you are doing.

Structure

The finest piece of advice ever given to scriptwriters is to be found on page 460 of William Goldman's book *Adventures in the Screen Trade*. Goldman, a gifted writer of over fifteen major scripts, including *Butch Cassidy*, says it all in three words: "Screenplays are structure."

As he puts it, "Nifty dialogue helps one hell of a lot. It's nice if you can bring your characters to life. You can have terrific characters spouting just swell talk to each other but if the structure is unsound, forget it."

For an architect, the structure is the shell of the building, including the foundations. For a scriptwriter, structure is framework, form, and modeling. By structure we mean a sound shaping of the story. It is the solid underpinning that will carry the story in the most interesting way from page one of the script to the end.

Structure is about order, and how to arrange your real-life story in the best possible way. It tells you where to place your sequences, your events, and your major and minor conflicts, so that the film becomes as powerful as it can possibly be. Structure is about finding a beginning, a middle, and an end. Jean Luc Godard is supposed to have said, "A film should have a beginning, middle, and an end, though not necessarily in that order." Most writers would disagree and maintain that those elements in that order are perfectly fine.

In film we call this the *three-act-structure*, or the three-act design. Most drama is based on that concept and it's been around for hundreds of years. The three-act structure doesn't cover everything, but it's a very useful starting point for a writer. In this system, each act serves a different function.

Act One

Act One sets up the premise. It can last twenty to thirty minutes in a two-hour screenplay and has to grab, or hook, the viewer. If you can't do that, then your film is dead before it's gotten off the ground.

Act One lets you know who the main characters are and the problems they face. It usually tells you something about the background of the hero, introduces his or her main antagonist, and hints or tells you directly about the main conflict of the story. It's like the catapult mechanism that shoots the plane off the carrier. It sets up the action, and gives the story direction and a strong push to get it going. Act One ends when you have set up very clearly the predicament facing your hero. Act Two then comes in to provide the complications.

In *Cliffhanger*, Act One stretches from the girl's climbing tragedy through to the hijacking of the banknotes. By that time we know who Stallone is, what he does, where he lives, and whom he loves. We also know about his personal sense of responsibility for the accident. At the same time we have met the villains, been introduced to the hijack story, and seen the loot tumble down the Alps. In *Dead Ahead: The Exxon Valdez Disaster*, Act One starts off by showing us the beauty of the Alaskan scenery, introduces us to the crew and voyage of the Exxon Valdez, and concludes with the crash of the ship against the ice and the escape of millions of barrels of oil.

In *The Fugitive*, the first act lasts through Harrison Ford's escape from the police van to his disappearance down the waterfall. We've discovered that Ford is a doctor, that his wife has been mysteriously killed, and that he has been sentenced to death for her murder. We've also seen him escape from custody and flee into the forest with his pursuers after him.

Act Two

Act Two contains the mass of your story. This is the section where complications set in and multiply. Here the hero gets deeper and deeper into his predicament. Often his goal seems harder and harder to achieve. The obstacles keep increasing. There seems to be no way out.

In *The Fugitive*, the second act shows us Ford trying to hunt down the killer, while at the same time he has to evade the police. Every few seconds a new obstacle is placed in his way. Every few minutes he has to come up with a new trick to escape Tommy Lee Jones. The twists and turns of the plot now keep happening at a fantastic pace.

The same situation can be seen in *Tootsie*. As the second act progresses, Dustin Hoffman (1) succeeds in becoming the nation's top woman TV star; (2) falls in love with Jessica Lange but can't reveal his love; and is himself pursued by (3) a male TV actor and (4) Jessica Lange's father.

Act Two is always about compounding the situation, putting on the pressure, and providing more complications and barriers.

In *Chariots of Fire*, we wait expectantly for Act Two to lead us into the Olympics and show us our heroes racing, but that is too simple. Instead, Eric Liddell refuses to run on a Sunday and all hell breaks loose. In *Moonstruck*, not only does Nicolas Cage fall more deeply in love with his brother's fiancee, but Cher's father is shown to be having an affair. In *Willing to Kill*, the story of the Texas cheerleading mother, Act Two deals with the focusing of Wanda Holloway's hatred on Verna Heath and the setting into motion of the death contract.

Operation Yonatan, the Israeli feature film about the rescue raid on Entebbe, also gives us a good example of the workings of a classic second act. The first act has ended with the hijack of an Air France airplane to Entebbe, with over 100 passengers on board. It has left us with a question: what next, surrender or rescue?

Act Two resolves that question, but only after agonizing dilemmas are portrayed on the screen. We see the hostages being questioned by the hijackers. We watch the debates of the Israeli cabinet. We watch Israeli shock troops in training. Then the word is given: "We're going for a rescue," even though the target is over 1000 miles away. And the second act ends with the massive Hercules planes heading off into the moonlit night.

In fiction films, the second act often complicates matters by offering a major revelation about one of the characters which changes his or her relationship with the others. This occurs in *Casablanca* when Ingrid Bergman tells Bogart she is married to Lazlo. It occurs in *The Firm* when Tom Cruise tells his wife he has been unfaithful. The revelation is a useful dramatic device, and it is worth checking whether the possibility for its use arises in your own real-life material.

Act Three

Act Three brings all the loose strands together. It resolves all the problems and provides the resolution. If Act Two lasted fifty or sixty minutes, Act Three is likely to last twenty or thirty. Act Three tells us what happened to the main characters, how they solved their conflicts, and how they overcame their barriers.

In *Chariots of Fire*, Act Three tells us that Liddell did not run on a Sunday, but competing on another day, unexpectedly won the gold medal in the 400 meters. Act Three of *Tootsie* centers around a bravura improvisational speech of Tootsie to her (his?) coactors, in which every single problem of the TV drama is neatly wrapped up. This still leaves the problem of the love story, but that is finessed in the last minutes of the film when Hoffman tries to justify his actions to Jessica Lange.

In the final section of *Moonstruck*, Cher's fiancee returns from Rome. The tension mounts as the family realizes he will have to be told that his brother has fallen in love with Cher. Then suddenly the problem is solved. The fiancee's mother is still alive and thriving, and therefore he cannot marry. If he cannot marry Cher, then the brother can. Fade out to embraces and the sounds of "Amore." In *Operation Yonatan*, the rescue is sensationally successful, except for the death of the Israeli commander, and the hostages return to Israel to be greeted by a riotous welcome.

Further Considerations

The Seven-Act TV Structure

Television drama differs from motion picture films in two important aspects that affect you very much as a writer. First, whereas the feature film can be any length, from say an hour and a half to two hours, a U.S. prime-time docudrama on network TV is usually written in two-hour segments. This really means about one hundred minutes a show, after allowing for commercial breaks.

The second point, which is a consequence of those commercials, is that the drama is structured in *seven* acts instead of three, with four of them coming in the last hour. This allows a major commercial break to be inserted after the conclusion of each act. The first act is normally the longest, about 25 minutes, and parallels the first act in a feature film.

Obviously the writing is geared so that there is a climax plus a question mark at the end of each act so that the viewer will be hooked, and resume watching when the commercials are finished. Another point to note here is that you should aim for a high point at the end of the third act, or first hour, as viewers often change stations on the hour, and you want to keep them with you for the remainder of the film. What should also be clear from the above is that in a four-hour mini-series you have to allow for 14 acts, with a major climax at the end of the seventh act, or first evening.

This doesn't really affect our basic theory of the ideal three-act structure very much. It merely means that your three acts are subject to a measure of subdivision, with minor conflicts, problems, and challenges now serving as the cutoff point for the end of your four extra acts. This is seen very clearly if one looks at the structure of *Diana: Her True Story*, which was a four-hour mini-series spread over two evenings.

DIANA: HER TRUE STORY. *PART ONE.*

Act One: Introduces the main characters and ends with Prince Philip stressing that it is time Charles got married.

Act Two: The romance starts with Diana, and the act ends with the Queen wondering whether Diana will be up to the task of marrying Charles, with all that it implies.

Act Three: The romance deepens. The act ends with Charles proposing marriage. (This is the high point at the end of the first hour.)

Act Four: This act shows the ensuing complications in Diana's life, and hints that there are likely to be major difficulties with Charles.

Act Five: The wedding hangs in the balance, but finally takes place.

Act Six: Major difficulties emerge between Charles and Diana. The act ends with him telling her she isn't his Princess, to which she replies, "Neither are you my Prince."

Act Seven: The difficulties increase, there are strong hints that Charles has a mistress, and the act ends with Diana throwing herself down the stairs.

The division is fairly straightforward, and even a superficial glance shows that what we are looking at is merely our old friend, the three-act structure, slightly chopped up into more convenient portions for commercial breaks. If the author had wanted to write in the classic structure, then it's easy to see that Act One would have concluded with the offer of marriage, Act Two with the wedding, and Act Three with the accident on the stairs.

Tidiness

Sometimes the three-act film structure or seven-act TV structure seems too neat, too tidy, too artificial. Life isn't set up in such a simplistic way. All this is true, but one has to remember that the structure is not a rigid framework. You play with it in the way that best suits you. It is a starting point when you are unsure of your techniques and capabilities, and it's a tremendous help even when you are experienced.

But these ideas on structure are not gospel. They are not a set of rules written in stone. The three-act structure, is merely a guide that seems to have worked from D. W. Griffith and Anita Loos to William Goldman, Lawrence Kasdan, and Joe Eszterhas.

Pace and Acceleration

Structure gives you the basics, the order of your scenes, and the development of your plot, but for film to work the scenes have to be paced. There has to be an acceleration of the drama. The viewer has to be drawn in more and more deeply. The rhythm has to quicken. One has to become more and more involved, and concerned with what is at stake. In slang, you have to up the ante.

Most of these things we'll deal with later, as we work through treatments and adaptations, but start thinking about them now. Without them, your neat structure will remain lifeless. Add these elements and your script will live and breathe.

Action Points

Most scripts depend on two or three major incidents or happenings to spin the plot in a different direction at a crucial moment of the script. Syd Field, in his book on scriptwriting, calls these plot points. Other people refer to them as the turning points. I prefer to call them action points. These action or turning points serve many purposes:

They propel the story into the next act.
They refocus the drama.

They raise the stakes.

They necessitate major action by the hero.

They demand major decisions and major actions.

Sometimes the points serve all of the above uses, but their main function is to move the drama from Act One to Act Two, or from Act Two to the conclusion.

In *Moonstruck*, the crucial action point occurs when Nicolas Cage takes Cher to bed. After that nothing will be the same. In *Barbarians at the Gate*, the first turning point comes when Ross Johnson, the CEO of RJR Nabisco, decides to put the company up for sale. In *The Fugitive*, the key moment is when Harrison Ford makes the decision to hunt for the real murderer. Nothing would have happened in *Diana* had not Charles proposed. In *Willing to Kill*, the vital moment occurs when Wanda Holloway decides to kill her rival. After that decision, the way down will become blacker and blacker.

The main function of the action point between Act Two and Act Three is to set up the climax and resolution, and you can see this very clearly when you analyze most popular screenplays.

In Peckinpah's classic *The Wild Bunch*, the plot point for Act Three comes soon after Angel, one of the Wild Bunch, is held prisoner by the Mexican bandit chief. The crucial decision for Holden and his friends is whether to ignore the action or go and release Angel. Once Holden says, "Ok, let's go," the die is cast for the brutal and horrific last shootout that ends the film.

Before you start your script, you are going to be asking yourself various questions. Two of the most important are going to be

Is my structure clear?

Are my turning points correctly positioned to act in the strongest way?

If you can say yes to both, you are in a good position to proceed.

The Sequence

Each of your acts is going to be made up of various sequences. These are units of the film, connected by place, idea, or action.

In *Cliffhanger*, the first sequence deals with the failed rescue. This is quickly followed by various sequences showing bullion being readied for transport, Stallone being rejected on his return home, the failed hijack, the loss of the money, and the calling out of the rescue team.

Taken together, these sequences make up the first act.

They all have their various crises and confrontations. Will the girl be saved? Will the hijacking be successful? Will Stallone and his girl get together? All the points are clear, and throughout the film the drama is expressed through action rather than dialogue.

The transition from Act One to Act Two is also clearly shown when Stallone is captured, then escapes. From then on, the issue is plain. It's Stallone against the villains, with death of one or the other being the only thing that will settle the conflict.

Within the overriding arch and premise of the film, one is constantly searching for interesting sequences that will hold the audience all along the way. Sometimes they are sequences of tension, such as the life and death struggle at the start of *Cliffhanger*. Sometimes they are sequences that prove the excellence of the hero, such as the race around the college yard in *Chariots of Fire*. Sometimes they are sequences of awakening love, such as those between Holly Hunter and Harvey Keitel in *The Piano*.

Your aim, however, is not just to make the sequences funny, tense, comic, or dramatic in themselves. They have to do more. They must show us something fundamental and important about our protagonists, and they must advance the story. In other words, each sequence must have a clear *function* that you should be able to plot. All this can be seen very clearly if one looks at the first few sequences of *Barbarians at the Gate*.

Sequence	*Function*
1: Ross and wife in limousine going to company party.	Give atmosphere of sex and luxury. Introduce Ross.
2: Party at Nabisco headquarters.	Show luxury style of company execs., and introduce secondary characters. Life is fine as TV shows cancer smoke trial fails.
3: Ross and other execs. talk between private planes.	Reveals *problem*. Stock price low. Reveals new cigarette is planned.
4: Tennis club. Fancy occasion.	Shows that shareholders are worried. Raises the question of a management buyout as an answer to the company's problems.

Here one can see, even from the few sequences, that the plot is evolving very fast. As soon as we are finished with the introduction to the main characters and story background, we get into the problem (seq. 3). Immediately afterwards we are offered a possible solution (seq. 4), which will lead to complications and battles. However, besides driving the plot forward, each sequence also emphasizes money, glitz, and luxury, which are the baubles tantalizing and bewitching every character in the drama.

When you come to write your own films, you'll find that it helps you a great deal to do exactly what I've done above. List your possible sequences, and also describe their functions in the plot. Also ask yourself, when you've inserted something for a purely technical reason, say to move the plot along, whether it is also really interesting. This process doesn't take long but reveals immediately whether there is a point and purpose to the sequence, or whether it's just put in as padding.

Character

A script is not often about an idea or a place. It's about a person, whom we usually like, who gets involved in a crisis or complex situation. Sometimes the crisis is of his or her own doing. Sometimes it's a crisis precipitated by someone else which gradually involves the hero. The hero takes action and the plot gradually thickens until the last act resolves everything.

So who are our heroes? What are they like, and what do we need them to do?

Larger than Life

In many films we require them to be larger than life. We want them to be able to do things we only dream about. We want to live vicariously through their courage and their actions.

Fiction scriptwriters are aware of our needs, and to satisfy us they give us Rambo, James Bond, and the actions of Schwarzenegger. When writers of docudrama want to do the same thing, they turn to history and give us Lawrence of Arabia, Malcolm X, Patton, Eisenhower, and the British heroes of *Zulu*.

Like Us but More Amusing

When we tire of the great heroes, we search for characters we can identify with easily. We want them to be like us so that we can empathize with their plight and their struggles, and yet their lives should be a little more amusing, a little bit more fascinating. If Quentin Crisp, the homosexual hero of *The Naked Civil Servant*, was just another gay man there would have been no story. It is his outrageousness and flamboyance that makes him interesting as a dramatic character. It is that same larger-than-life quality that attracts us to Ross Johnson in *Barbarians at the Gate*.

When you work in docudrama, the real-life characters you've found in your research will often lack the dramatic qualities you need for a strong film character. They may be nice people but a bit bland, who perchance have been caught up in a strange situation. Your task then is to add something in your writing which will sharpen our interest in them as screen heroes. This can be seen in HBO's version of the Wanda Holloway case, where Wanda herself is portrayed not just as a vindictive would-be murderess, but also as a complex, sharp, brittle, funny, and even occasionally philosophical woman. This raises a question of how far we can distort reality, and that's all discussed further in Chapter Twelve.

Fascinating Villains

There is one rule which every scriptwriter knows. If you have to choose between telling the story of a saint or a sinner, take the sinner. The story of Mother Teresa may uplift you, but if you want a good screenplay, you make a film about Tammy Faye and the Reverend Jim Bakker.

This rule is particularly applicable to television and docudrama. In most years, it's the movie with the best villain or the best sinner that tops the ratings. In 1991 it was *A Woman Scorned: The Betty Broderick Story*, in 1992 any of the Amy Fisher portrayals, and in 1993 the story of Wanda Holloway. *Citizen Cohn* told the story of an utterly detestable character, yet he was so compelling one couldn't move away from the TV set.

But we don't just want villains as protagonists. We want them, in fact must have them, as suitable opponents and antagonists for our heroes. Steven Seagal presents the guy we can root for in *Under Siege*, but his portrayal takes on an extra power when he is opposed by such a wonderful villain as Tommy Lee Jones. *The Raid on Entebbe* gave us simple heroes, but in many ways we were much more fascinated by the terrorists, particularly the German woman, who was very well written as a character.

The Character Dimensions

To be interesting, your characters must have dimensions. They must have aspirations and goals, needs and demands, virtues and defects, and on the whole they must be real and believable. Above all, they must have a certain magnetism or charisma that makes us interested in their plight. To a certain extent this is provided by good casting, but the basic quality must be there in the way the characters are written. We must be able to empathize with them, and we must be concerned about them. If we are not drawn to them, if the characters leave us cold, there is no drama.

Motivation

We are going to follow your hero for an hour or so and watch him or her get in and out of various scrapes. He's going to act and he's going to react, and we must know why. We must understand the basis for his actions. We must understand what motivates him. Is it greed? Is it power? Is it revenge? Is it money? Is it sex?

When the motives of all your characters are clear, the film will proceed very easily, but forget motivation and your script will begin to leak like a sieve. This was one of the faults of ABC's *Willing to Kill*.

The real-life TV movie traces Wanda Holloway's obsession in getting her daughter onto the school cheerleading team. The obsession is so strong that she is even willing to go and take out a murder contract on the mother of her daughter's rival. This is quite fascinating in its own way, until we begin to ask, "Why?" Why would a woman go to such ridiculous extremes merely to get her daughter onto the school cheerleading team? It's a critical question and the film never quite answers it.

The same question, "Why bother?" also occurs to us in *The Fugitive*. Even after Harrison Ford plunges down a mighty waterfall, pursuer Tommy Lee Jones insists, against all evidence, that Ford is not dead and the hunt must continue. Well, we know it must go on—otherwise there would be no film—but it might have been interesting to give Tommy Lee Jones a more powerful motive than merely that the law must out. The murdered girl could have been his sister. Ford could have been his best friend, whom he had to pursue in case he was thought soft. There could have been a hundred different motivations for Jones' actions, but not one is offered.

The Elements Combined

What I've presented up to now is a survey of the key elements in your script, from story through character. I've tried to get you to think about their use in a logical way and to see how each element relates to the others. But I realize there is a danger of making everything too schematic, and filmmaking isn't done that way. There is no such thing as writing by numbers. However, analyzing the key elements allows you to clear your head before getting down to the real work. The process helps you organize your thoughts, and suggests areas that you ought to consider before you commit yourself to the script.

7

□ □ □
□ □ □
□ □ □

Shaping the Film

After considering the elements of story, conflict, and character, there are still a few questions you have to answer before tackling the script. Your concern is how to shape the film into a logical and emotional whole. Here you are concerned with problems of approach, framework, attack, and rhythm. You are taking another look at structure and form but from a slightly different angle.

Approach

Writers tell stories in different ways. Some simply go from A to Z. Others tell the story in flashbacks. Others invent the outsider who views the events from a distance. Whatever the method used, the writer has to consider and define his or her basic framework and approach to the story before he or she writes a word.

The challenge is to tell the story in the most interesting manner. The majority of TV movies use a simple linear and chronological approach. This is the oldest form of storytelling and the most frequently used, because it satisfies our natural curiosity to see what happens next.

If we are introduced to the gifted kid who sings all day, we want to know what happens to him as an adult. We want to see the nun in the cloister, then follow her progress when she gives up her vows and returns to the secular world. We know Stalin ruled half the world, so let's see how he got there after an insignificant beginning. And let's have a look at Gandhi's work as a humble lawyer before he galvanized India with his national marches.

Chronology gives us a chance to observe process and growth. It helps us understand how incidents in a career, home tragedies, and professional obstacles shape and form our main characters. Seeing where they come from, and what they had to battle against, we appreciate their final triumphs even more.

The simple linear approach is also the attack most used in the films dependent on crisis, conflict, and resolution. In *Everybody's Baby: The Rescue of Jessica McClure*, we simply follow the crisis and the rescue. In the Entebbe films, we see the hijack and follow through all the complications to the rescue.

The chronological approach is simple, effective, and usually gives us a good story with a defined beginning, middle, and end. But there are many variations, and some of them can be quite effective.

Parallel Stories

A fairly common approach to narrative form is to tell two stories at the same time. They are usually about the same person, but one story takes place *now*, and one story is set in the *past*. However, as the current story proceeds, our understanding of the actions, motivation, and character of our "hero" keeps changing as more and more information is revealed from the past. In most cases, the *present* story proceeds in a chronological fashion, but the *past* story may move in all directions.

This approach is seen very clearly in Bergman's *Wild Strawberries* and in *Breaker Morant*. It can also be seen in the Merchant-Ivory film *The Remains of the Day*, which was based on the book by Kazuo Ishiguro.

At the start of the film we see Stevens, an old-fashioned butler, setting out to drive to the west of England. We watch with interest as various things happen to him along the way, but our main attention is focused on the past and how Stevens behaved in the "great days" of the thirties. This interaction of past and present keeps deepening our understanding of Stevens, setting us up for the moving final episode of the film.

This "then and now" approach also dominates the structure of Michael Eaton's docudrama *The Enemy Within*. *Enemy* tells the story of Michael Betteny, who worked for MI5, the British internal security agency, and offered his services to the Russians. In the end Betteny was caught and sentenced to 25 years in jail.

I asked Michael to give me the rationale for his structure.

Now remember, the public knew a lot about the story. If they knew anything they knew that there was an MI5 officer who had passed over secrets. So I decided to enter from there. I decided the best way to do the film was to start the story at the moment of his decision to give information to the Soviets.

So, as it were, there was a *present* to the story, a *now* to the story, from the time he decided to give the secrets to the time he was caught. That made it into a kind of thriller structure. Finding out there is information being leaked, and tracking it down.

But at pertinent moments of this *now* there were flashbacks into the *then*, into the past. We would see Michael at the time of his recruitment into the service. We would see him serving as field officer in northern Ireland. We would chart his growing disillusionment, his inner anxiety and the turmoil that made him take this dramatic step. The *now* of the thriller story was also being set against the past. This helped shed light on the institution of MI5 and also on his motives for the betrayal.

Though the parallel story, the *then* and the *now*, is a good device, it also presents a number of problems. If handled badly, it may confuse the audience, lessen tension, and give away too many secrets. It has to be handled with finesse and subtlety.

After discussing *The Enemy Within* and the use of the parallel story, Eaton went on to tell me why he *rejected* the device in another TV movie of his, *Shoot to Kill*.

Shoot to Kill, which was done for Yorkshire TV, tells two intertwined stories. Their setting is Northern Ireland and the Protestant-Catholic conflict. The first story involves three incidents in 1982 when armed military units of the Royal Ulster Constabulary ambushed and fired on people who turned out to be unarmed. A number were killed and several turned out to have absolutely no connection with the paramilitary Republican groups.

The police produced a plausible cover story, which was broken when one policeman related what really happened. This caused a major scandal, because the police seemed to be inventing a set of stories to cover up a very different reality. End of story one . . . the *happening*.

Real-life story two began with the appointment of a man named John Stalker, the Assistant Chief Constable of Greater Manchester, to head an enquiry into the incidents. Michael Eaton takes the problem from there.

So it was a double story: a set of crimes, and an investigation. Now there was some discussion whether we could deal with the incidents themselves through flashbacks, so that the Stalker Enquiry and the audience learn what has happened at the same time.

The great argument against using this kind of structure was that if my audience knew anything it was that *Stalker was unsuccessful* . . . that he was taken off the enquiry before it was finished. So I knew as it were that there was *little suspense* to the story because everybody knew the downbeat ending.

In the end I decided it was easier to present things *chronologically*. I would show the incidents and then show the way the police construct a cover story.

The result is the audience knows what really happened, and also what the police *said* happened. So when the enquiry starts the audience knows *more* than the investigators. And to that extent one has created a situation of suspense, because as we see the first faltering steps of the enquiry to get at the truth the audience knows when they're going in the right direction and when they're going wrong.

Time Frames

Sometimes one wants to use time variations not just for telling parallel stories, but as a distinctive framing device for the film. The simplest examples can be seen in *Lawrence of Arabia* and *Chariots of Fire*. Both start off with the funeral of the hero, and then go back to tell you his story. In *Little Big Man*, we are introduced to Dustin Hoffman at the age of 110, who then proceeds to tell us about the great moments of his life.

This question of time frame was one I had to consider very seriously in a film I wrote about the British Sinai explorer Edward Palmer. The facts of Palmer's life are fascinating. He was a nineteenth-century Cambridge don, or university professor, and one of the greatest linguists of his day. With the support of the British Biblical Society he went to the Holy Land, then under the Turks, and spent years exploring the Sinai desert.

He returned to England to great acclaim, and wrote a classic book on the unknown Sinai. In the mid-1870s, he set off once more for the Holy Land to do further explorations, and also to spy for the British on the Turks. When he disappeared in the desert, a rescue party was sent after him under the leadership of a Captain Charles Warren. But Palmer was already dead, murdered by Bedouin, who were caught by Warren, tried, and hung.

My problem was to find the proper attack and entry into the story. On the surface there were two obvious approaches: (a) tell the story chronologically; (b) start with the trial and then relate the events that lead up to Palmer's death. Neither approach satisfied me.

The problem with the chronological approach was that we had a slow beginning—Palmer in Cambridge, Palmer the don—till we got to the more exciting part of the film, which was the first Sinai trip. This meant that in a TV movie about an unknown British explorer, people might well move to another channel before the story hit its stride.

Starting with the trial had the disadvantage of giving the whole game away. Assuming there was a mystery in Palmer's disappearance, and a mystery that would fascinate an audience, we would be wasting our best dramatic shocks too early in the game. There also wasn't the fascination of a great trial, as in *Breaker Morant*. Here there were no facts in dispute, and the trial was relatively short and unspectacular.

My ultimate solution, which I was pretty happy with, was to start the film with the British search party under Captain Warren going out to hunt for Palmer. This gives you a search, a goal, and a mystery right at the beginning. The audience wants to know who *is* this man you are looking for, and you retrace Palmer's story. Eventually *past* catches up with *present* as we discover the murder, and the mystery is solved.

The concept of the time-framing device is very simple, but often adds immensely to the story. In *Citizen Cohn*, the framing device is the hospital deathbed. Cohn is dying and we continually flash back from the hospital to major episodes in his life. At the end of every episode, characters appear from his past, like atom spy Ethel Rosenberg, to talk to him and comment on his actions.

Experiments with Form

Many filmmakers think there is a standard pattern for writing scripts. Nonsense! What should dominate your thinking about form and style is that there is no prescribed, hallowed way of doing fact-based dramas, or for that matter, any drama.

For starters, give your approach a bit of freedom. Remember, the only boundaries are those of your imagination. I know the form used in most films and TV movies is straightforward, realistic, and prosaic, but think for a moment. You could opt instead for fantasy, humor, farce, or parody if you believed that approach or style would make for a more interesting and successful script.

In *Citizen Kane*, writer Herman Mankiewicz and director Orson Welles have great fun playing around with form. They take Kane's story and then examine it and reexamine it from four or five different angles as the story is told, and retold, by different characters. The film uses black humor. It uses realism and expressionism, and it plays around with editing. It takes chances and it works.

This experiment in multi-faceted storytelling was used in *Rashomon* to great effect, and also surfaces in Antony Thomas's *Death of a Princess*. In Thomas's film, we are presented with a problem. A reporter knows a Saudi Arabian princess has been executed. But why? What happened? And who is this girl who brought such a drastic punishment on herself? The questions haunt the reporter, and to answer them he embarks on a journey of discovery. Eventually half a dozen characters all give a different version of the truth, exactly as in *Rashomon*.

One of the best examples of experiment in form is undoubtedly *The Singing Detective* series, written for the BBC by Dennis Potter. In *Detective*, Potter tells the story of a mystery writer who is hospitalized with a very painful skin disease. It doesn't seem like a great subject for a series, but some regard it as the best thing ever done on British TV.

What Potter does, first of all, is play around with past and present. So we see the writer in the hospital, and also flashbacks of him as a child. After that, Potter takes off into a fantasy dimension, giving us slices from the writer's novel. To complicate things further, Potter breaks out of realism and has his characters sing and dance to the pop music of the forties. It's an experiment which in lesser hands could well have bombed on takeoff. Piloted by Potter, the drama soars off into clouds of applause.

The Singing Detective was created for British TV and it might be that experiment is much more encouraged in England than in the States. It's also possible that Americans are more conservative as regards form, and it could also be that British producers are more open to oddball approaches. Whatever the reason, England definitely seems to take more chances than the States.

For example, it would be hard to imagine *The War Game* getting through an American producer's hands in its original form. Peter Watkins's controversial 1965 film envisioned a nuclear bomb being dropped on Kent, not too far from London. Although a drama, the film is shot in grainy documentary style and follows the fate of four or five people before and after the holocaust. What makes the form so challenging is that Watkins occasionally leaves the story and inserts interviews and comments from fictitious experts. In theory one would think these interruptions would ruin the drama; instead they enormously enhance it. By way of contrast, it is interesting to note that ABC's film *The Day After* follows a similar story of a nuclear holocaust, plays everything very straightforwardly, and in my opinion is much less successful as a film.

When one does see experiments in form in U.S. features, or on American TV, they are usually the work of people outside the main studio system, or people working for HBO. *The Thin Blue Line*, for example, was a marvelous independent production that combined elements of documentary with staged reenactments to investigate a murder. As a result of the film, the police instituted a new inquiry into the murder, while the original "convicted murderer" was released.

HBO's finest contribution to variations in form can be seen in *The Positively Amazing True Adventures of the Alleged Texas Cheerleading Murdering Mom*. The film, whose plot I mentioned earlier, is based on the true story of a Texas woman who allegedly took out a contract of murder on the mother of one of her daughter's friends. Here the film flits between the framing device of a TV documentary interview of Wanda (post-trial), and a rather humorous recounting of the original story. What makes the case especially interesting is that a straight version of the story was made by ABC, entitled *Willing to Kill*. Because the variations in the form and approach of the two films are so striking, I've analyzed them in detail for you in Appendix B.

Beginnings

You have your form, your characters, your incidents, and your conflicts, but how do you begin to tell your story? By paying attention to two points. The opening of the film has to do two things very fast. First, it has to catch, or "hook," the viewers' interest, and second, it has to define very quickly what the film is about and where it's going. These are good artistic rules and also good practical rules in a world where your films will primarily be seen on television and have to compete with many other programs for viewers.

The only real exception to these rules, at least in the television sphere, is when you are dealing with a very well-known, totally pre-sold subject. In the *Sinatra* TV mini-series the beginning was appallingly slow, but it didn't matter because we knew the payoff would come fairly soon.

The opening "hook" should play into the audience's curiosity. You present an intriguing situation and you say, "Watch me! You'll be fascinated to see where I'm going to take you." Let us imagine, say, a film that opens with a very serious middle-aged man dressing up as a woman. In another film, a rather prim and proper teenage girl is seen loading her revolver and then shooting at objects in her basement.

Immediately we are struck by the strange, even bizarre quality of these situations. We want to know who the man is and what he is doing. Is he an actor, a transvestite, a spy? And what about the girl? Is she merely practicing self-defense? Does she want to commit suicide? Is she the best revolver shot in the States? What is she going to do?

At this point the curiosity is piqued, the imagination stimulated. We want answers to our questions, so we decide to stay with the film for a while, but only so long as there is a payoff from the first few shots. They had better be leading somewhere interesting.

This provoking of your imagination and curiosity is seen very clearly in *Prick Up Your Ears*, a film about the life and death of the British playwright Joe Orton. The film opens with the discovery of a gory murder . . . Joe's. We soon discover he was famous, gay, and extremely unconventional. Scriptwriter Alan Bennett thus intrigues us with two questions. How did Orton live, and who killed him? Having successfully ensnared us, Bennett then leads us through a fine, often funny, and often desperately moving drama.

With theatrical films, you are theoretically in a slightly better position than with TV. People have paid good money to see the film. Some friend or a critic has probably recommended it, so the odds are the viewer is not suddenly going to get up and walk out. But even so, if your film is not working in the first ten minutes, you are in dire trouble. Even when your subject is highly popular, like Elvis, and the audience well disposed to see something about it, you are advised to get in there fast, grab your viewer, and hold him or her to the end.

Producers know this and the fast beginning is normally the one they urge on their writers. In the TV docudrama *The Tragedy of Flight 103: The Inside Story*, about the terrorist attack on a Pan Am jumbo jet, the first version of the script started very slowly. It was OK, but took a lot of time establishing minor Arab characters and security agents. By contrast, the shooting script allows the film to explode into action with a bomb immediately being placed on a Pan Am flight. Here there's no playing around. We are right into the heart of things from the start, and stay riveted to the screen to find out what happens next.

Bernard Maclaverty's film *Hostages*, about the hostage crisis in Lebanon, also catapults into action from the start. Here the film opens to a news montage illustrating the chaos and anarchy of Beirut in the early eighties. Bombs are exploding. Gunfire is heard, and a news voiceover says, "When the fighting reaches its fiercest, Beirut looks like hell on earth." Immediately after that we see the abduction of Terry Anderson and Tom Sutherland. You are, as they say, in with a bang!

Antony Thomas's *Death of a Princess* starts slightly slower, but what it lacks in speed it most certainly makes up for in fascination and in capturing your curiosity.

DEATH OF A PRINCESS: SCRIPT.   Antony Thomas.

SEQUENCE 1

A VAST CONSTRUCTION SITE.

EDDIES OF SAND WHIPPED BY THE DESERT WIND...

AN OPEN-AIR CAFE LASHED BY WIND...A FLAPPING TENT...

A DESERT FORT, SQUAT AND MENACING. A SINGLE GATE.

THE GATE SLIDES BACK. A CONVOY OF VEHICLES (CRUSHED BY THE LONG LENS) NOISELESSLY DIPS AND TURNS.

FLAT ROOFS. NARROW ALLEYS...IT IS THE TIME OF PRAYER.

THE SOUK EMPTIES FOR WORSHIP. A CACOPHONY OF PRAYER FROM A DOZEN MOSQUES.

THE CONVOY APPROACHES THE TOWN ALONG A DESERT ROAD.

THREE LIMOUSINES. TWO COVERED VANS.

A DETAIL. THREE VEILED WOMEN JUST PERCEPTIBLE THROUGH THE GLASS OF THE LEADING LIMOUSINE.

A NARROW ALLEY. A WATER CARRIER SPLASHES THE DUST.

HALF A DOZEN SAND-CAKED EUROPEAN WORKERS IN A TOYOTA ARE STOPPED AT A ROADBLOCK . . .

MOSQUE INTERIOR. CONGREGATION AT PRAYER.

THE CAR PARK. A PICKUP TRUCK DUMPS A PILE OF SAND.

IN A CHEAP HOTEL A EUROPEAN WORKER PULLS ON A CLEAN SHIRT.

CROWD COMES OUT OF MOSQUE...

CONVOY PASSES THROUGH ROADBLOCK.

CONSTRUCTION WORKER FIGHTS WAY THROUGH CROWD.

DETAILS IN THE CAR PARK. A BOY WITH A BICYCLE. TWO MEN CLIMB ON A WHEEL. ARMED MEN HARRY THE CROWD, FORCING THEM BACK. THE SAME CONSTRUCTION WORKER STRAINS FOR A BETTER VIEW.

THE VEHICLES OF THE CONVOY ARE IN POSITION IN THE CAR PARK AT THE CENTER OF RESTLESS SPECTATORS. AN OLD MAN WEARING A WHITE THOBE AND SCABBARD KISSES AND HUGS A DIGNITARY.

GLIMPSE VEILED WOMEN IN LIMOUSINE.

THE OLD MAN DRAWS HIS SWORD AND CUTS THE AIR.

VAN DOORS ARE UNLOCKED. TWO FIGURES STUMBLE OUT, A VEILED WOMAN IN BLACK AND A 22-YEAR-OLD MAN. TWO SOLDIERS LEAD THE WOMAN TO THE PILE OF SAND AND FORCE HER TO KNEEL.

6 MEN SIT ON THE SPOKES OF A GIANT WHEEL, MOTIONLESS.

THE CONSTRUCTION WORKER HURRIES AWAY FROM THE CROWD. FREEZE ON HIS FACE. SIX PISTOL SHOTS SLOWLY DIE AWAY.

MONTAGE OF HEADLINES AND PRESS PHOTOS. "GIRL SHOT FOR LOVE;" AND "THE BOY WHO WOOED HER EXECUTED BY THE SWORD."

It's a hypnotic beginning, the suspense building as we gradually realize what is going on: that we are going to witness an execution, a ceremonial death. At first the details are deliberately blurred ... the convoy seen in the distance, everything a little hazy. Then it becomes clear and we are horrified at the implications of the scene, and the indifference of the spectators.

The scene is actually repeated a little later in the body of the film, with more depth added. We see the worker surreptitiously taking photos. We see the execution of the boy in all its gory detail. And we see the convoy depart. It's a bloody but wonderful opening with only one problem. It's clearly the strongest and most fascinating scene in the film. And because it comes at the start, it creates a hard act to follow.

If the film is about some charismatic figure...a historical personality, a famous singer, a champion athlete...it helps to introduce these characters very early and hint at the conflicts surrounding them. It's also useful to surprise the audience and let the viewers know they are going to see sides of this well-known character they never even dreamed about.

This is very much the line taken by Paul Monash in his *Stalin* script for HBO. He needs to get us into the film, but also show us a facet of Stalin which will intrigue us. How does he do this? By showing us a brief scene at the Imperial Military Headquarters, where Stalin is being examined by a doctor before army induction.

The first lines of the doctor tell us that Stalin is 38, is called Joseph Vissarionovich, was born in Georgia, and was exiled to Siberia for revolutionary activities. So far so good. This is information that we need put over in a fairly quick, painless, and not too obvious way. But the Doctor's next remarks really surprise us.

> DOCTOR
> Conscript has the following deformities. Left arm two inches shorter than the right, possibly congenital defect...Second and third toes of left foot webbed and joined, skin pockmarked.
>
> OLD MAN
> The mark of the devil!
>
> OFFICER
> Rejected!

This really shocks us. That Stalin, who supervised the battles of Stalingrad, was rejected by the army. Well, who would have thought it? Interesting! This scene is immediately followed by one telling us that the Tsar has abdicated, and we are into the body of the film without any time being wasted.

The first remarks of the doctor, telling us where Stalin comes from, are short but relevant. They help us get over the problem of *backstory*. By backstory, we mean the necessity of giving the audience sufficient information about what has happened before the film started so that the events of the film make sense.

Backstory tends to be a problem, and there are ways of solving it subtly or crudely. Crude backstory might go as follows:

                    JOHN
          Ah, Richard. Aren't you the new
          boy from Australia? They told me
          you were very rich, your father
          was a banker, your mother had
          died, and that you're a tennis
          champion. Oh, and that the girls
          adore you.

A fractionally more subtle way of presenting the same information might be

RICHARD GETS OUT OF TAXI. HE GIVES THE DRIVER THIRTY
DOLLARS, THINKS, THEN ADDS ANOTHER TWENTY AS TIP. AS
HE CARRIES HIS CASE UPSTAIRS, THE MAIDS LOOK HIM UP
AND DOWN IN SEXY APPROVAL. IN HIS ROOM HE TAKES OFF
HIS JACKET AND WE SEE HIS BLACK ARMBAND. HE QUICKLY
ARRANGES TENNIS PHOTOS, AUSTRALIAN PENNANTS, AND A
FEW TROPHIES. HE FINALLY ARRANGES THE FAMILY PHOTOS.
PARENTS, BROTHERS AND SISTERS, AND THE HARDEST ONE,
THE SINGLE SHOT OF HIS MOTHER.

You *can* reveal backstory by dialogue, and it can be done well, but my own preference is to make it short, and reveal it by action. The same thing applies to character depiction.

Throughout your script, you will be telling us about your characters by their dialogue and by their actions and reactions. However, we need to know fairly quickly at the beginning of the film exactly who we are dealing with, so that we can get a fix on the characters. The very first scene in *Stalin* actually shows him shooting a rabbit and dragging it off, leaving a trail of blood. The message is clear, a bit obvious, but maybe necessary for TV . . . that Stalin is going to be soaked in blood all his life.

One of the most amusing scripts for establishing character fast is William Goldman's *Butch Cassidy and the Sundance Kid*. Do you remember the first scene? Butch enters a newly fortified bank and looks wistfully around. He watches the guard working and then says sadly, "What was the matter with the old bank? It was beautiful." To which the guard replies, "People kept robbing it." From which we gather that (a) Butch is probably a holdup man, and (b) he has a droll sense of humor.

The humor is also a vital element of the second scene, which introduces Sundance. A card game is going on and Macon, the saloon keeper, accuses Sundance of cheating. Sundance denies this, but says if he's invited to stay, he'll go quietly.

Macon refuses and seems intent on a shootout. Butch keeps begging Sundance to back down and tells him he's over the hill. Macon might be good. He might be very fast. He tells Macon the two of them will behave if he asks them to stay. But Macon gets bolder and bolder, till Butch says, "Can't help you, Sundance."

The word "Sundance" changes the direction of the scene. Macon realizes he's facing the finest gunman in the west. He backs down and abjectly asks Sundance to stay. It's a very funny reversal, but hasn't yet reached its climax. This happens when Macon says, "Kid, how good are you?" On this Butch jumps for safety as Sundance whips out his guns, shoots off Macon's gunbelt, and puts three bullets into it as it snakes across the room. Then Butch and Sundance leave, with Butch's parting words being, "Like I've been telling you . . . over the hill."

When writing is as good as Goldman's, it moves from art into ecstasy.

Rhythm and Pace

A good beginning takes you into a film with a bang, with a sense of expectation. The problem then is how to sustain interest through the next hour, through the second act. Most of the problem is solved if you have provided yourself with a solid structure, interesting incidents, and a fascinating plot. Even so, there will be pitfalls, and many of them have to do with *rhythm* and *pace*.

These are not just elements of films but problems that every writer—novelist, playwright, or feature filmmaker—has to worry about. How often have you heard someone say, "Well, the book runs out of steam halfway through," or, "It started dragging and becoming boring in the middle and then never seemed to come to an end"? This complaint of a slow, dragging film is unfortunately too often made about reality-based dramas, particularly those determined to give you every fact about a person, whether it is interesting or not.

What do we mean by good rhythm and pace? Quite simply that a film should have a logical and emotional flow, that its level of intensity should vary, that it should hold our interest all the time, and that it should build to a compelling climax. Unfortunately, it is easier to point out the problems than it is to offer all-embracing solutions. Here are just a few of the most common problems.

1: Sequences that go on too long
2: Lack of connection between sequences
3: Too many similar sequences following each other when we thirst for variety
4: Too many action scenes and too few reflective scenes
5: No sense of development or logical or emotional order to the sequences

Are there any hints about rhythm and pace? First, *get into the film fast*. Establish what you are going to do, then do it. Second, *build the film with variety between the scenes* and a gradual crescendo of climaxes. By crescendo I am talking about the *intensity* of your crises and problems. The confrontations and difficulties should probably be small at the beginning of the film but of major consequence at the end.

Where you may have to modify some of the above ideas is when you come to write TV dramas, and have to allow for the seven-act structure and the disruptive effect of the commercial breaks. Here your need for sequence variety stays the same, but your films are probably built up of a number of mini-crises, rather than evolving to one grand finale.

This can be easily be seen when you look at the 1992 Sinatra mini-series for CBS. Instead of one major drama, the series proceeds through a variety of challenges and confrontations, such as

1: The young Frank versus family
2: Frank's struggle for first jobs
3: Frank's battles with Tommy Dorsey
4: Frank's wife versus the women in his life
5: Frank's battles over Ava Gardner
6: Frank's battles with the studio

Each story is sufficiently interesting to sustain us for ten or fifteen minutes of screen time, until the commercials, and then we gratefully move on to the next incident. Here we are not looking for much more than a few good songs, and some compelling scenes from a widely lived life.

If there is any one point which needs stressing, it's the need for variety in the type and tempo of the scenes you are writing, and *Butch Cassidy* provides excellent instruction on the issue. *Butch Cassidy* was one of the most successful "buddy" movies ever made. A lot of the success was due to Goldman's superb sense of structure and his marvelous feeling for variety and tempo.

The film is full of sequences of action, pursuit, and gunslinging, but Goldman knows even these can get boring. So in between everything he inserts an idyllic scene of Paul Newman bicycling around with Sundance's girlfriend in between the trees, while the music plays "Raindrops Keep Falling on My Head." It's a light, funny scene that allows us to breathe and relax before we return to the chase. The love of bicycles, incidentally, is faithful to the original Butch Cassidy character.

Joe Cacaci's script for *Her Final Fury: Betty Broderick, the Last Chapter* is also very instructive in showing what can be done in playing with mood, action, and tempo. This 1992 film tells how ex-socialite Betty from La Jolla murders her ex-husband and his new wife, gives herself up to the police, and stands trial. Betty's first trial takes place around the middle of the film. There is a hung jury, which is a triumph for Betty. The scenes after that go as follows.

SC. 102: A REPORTER, NATALIE, TALKS TO BETTY'S FRIEND KAREN IN A CAFE.

SC. 103: KERRY, THE PROSECUTOR, IS SEEN AT THE DRY CLEANERS. SHE DECIDES TO PROSECUTE A SECOND TRIAL.

SC. 104: BETTY TALKS TO REPORTER NATALIE IN JAIL.

SC. 105: BETTY LIES ON JAIL BUNK, READING ARTICLES ABOUT HERSELF.

SC. 106: DA'S OFFICE. PROSECUTOR KERRY DECIDES NOT TO ACCEPT A DEFENSE DEAL WHERE MURDER CHARGES ARE DROPPED, AND BETTY ACCEPTS TWENTY YEARS IN PRISON.

The mood of these scenes is very sedate and very civilized. The tempo is relaxed, the physical action minimal. This all changes in Scene 107, when Betty is insulted and roughed up by another prisoner. But so far the action is minimal, and Scenes 108 and 109 are again quiet scenes. However, the violence only hinted at in Scene 107 breaks out in full fury in Scene 110.

110 INT. PRISON CORRIDOR - DAY

Deputy 2# unlocks the door to Betty's cell. She's on her bunk reading. Deputy 2# comes in....

> DEPUTY 2#
> Your little tantrum yesterday
> earned you two days in lockdown.
> Starting now. C'mon.

> BETTY
> Nobody told me.

> DEPUTY 2#
> We gave you verbal and written
> notice. Now get off your bunk
> and let's hustle it up.

> BETTY
> I'm not going anywhere.

The deputy grabs her. Betty violently pulls away.

                    BETTY (CONT'D)
          No, get your stinking hands off.

Deputy 1# comes in.

                    DEPUTY 1#
          Okay. We're going to do this the
          hard way.

Other DEPUTIES enter. They all try to restrain Betty and pull
her off her bunk.

                    BETTY
          Nah uh...get out of here....

                 ANOTHER DEPUTY
          I got her...

Betty resists. A SCUFFLE ensues, with the deputies CLIMBING
up on to the bunk and literally PRYING Betty's hands off the
post. Betty is KICKING and resisting vehemently.

                    BETTY
          No, you don't.

Eventually it takes FIVE deputies to pull her out, along with
one DEPUTY who is filming the entire encounter on video.
Betty is finally DRAGGED from the cell, and carried off up the
corridor. The other inmates laugh, yell, and catcall.

Scene 111 shows Betty's sons watching television as a series of photos flash
on the screen: their parents' wedding pictures; their house; their father. The final
pictures are of their dad and his wife Linda, murdered. Over it all the announcer
drones on.

                    ANNOUNCER
          ...as she struggles here with
          deputies at Las Colinas Women's
          detention Center. She had a story-
          book marriage...money...man-
          sions...beautiful family. Dan
          Broderick was a powerful lawyer,
          Betty Broderick was a superior
          mom and country club socialite.
          Then it went tragically wrong.
          Dan married his beautiful young
          assistant and Betty got a gun. Did

> she murder in cold blood? Did he
> drive her to it...? Watch "Amer-
> ica Reports," Friday at ten.

GRANT, the son, puts his head down on the table.

Scene 110 is extremely powerful, but a lot of that power is due to its placing. Scenes 102 to 109 were basically calm, and therefore the contrast with Scene 110 becomes very strong.

Scene 111 then acts as a final wrapup and closes off the act. Once more the scene is calm. Once more we can relax slightly, but the scene has an extra function. It *summarizes* everything. It brings everything together. It tells us where we have come from, and then asks, "Did she murder in cold blood? Did he drive her to it?" These are crucial questions that very neatly project us into the next act, where a second trial finds her guilty.

Rhythm and pace are, in many ways, the most difficult things for a beginning writer to handle well. One of the reasons is that they are such nebulous and insubstantial concepts. Yet they are two of the secrets of good scriptwriting.

One of the most effective methods to help you with the problem is to make a simple graph of your script. You then plot the rise and fall of the action and confrontations as points in a curve. You should arrive at a picture of mountains and valleys, with the mountains getting higher and higher as you proceed towards the climax. If your graph gives you a straight line, or a very gently modulating line, you are probably writing a bedtime story rather than a Rambo movie. If your graph is a roller coaster, then you may have written an action movie with no letups.

Another thing you can do is mark your action scenes in red, and quiet or contrasting scenes in blue or green. This will give you a quick visual picture of the contrast in moods in your film. When you've charted both the action and the moods, you should be able to spot very easily where the problems lie in the film.

You can work out endless variations on this idea of graphing the script. You can plot when characters come in, you can star the turning points, and so on. For myself, I'm a little bit wary of all this. If you are not careful, it can reduce scriptwriting to a very mechanical formula, whereby technical data is fed into the word processor and the script emerges. That's the way to hell. However, the graphing of climaxes and moods can be of some assistance in the beginning. If you have a problem, try it out and see if it helps.

Endings

We all know what should happen in the ideal ending. There should be a big climax and then maybe a short scene before fadeout, allowing us to breathe just a little bit easier. Everything should be clear and unambiguous. There must be no loose ends. All issues should be resolved, and our hero and heroine should go off triumphant. They said he couldn't do it, but he did it! They said she'd never get the boy, but she did!

These are endings we love. Harry marries Sally. Fugitive Harrison Ford tracks down the killer. Mountain climber Stallone kills the villain. Liddell and Abrahams win the Olympics. These are clean, affirmative endings, satisfying our need for "happy ever after."

We've shared the emotions of the characters in the film. Very often we've identified with them. We want them to win, and unless you give us that ending, we are going to go home dissatisfied.

Yes, you can give us a tragic ending, but do that and you risk losing your audience. In the Peter Viertel's novel *White Hunter, Black Heart* (based on John Huston's experiences in Africa), the young scriptwriter begs his director not to kill off his main characters. The words are from a novel, but could have come from any book on scriptwriting.

> I'll say it in Hollywood terms . . . you've gone through hell with these two
> people . . . You've improved their characters, made them see life with a
> humane, decent point of view, then you kill them. And you kill them bru-
> tally, uselessly. I don't think an audience can stand that.

The scriptwriter is correct. Films are our dreams, our escapes, and we want the dreams to come true, characters to triumph, love to be complete, and evil to be vanquished. Even when death of necessity rears its head, we want to believe that too can be vanquished. So Butch and Sundance don't die, but live immortally in freeze-frame, as do Thelma and Louise.

Well, all this theory is fine for the normal fiction film, but often *very difficult to put into practice in reality-based scripts*. Very many times *real life* has neither a conclusive ending, nor a happy ending. Which can make a scriptwriter's task complicated, to say the least.

Part of that problem is overcome by simple subject choice. The Entebbe hostages *are* rescued. The Beirut hostages return to their homes. Baby Jessica *does* live to cry another day, and the siege of Waco does have a clear end. Again, in all the current murder stories around Amy Fisher, Carolyn Warmus, Wanda Holloway, and Betty Broderick, their trials give us a convenient climax.

Yet what of the more complex stories, such as the story of Yuri Nosenko, or the Exxon Valdez, the Stalker enquiry, or Lockerbie? It can be extremely difficult to find endings to stories like these. Often there is no obvious strong climax, no clear cutoff point, and no resolution of issues. What can you do in these cases?

Very often, you look for a link that will connect the beginning and the end that is not that obvious from the story itself. This link can be a physical situation, an idea, or the words of a character. The point is that the link will clearly inspire thoughts of *before and after*, or *cause and effect*, or will sum up the film's message.

This was the solution favored by Michael Baker in rounding off *Exxon Valdez*.

The end was a huge problem all the way through. There was no end in the sense that the story just went on and on and on . . . I eventually decided there had to be a very early cutoff point, and that would probably be within days of the spill. Also, Iarossi had been called back after a week, and later on Dan Lawn was fired. So my main characters left the scene early.

That was the "cutoff". But there was also the question of shape. Once I knew the opening would be the beauty of the Sound, it was clear how the story would be enveloped. The pristine Sound at the beginning. The tarnished Sound at the end.

The speech of President Bush that went over the ending was also important. He says, "I am the environmental President," and originally I had put that at the beginning. But I think that gave the game away. Putting it at the end sort of involves everybody. [The film] isn't just the story of the Sound. It's about oil transportation, and that we are all responsible to some extent.

This is the way the end sequence appears in the script:

166. END SEQUENCE.

A dead and badly oiled bald eagle opens a montage of archive footage depicting heavily oiled beaches, stagnant oiled pools, oiled birds and mammals; the visual tally of the death and destruction wrought by the spill.

NARRATOR
(VOICE OVER)
The commercial fishing season
was closed down and the slick
went on to oil over 1000 miles of
Alaskan beaches. Upwards of over
400,000 birds and many hundreds
of mammals died in the spill,
making it one of the most lethal
on record.

After an interval, we hear the words of President Bush, addressing a White House luncheon in 1989.

BUSH
(VOICE OVER)
The Arctic National Wildlife Refuge

in Alaska contains huge reserves
of oil and it would be irresponsible to ignore those. We have to
transport oil. We are becoming
increasingly dependent on foreign
oil and that is not
acceptable...What you do is
express the genuine concern you
feel on the environment, and I do
feel a concern, but not take irresponsible action to guard against
an incident of this nature...

Where it is impossible to find this wrapup link, and there is no easy ending, you have to ask yourself, "What more would the viewer really like to know?" This usually amounts to

1: What were the immediate and long-term results of the main events of the film?
2: What happened to the characters whose lives we have been following?

Following the questions you give the answers. It may not be the greatest solution, but it is one which is relatively satisfying and ties up the loose ends.

Take the ending of Paul Monash's film on *Stalin*, for example. After passion and fury throughout the film, it all ends rather weakly. Instead of being assassinated, which would have given us a nice Julius Caesar scene, Stalin falls ill and dies quietly, surrounded by his ministers. To get over the letdown, Monash then gives us an "update."

THREE MONTHS AFTER STALIN'S DEATH LAVRENTI BERIA WAS
EXECUTED BY HIS FORMER ASSOCIATES.

THREE YEARS LATER NIKITA KHRUSHCHEV BEGAN TO REVEAL
THE NATURE AND EXTENT OF STALIN'S CRIMES, WHICH
CAUSED THE DEATH OF 40 MILLION SOVIET CITIZENS.

NINE YEARS LATER VASILY STALIN DIED OF ACUTE ALCO-
HOLISM.

SVETLANA ALLILUYEVA NOW LIVES IN ENGLAND.

This brief roundup of events was also the only solution left to Michael Eaton in ending his film on the Stalker enquiry into the killings in Northern Ireland. What had happened was that once Stalker got too close to the truth, the powers that be stepped in and closed his investigation. Stalker was suspended and his team disbanded. This was a terrible finish for Stalker. And for Eaton, not the greatest material for the conclusion of a detective film.

Eaton's signing off went as follows:

SC. 279 INT. THORBURN'S OFFICE. NIGHT

Thorburn, Stalker's assistant, sits alone in his office as night falls. He is shocked by the news on the front page of the paper.

A quiet knock, and Sergeant Eileen puts her head round the door . . .

                EILEEN
      Come on, sir. I think it's time
      you went home. There's no truth
      in any of this, is there, sir?

Thorburn looks up at her as if to say: how can she even ask?

She is reassured.

                EILEEN
      If they'd have wanted a white-
      wash . . . well, they've picked the
      wrong team, sir.

He stands up and takes his coat from a peg behind the door.

                EILEEN
        (ALMOST TO HERSELF)
      We were so close.

              THORBURN
         (IRONICALLY)
      Aye. Weren't we just?

He turns off the light and they leave the office.

                    FADE TO BLACK
                    END CREDITS
           CAPTION
      JOHN STALKER was reinstated as
      Assistant Chief Constable of the
      Greater Manchester Police after a

3-month enquiry could find no evidence of misconduct against him...BUT he resigned from the force a few months later.

JOHN THORBURN took an early retirement from the GMP.

THE SAMPSON ENQUIRY supported Stalker's recommendation that senior Special Branch Officers should be prosecuted for conspiracy to pervert the course of justice...BUT in 1988 the Attorney General announced that in the interests of national security, no such prosecutions should take place.

Endings are difficult, but you try as best as you can. And if you can't think of anything, you tell your producer to make a film on Hitler instead of Stalin. He and Eva commit suicide. Their bodies are burnt. The Allies advance. Their tanks are all over Berlin. The Reichstag is in flames. The sky is blood red. Now that's an ending a writer could really go to town on!

Additional Dramatic Devices

A lot of people write good beginnings and endings, but face difficulties in making the middle of the script really work. Act Two tends to be a long act, and unless you are careful, this can be the place where the script begins to sag. At that point, fiction writers occasionally use one or two dramatic stratagems to help speed things along.

The most commonly used device is the *reversal*. This is the place in the script when the hero's plans collapse, when the simple solution is seen to be out of the question, when unexpectedly the villain or antagonist gains the upper hand, when support disappears and one is left to face the enemy alone. The reversal causes the protagonist to assess the situation totally differently, and causes him to move in a new direction. In *Her Final Fury*, the reversal point for the prosecutor is when she loses the first action. She then has to decide whether to abandon the case or continue. She decides to go on, and the script moves forward with increasing vigor.

Reversals are very close to *surprises*, but whereas the former is usually negative, a surprise can be negative or positive. The surprise is when the hero suddenly wins a million dollars, when the most beautiful woman in town turns out to be his long-lost cousin, and when the dream holiday he arranged from a newspaper ad takes him to the biggest dump he's ever seen. Both reversals and surprises are species of action points that can help you when you are in difficulties.

Another device of considerable help is raising the ante, or increasing the stakes, for both your hero and your villain. This is the point in the film where you reveal that you are not talking of the loss of a few barrels of oil, and the ruin of a few beaches, but rather of the loss of ten million barrels and a major catastrophe. This is also the point when you realize that the water will submerge the trapped miner in hours rather than days.

Your task in docudrama is to see where your true-life story offers possibilities for the use of these stratagems. In many stories, like the Exxon Valdez case and the Baby Jessica situation, the opportunities for reversals or raising the ante are inherent in the original material. If so, think of using them. If they are not there, then be careful, because if the gimmicks seem too contrived or artificial, the audience will reject them out of hand.

Script Examples

Earlier in this chapter, we looked at some experiments in form. On this score it's worth looking at Thames TV's *Letters of a Bomber Pilot*. The script was written by David Hodgson and is another excellent docudrama from England.

Hodgson's elder brother Bob was a pilot in the Royal Air Force, and was shot down over Europe in March 1943. On his mother's death in 1978, David found a bunch of his brother's letters at the bottom of her wardrobe. All were written between 1940 and 1943 and describe the experiences of a young airman during the early years of the war. Written with humor and honesty, they described the training, the friends, the drinking, the crashes, and falling in love.

Using the letters as the basis of his script, Hodgson started tracing what happened to many of the people mentioned in the letters.

It's a brilliant film, but its method is simple. Narrated by Hodgson, the film is grounded in a personal point of view. The letters, which form the basis of the script, are sometimes illustrated by library footage and sometimes by acted scenes. Thus occasionally an incident or a mood suggested by a letter will be fleshed out in a short dramatized scene. What gives the film its poignancy is that a number of the people mentioned in the letters are traced down and interviewed by the author. So a friend appears in an on-screen interview, which then dissolves into a reconstructed scene with actors.

The techniques are simple but work very well, as can be seen below.

Visual	Audio
Stills of Hugh Feast	NARRATOR: Hugh Feast became one of Bob's closest friends. Like Bob, he
Stills of Bob, Alf and Hugh.	came from London and was just the same age. Just twenty.

Archive footage of WAAFS (Women's Auxiliary Air Force) Hugh shuts door and walks to the bathroom watched by his friends. Derek, Alf, Bob and Bob Wells.	In November they were posted to RAF Shawbury to learn advanced night flying. Most RAF stations employed WAAFS in ground jobs, and not surprisingly romances blossomed. Hughie Feast was the first to be bowled over. Something that amused his friends. BOB: Now what's Mr Feast getting dolled up for? ALF: He's meeting his WAAF. BOB: Again? BOB WELLS: This is the third time this week. It's serious stuff, isn't it? Let's lock his door.
Close-up of hands locking bathroom door. Medium shot of Hughie shaving. Bob peers at him from door. Lads run into dorm, followed by Bob.	BOB: (Voice over) Dear Joan, Hughie is going out with a girl from sick quarters. I believe he's taking her seriously.

What we see here is a fusion of three techniques: (a) voice over archive footage and stills, (b) a dramatized scene, and (c) a letter voiced over a dramatized scene.

As the film proceeds, various people are interviewed about their memories of Bob and how they met him. The interview with Bea Cauldrey demonstrates how such interviews are integrated into the film.

Visual	Audio
Still of Bea.	NARRATOR: At the beginning of September, Bob came on a 48-hour pass, and went to a local dance. There he met a girl called Bea Cauldrey.
Medium closeup of interview with Bea.	BEA: My friend Doris and I went to this dance held by the Home Guard. Not many people came to
Pan with dancing couple to see Bea (actress) talking. Bob and his brother and sister enter.	these dances because the hall wasn't terribly big. I remember sitting on the side and then I saw this very tall man coming through the door.

We also discussed endings in this chapter, and I suggested that trials tend to give a convenient climax. Even then they can be handled well, or ruined, according to the writing. The trial scene in *Her Final Fury: Betty Broderick, the Last Chapter* is particularly well done because the writer, Joe Cacaci, had the sense to save some of his best material for it . . . namely the murder itself. The murder is indicated to us at the beginning of the film, but never actually shown. We see Betty in the murder room holding a gun on the sleeping couple, but are actually looking at the house from *the outside* when we hear the shots.

At the trial, Betty's defense is that she never intended to murder her husband Dan, but only took the gun "to make him talk to me." By using *flashbacks* to the actual murders under the voices of Betty and the prosecutor arguing, Cacaci shows how the defense is impossible.

The flashbacks, so often badly used, work as a wonderful dramatic device, strengthening an already high-powered scene. The crisscross between courtroom and flashback takes us from Scene 121 through Scene 139. Below, Scenes 127 through 132 show how effective the flashback can be when used well.

Sc. 127. <u>FLASHBACK</u>. INT. BEDROOM. CLOSE ON BETTY as she watches

>   KERRY (Prosecutor)
>   VOICE OVER
> You brought the gun as a show
> of force to. . .

PULLBACK TO REVEAL Dan and Linda asleep as Betty stands over them.

>   BETTY
>   (V.O.)
> ...to talk...to make him talk to
> me...

>   KERRY
>   (V.O)
> ...to make him listen. And yet
> you didn't use the gun to say,
> "Hold it, buster. I want to talk to
> you."...You just shot.

>   BETTY
> I never had a chance.

>   KERRY
> What do you mean you never had
> a chance?

> BETTY
> Well, it all happened so fast.

Kerry moves to two mannequins which are marked with places that the bullets entered Dan and Linda's bodies.

> KERRY
> Obviously it didn't. It took five shots for you to shoot these people. It could not have happened just like that, as you have indicated.

> BETTY
> It did.

> KERRY
> It does not take that...

Kerry snaps her fingers, then indicates on the mannequin the place where Linda was shot.

> KERRY
> (CONT'D)
> ...to shoot Linda in the chest.

SC. 129. <u>FLASHBACK</u>. INT. DAN AND LINDA'S BEDROOM.

THE SOUND OF A GUN GOING OFF.

A bullet hits Linda.

SC. 130. INT. COURTROOM.

> KERRY (Cont'd)
> ...then shoot Dan in the back.

SC. 131. FLASHBACK. INT. DAN AND LINDA'S BEDROOM.

THE SOUND OF A GUN GOING OFF.

A bullet hits Dan.

SC. 132. INT. COURTROOM.

> KERRY (Cont'd)
> ...Then re-aim and shoot Linda in the back of her head.

The flashback works superbly here, but there is also another element which contributes to our enjoyment. At the start of the film, when we only *heard* the murder, there was probably an element of voyeurism in us that was left unsatisfied. By showing the murder in the last act, Cacaci probably satisfied all his viewers' wishes.

This kind of flashback is something you use with caution. In *Fatal Memories*, we are told about a young girl witnessing her father's murder of her nine-year-old friend. Again we have a trial, but this time there are no flashbacks, and rightly so. The murder is graphically described in the dialogue, but to have shown it would have been in absolutely bad taste and probably revolted most viewers.

So it's not simple . . . but it never is.

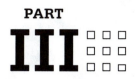

PART

III

From Treatment to Script

8

□ □ □
□ □ □
□ □ □

The Outline Treatment

You don't have to do a treatment, but it helps, especially in fact-based films. The treatment is your first attempt to outline the drama. Its purpose is to show

1: The way the story develops
2: Who your main characters are
3: The situations they get caught in
4: The actions they take and the results
5: The focus at the beginning and the end
6: The main confrontations and resolutions
7: The main action points
8: The sense of the overall dramatic buildup and pace

The treatment is normally written as a series of loosely sketched *sequences*. They can be numbered or not, according to your fancy, and they indicate a location and the action of the characters. Occasionally they may contain dialogue or scraps of dialogue. Otherwise, they may indicate what the characters are talking about.

The opening sequences of my treatment on the British explorer, Edward Palmer, go as follows:

1: Lawns of Cambridge University, 1865. Crowds of students and lecturers in 19th-century dress. Kings College dominates.
Voice of PALMER. Inside the college PALMER thanks audience for making his trip to the Holy Land possible.
2: A desert oasis. Three British army officers stretched out in the sun. Officer arrives on camel and dismounts. He indicates that there is no word from Palmer, and he may be lost.
3: Dining room in luxury house. Dinner is over. Men in evening suits. PALMER is standing, pointing to map. He indicates that this is Sinai, an unknown desert. Here the Children of Israel wandered for forty years. "Gentlemen, with my time and your money, I intend to bring God to the heathen and make the darkness visible."

4: British headquarters, Jerusalem 1878. Drinks on table. Officers looking at vague Sinai maps. Silence. An orderly enters and clears the cups. BAGLEY worries that the Turks may have Palmer and the gold will be lost. FRANKLIN suggests he's already dead, that Palmer was mad ever to go into the desert. BAGLEY, decisively: "There will be hell to pay if the story gets out. Palmer must be found."

As you can see, the treatment is written very much in a shorthand form. It's not a literary document. It's not for publication. It's merely a device to help you and the producer see where you are going and what you want to do.

What I mean by *sequence* was discussed briefly in the last chapter, but needs a little elaboration, even though the Palmer sketch shows clearly what I have in mind. It is a series of shots joined by some common elements—a series of ideas, a visual setting, a series of actions—that make one or more specific points.

The shots in a sequence may be unified by

1: *A central idea.* We see children playing football in a park; a woman throwing a javelin; a wrestling match. The sports motif is the unifying element, but the central idea you might want to make is that sport originates in war.
2: *Setting.* We see huge mountains. Immense seas. Whales spouting. Dolphins playing. Ships passing. Here the common element is the setting and the grandeur of nature.
3: *Action.* A student leaves her house, goes to the university, greets her friends, has coffee, enters class. All the shots up to the class entrance have a certain unity, whereas the classroom shot would probably begin a different sequence.
4: *Mood.* War has begun. Tanks are advancing. Women are weeping. A destroyed building is seen in silhouette. A boy wanders forlornly in a street. Here the binding element is not just the start of the war (idea) but also the gray, bleak mood of the people and the setting.

Obviously there are more categories and they overlap considerably. Ideas, actions, settings, central characters, mood—all these things may join together to unify a sequence. Put your sequences together and you have not just a treatment but a *step outline*—a document that will show exactly how your script is built and how every sequence relates to the development of action, mood, and tension. With this step outline as your base, you can see very quickly the *function* of each sequence, whether it is necessary, and whether it is in the right place.

To show you an example of this, I analyzed the TV docudrama *Her Final Fury: Betty Broderick, the Last Chapter*, mentioned previously, to give you the first sequences in shortened step outline. The script is made up of about 56 sequences, and below I've set out a few of them, together with their function in the script.

Sequence	Function
1: Murder	Introduces Betty and action
3: Betty phones parents	Shows her emotional state
4: Police at scene	Murder is known
5: Husband's brother phones police	Introduces Betty's first opponent
6: Betty tells kids	Introduces her family
8: Betty turns herself in	Law has taken over
9: Woman goes to work	Introduces woman DA, Betty's chief opponent
10: Betty in jail	Loneliness, depression
11: Brother arrives	Introduces funeral element
13: Visit in murder house	Atmosphere
16: Funeral of husband & wife	Sadness, loss. Husband's family
17: Betty denied bail	This and following sequence show
18: Betty demands new lawyer	the ugly sides of B's character

So far the sequences introduce the characters and give us two clear sides. On the one hand stands Betty, and on the other, her husband's family and the district attorney. As the sequences proceed, we gradually realize that the main battle is Betty versus the woman DA. We also have a number of action sequences which contrast with quiet emotional sequences, and as the film continues we will get more and more juxtapositions of fury and calm.

The step outline, or treatment, also gives us a good sense of where the *turning points* that I referred to earlier are placed. In *Final Fury*, the most obvious turning point is at the end of the first trial. The jury cannot reach a verdict and Betty is triumphant. The prosecutor refuses to accept defeat and by her actions sets the scene for a spectacular second trial.

Some writers swear blindly by the need for treatments. Some view them very skeptically, like Stephen Davis, whom I spoke to about the making of *Yuri Nosenko, KGB*.

I regard treatments as a bit of a nuisance. If you write a three-page treatment you'll be asked why didn't you write a thirty-page treatment. And if you do that, your producers will ask you why you didn't reduce it to three. If you write a detailed plot scenario you'll be asked if you could write an impressionistic, subjective, creative document. And that's the way it goes.

I regard treatments with absolute dread. I think they are designed to win a consensus of some sort, at which point the writer can go away and do the real writing.

Most producers do in fact demand a treatment, and one can see why. The point of the treatment is to help you find the body of the film and start writing the script. Besides helping you clear your own mind, the treatment helps the producer see exactly where you are going.

For many films with simple plotlines and clear action, the process of writing the treatment is relatively easy. This applies to Hollywood epics as much as to throwaway TV movies.

Patton is a fairly good example. Think what Coppola had to hand when he wrote the script; a famous general, who masterminded some of the U.S.'s greatest tank victories over the Germans; a controversial general, who had assaulted one of his own men; a loner, a maverick, and (so it's reputed) a lover of Marlene Dietrich. A treatment, whether by Coppola or anyone else, would probably go in a linear way, progress from minor to major triumphs, and show some of the human failings along the way. Here we had a life full of color and incident, and the writer's task was almost "select the best and head for home."

The Israelis' rescue of the hostages at Entebbe is another case where it seems in retrospect that writing a treatment must have presented few problems. Here we had the simplest of all action stories. A plane takes off with over 150 passengers and is hijacked. Rescue seems impossible. The hijackers preen themselves while diplomatic talks go on. Secret plans are made to solve the crisis. In the dead of night, and against all odds, four Hercules planes with Israeli troops fly over 2,000 miles and effect a spectacular rescue.

Again it's clear that the simplest way of doing the treatment would be to go in a linear way, from hijack to rescue. It is also obvious that the essential blocks would consist of (a) the hijacking; (b) the state of the hostages in Uganda and their treatment by the hijackers; (c) the discussions in Israel; and (d) the rescue.

As it turned out, three films were made on the Entebbe rescue and all of them followed the above sequence. Where the films varied was mostly in matters of emphasis and order of sequences.

The Problems of Docudrama

At first glance, writing the treatment for a docudrama seems fairly simple. You select your most interesting events and episodes and then order them in the most dramatic and compelling way. Unfortunately, the problem is far more complex. In many cases you know what attracted you to a story...the sheer newsworthiness of the blowing up of Yankee Stadium or the assassination of the Pope...but apart from that, all is jumbled and confused. You cannot see

1: What the *focus* of the story is
2: Who your main *characters* are
3: What the *conflicts* are

And underlying everything is your central problem, that your hands are tied. You can't just invent. You can't just neatly sort everything out in the way a fiction writer can because you are dealing with *true events*, and *real people*. Given all that, the writing of the first treatment becomes a little more problematic. There really has to be a very thorough clearing of the decks. How do you start?

My own method is to *list on a few sheets of paper*

1: The factual progression of the story, with all key dates and times included. (You should actually have done this during research.)
2: A few notes on structure and form, and possible approaches.
3: *All the elements* that have caught my eye in research; interesting incidents, fascinating characters, main problems, conflicts between people, and so on.

Obviously I will have been getting some idea of the story in the research. In the assassination of the Pope, I would have known from the beginning that I was doing a detective story, so my listing wouldn't have been random. My sheet of paper would probably have headings like "suspects," "motives," and "movements."

You can see below that this is very much the method used by Michael Baker when he started thinking about the scripting of his Exxon Valdez oil disaster movie.

I don't see how you could have done without a treatment on this film. I wasn't *required* to do one but in fact I did several. The first treatment was just looking at the story as a whole. It was a very long thing in which I just picked out salient sequences and scenes for a possible drama. What would be the entertaining scenes? What would be the revelatory? What were the details that were funny, or gripping, or made you laugh or cry? In other words, I was trying to find what was generally dramatic about this story without attempting to find the key that would take me from beginning to end.

The treatments that followed were largely a process of whittling down the length, and getting it into shape, and that's what I think a treatment is for, *to find the shape so you can start writing.*

Focusing the Story

After laying out your lists, you try to *focus* your story. This means knowing what your story is about and where you're going with it. In most character stories this is relatively easy, and you should be able to answer the question of story and focus in one or two sentences. For example:

1: *Mountains of the Moon*: This is about two men trying to find the sources of the Nile. Its focus is on rivalry in the quest for fame.

2: *The Jazz Singer:* This is about a young man climbing the ladder to
become the most popular singer in America. Its underlying conflict is tra-
ditional Jewish family values versus modernity and assimilation.

Before you start doing your treatment, you must also know very clearly what
the underlying conflict is about. Sometimes it's very clear, but often there is a hidden agenda in your script which nevertheless sustains the whole scenario. A very
good example here is *Her Final Fury: Betty Broderick, the Last Chapter.*

In *Broderick,* the body of the film is taken up with how Betty comes to trial
and the nature of the trial itself. What you sense after a while, however, is that
there are two conflicts, one apparent, one hidden. The surface one is between the
woman DA trying to get Betty convicted and Betty trying to defend herself with
a plea of justifiable homicide. The more subtle battle is between the DA and Betty
as champions of women's rights, when only one can hold the title.

Betty Broderick, Malcolm X, The Babe, and *Mandela* all are personality-cen-
tered films, where it was easy to find story and focus. Where the going gets rough
is in films dealing with *issues, disasters,* and *public events.* The story may have
captured the headlines but it can be murder trying to find what the *best* story is
for the TV or feature film. The only way out is to consider a number of possibilities, and then go for the most dramatic, interesting, and entertaining.

Let's look, for example, at the case of the Lockerbie air disaster. In 1988 a Pan
Am jumbo jet was blown up over Lockerbie, Scotland, with the loss of over 200
lives. The killers were thought to be Syrians or Libyans. As a result of Libya's
refusal to hand over suspects, sanctions were imposed on the country by the U.N.
Millions were sought in compensation by relatives of the victims.

Problem: what story would one pursue for television?

My writing students came up with various answers:

1: The lives of five victims before the tragedy
2: The assassins, the plot, and the getaway
3: The town of Lockerbie, before and after the disaster
4: The relatives versus Pan Am

The eventual film that was made on the bombing for HBO and Granada was
called *The Tragedy of Flight 103: The Inside Story* and, as mentioned, was
scripted by Michael Eaton. When I spoke to Michael, he told me that at first he
thought the film would be about the terrorist groups who made the bomb, and the
police operation against various Palestinian groups in Germany.

As the research came in, he and his executive producer realized there was a
second vital story, that of Pan Am and the increasing breakdown of its security
measures. The film could then be shaped as two stories, which eventually meet
in the explosion and conflagration.

As Michael put it:

It then became a story about two institutions. It was a story about an international airline corporation and about an international terrorist organization.

And the way I wanted to tell the story was to look at those organizations from the top to the bottom; from the boardroom to the people who sit by the X-ray machine and examine your tickets and luggage when you go to an airport for a flight; from the people who go around the world looking for sponsorship for acts of terror down to the soldiers who carry the bags with the bombs.

So what the film would be was a juxtaposition between the way these two organizations work. And the chill of the story is that in many ways they are not too dissimilar.

The problem of finding the story, or the right story, also confronted Michael Baker when he came to work on the Exxon Valdez oil spill story. Here I asked Michael whether the two sponsors of the film, HBO and the BBC, laid down an approach for him.

Not really. I think all they knew was that this was an incident that had made a big impact in the States and they somehow wanted to recreate the story. But they didn't know how . . . As I went on with the research it became more and more apparent that the story we were going to do was certainly not the environmental story because I'd watched twenty documentaries on that and there was no point in doing it again. That's another important thing about doing drama-doc. You should always go for an angle that couldn't be done any other way. Otherwise what is the point of doing this as drama?

Anyway, it soon became apparent to me that the real story we were looking at was *the political story* behind the disaster. The backsliding. The cockups. The Government trying to renege on its responsibilities. In other words, a fairly explosive story in journalistic terms, but also one that would be very dramatic if you could carry it off.

In the chapter on research I mentioned the Nosenko story, written by Stephen Davis. What attracted the BBC about the Nosenko story was that it was the only defector case that had got into the press in spite of the CIA trying to keep it quiet. Fine! You had a defector, but where was the real kernel of the story? This was one of the first questions I put to Davis.

After having done some research I knew very quickly what my basic line through the story would be. It was a confrontation between two men, defector and investigator, and a confrontation that would go on for years.

I further knew I had to explore an enormous paradox about the two men. About the way the man handling the case was in a sense professionally broken and ended up to a certain extent professionally stigmatized. Around that basic confrontation I had to explore all the details of Nosenko's defection, incarceration and hostile interrogation.

The story of the two men and their confrontation also raised the question of what I should do with their private lives. There is still a sense that you can't just give the audience the main story, but also have to give them the characters' background and private lives. That's why I gave the background of the case officer, which I know is marginal to the story but still needed to be there.

Shape and Form

Though you have many things on your mind when you start your treatment, the questions of shape and form may be the least of your worries. This is because the answers to both tend to crystallize in your mind through the whole process of research. By the time you come to do the hard work on the treatment, you will almost certainly have committed yourself to a straightforward linear approach, or much less frequently to a more fanciful and inventive approach.

The nature of the material will also have helped determine your approach to shape and form at a very early stage. Thus if you are doing what almost amounts to a hard news investigatory story, you will probably opt for the simple chronological unfolding of the story. I said "probably" because, of course, *The Thin Blue Line* shows how effective an imaginative use of form can be, even in a police story.

If you are doing a biography, then you may have started thinking of a few variations, such as the framing device in the present, while you tell a story in flashbacks, as in *Marilyn: The Untold Story*, or as in *Prick Up Your Ears*, about playwright Joe Orton. Thus while you may query and slightly change your approach to form as you work through the treatment, your initial choice of approach will most likely have been made much earlier.

Choosing the Characters

Drama demands conflict and heroes, strong characters whose actions push the story forward. In fiction, you can invent characters to suit your needs, from Rambo and Bond to Harry and Sally. In docudrama, you have to select your characters from real life, and sometimes your choices are extremely limited.

The commonest problem is that you know the story, yet the central characters evade you. Ideally, you want a "hero" who will carry the story in the direction of your choice. Yet very often that character just doesn't exist. Besides story, that was the second problem of the Lockerbie film for Michael Eaton:

We simply didn't have a central protagonist. There were several people who potentially arose to play that role but *as real life doesn't follow the rules of drama* they soon found themselves out of the picture.

There was a man called Fred Ford inside Pan Am who was put in charge of beefing up Pan Am's security. But you quickly realized this was a cosmetic exercise. In a fictional film he would be the perfect dramatic protagonist. He would be the man who would fight the bureaucracy, fight the institution, go out on a limb, sacrifice his home and career so that truth will out.

What happened in reality was the moment he started blowing the whistle on Pan Am's poor security he was given the boot. Fired! He would have been the perfect protagonist but was kicked out at the end of Act One. At that point I went back and looked at all the material very thoroughly. *And this is where the idea of a treatment is so useful.* I looked at the material and it seemed to me the only way we could tell the story was to center it around two institutions, Pan Am and the terrorists, because there wasn't one character who stayed the whole course of the drama.

The need to find the central character who could carry the story was also one of the key problems for Michael Baker in the Exxon Valdez film.

For a long time we were interested in a fisherman who we thought would be a focus of tension. There was also a guy called Kelly Weaverling, who almost single handed, launched a kind of wildlife rescue operation which ran into the most appalling bureaucratic obstructionism. So I began to wonder if maybe we could reduce our canvas and look at the film through a Kelly story. Or should we do the captain's story . . .?

And one by one these stories were jettisoned. Kelly's was too environmental. With the captain's story there wasn't a real thread all the way through. He got taken off the ship and then was out of the story till the trial.

When the search for the right "hero" still fails to turn up a plausible central character, he or she may have to be created out of the author's imagination. This was the ploy used by Ernest Kinoy when he wrote *Skokie*. In the film the central character, played by Danny Kaye, is a fictitious Holocaust survivor who objects violently to neo-Nazis parading through Skokie. The technique works well, and gives us a sympathetic main figure who represents in himself the thousands of objectors to the march. The problem, though, is that the use of this device can blur the boundaries between fact and fiction, and raise questions of credibility relating to the rest of the film. When you use it, do so with caution.

Skokie also raises the question of the relationship between character and conflict. Do you look for the conflict in docudrama and find the character to carry it, or vice versa? Again Michael Baker was very perceptive about this dilemma, which can be central for the writer.

> The *Exxon Valdez* story followed conflicts. Looking at the facts you saw that everybody had been in conflict. What I was looking for was the *right conflict*, one which wasn't black and white.
>
> I was very concerned that we show a story in which human beings were presented with a crisis and we could see what happened to them. And most of the time they screwed up. Almost the bottom line of the Exxon Valdez story was "give human beings a crisis and they'll screw it up."
>
> I think for me the film was not so much a search for conflicts, but because the story was such a sprawling one, a search for characters who could carry the audience through from beginning to end. But it had to be the *right* characters. The right spread of characters to give you enough of the whole story. You couldn't be playing around with a character who was really a side show to the main attraction.

The story of the Exxon Valdez is, finally, not about the crash, nor about environmental pollution as such, but about the appalling human failures to stop the spread of the oil in the first three days. The failures embrace Exxon, officials from the State of Alaska, environmental protection agencies, and the company responsible for the first limitation actions. No one comes off well.

In the end the story focuses on the actions of two men, Frank Iarossi from Exxon and Dan Lawn from the Alaska Department of Environmental Conservation. How did Baker see them?

> Not as heroes. I wanted them to be human beings you could sympathize with. People whom the audience would root for but were also fallible, faced with a crisis. Why the choice of Dan and Frank? First because they were on different sides and presented the axis on which the story could hang. In fact they never even met, which presented its own problems. Secondly it struck me that while they were people with different problems and agendas, they had a lot of affinities. They were both isolated in their own camp and both basically trying to do a good job.

Eaton, Davis, and Baker have all, in their different ways, summed up what you should be looking for in your characters when you come to do your treatment. For your own purposes it may be worth making a checklist of the essential points or questions, and then seeing which of your own characters scores highest. Your list will probably look something like this:

1: Can he act as axis for the story?
2: Is he with the story from beginning to end?

3: Is he sympathetic?

4: Is he at risk through the story developments?

5: Does he take action, or just observe events?

6: Does he change in any way, or do we get to know him in a more meaningful way as the story progresses?

7: Do we need another main character to show an alternative view?

Revising the Treatment

The treatment is an argument for your approach to the material. As I've said, it lets you and the producer see very clearly where you want to go and how you intend to get there. It shows how you intend to solve the problems of story, character, and structure. It shows you your entry into the drama, the growing complications, and the climax and resolution. And it shows you all this without your yet being committed to the script.

Most treatments are written out in the form I showed you with my Palmer story, but it doesn't necessarily have to be that way. Many writers jot their suggested sequences down on cards, pin them to a wall, and start playing around with the choice and the order. Both ways work, and it's up to you to choose the one which best suits your temperament. I tend to choose the first method, if only because it gets a little wearying to keep inviting the producer up to your apartment to see a wall outline.

Treatments are not static. You will often write three or four until you are satisfied with what you've done. The first treatment of the Lockerbie disaster centered on the story of the terrorists. Only in the second or third treatment did the emphasis of the story shift to Pan Am's security failures. *Death of a Princess* started out as a straight dramatization of the princess's story. After a few months that approach was discarded by Thomas in favor of a journalist's search for the truth *behind* the main story.

As you proceed from treatment to treatment, you keep playing around with scenes and characters, testing and retesting their necessity, their use, their correct placing. Your search is to find the correct *action* logic that will propel your story forward, the correct *incidents* and events that will give texture to the script, and the correct *emotions* and rhythm that will take you to the climax.

Sequences and characters will be continually in and out of your treatment. For example, I asked Michael Baker what scenes got dropped as he progressed with the Exxon Valdez film.

The fishermen were the main story element we juggled with for ages. And even at the end there were people who wanted more of them while I wanted less. There were also a lot of individual scenes that stayed in for a long time and then got dropped, like a meeting of the subcommittee of the Valdez

Council. And the sort of ironic reason we dropped it was that although it was real, it was incompatible with dramatic reality.

What happened was that many people were beginning to get concerned about tanker safety. They were saying that everyone was getting complacent and that inspections at the terminal were lax. And that the Coast Guard weren't doing their job properly. And someone said at this meeting, "Gentlemen. It's not a question of *if* we are going to have a major spill, but *when*." Then a few hours later the Valdez ran on the rocks.

Initially everybody thought, "Great! This happened on the same night." But if you think about it, had you kept the scene in we would totally have undermined what was to come. So it came out of the script.

If you are lucky, you and the producer will see eye to eye on how the film should go. You discuss your approach with the producer—your angle on the story, and your selected characters—and he or she says, "Good! Go ahead, and let's see what you come up with." Occasionally, though, it can be quite sticky, as Stephen Davis relates:

In *Nosenko* I recall that my problems were more with the producers than my internal problem, how to make the script work. There were battles over accessibility and audience understanding. I think western audiences are very sophisticated. They understand images and digest things quickly. Well, my American producers were firmly of another opinion. They wanted things to be slow, clear, and almost pedestrian lest the audience fail to understand what was happening.

There were battles over the complexity of the intelligence case, and the number of characters. And there was a demand to simplify the narrative line. For example, the film seems to show that Nosenko was taken immediately to a secure facility when in fact he was held for a long time in an ordinary house.

Docudrama Versus Fiction

Before plunging into the writing of your treatment, stop a moment and ask yourself what you are really trying to do. Are you clear about your objectives? What is your perspective? And it very much helps here to understand one of the crucial differences between writing fiction and writing fact-based dramas.

One of the key attractions of fiction films is that usually the viewer *doesn't know the end of the story*. He does not know who killed Joe Smith. He does not know whether Harry or Bob gets Evelyn. He does not know which candidate will become President. He waits for the denouement and then smiles in satisfaction when he finds out that Henry is the killer, or that Evelyn really loves Michael.

There is immense pleasure in the final discovery of plot solutions, and many films ads warn us not to give away the end. Because of this, everyone keeps silent about the identity of the girlfriend in *The Crying Game*. Again, you would be furious at a friend who told you who the murderer in *Psycho* was.

Reality-centered films usually lack this basic appeal. Unfortunately, *we already know the endings*. We know a jumbo jet was blown up over Lockerbie. We know that Diana leaves Charles. We know that the Exxon Valdez crashed, and that David Koresh died. So the films have to give us something else.

That usually amounts to an exploration of

1: Why something happened
2: How something happened
3: Character behavior

The first two elements satisfy our curiosity to get to the heart of things; to go inside closed doors and see how things operate, to investigate the secret working of organizations, governments, and bureaucracies; to gain access to the forbidden, to penetrate, to overhear, and to spy in silence.

An exploration of character allows us what we've always desired . . . to get inside someone else's head; to look at emotions and actions that are often alien to us; and to explore thoughts and passions that are very different from ours.

Obviously, these elements also appear in fiction films, but in docudrama they provide you with your basic approach to the script, as opposed to being peripheral considerations. It all seems simple, but you neglect this at your peril.

Overall View

Writing a treatment is about *persuasion*. It is an argument for *your* point of view on the story. It is also about *planning*, about how to shape your script in the best possible way. But it's also about *creativity*, and about giving the reader the experience of the story and the feel of the people in it.

One of the mistakes you can make with a treatment is to work too hard on it, and to be too methodical. You may know all about story rules, conflict, character choice, and focus, but there has to come a time when you let go. As author Dwight Swain put it in a very good book on scriptwriting:

> The less attention you pay to mechanics when you sit down to do your first treatment, the better. Write from the moment's impulse. Get down everything in the wildest rush of enthusiasm you can muster. Hunt for the aspects that intrigue you, excite you, turn you on.

In other words, absorb the rules, but then take chances, let go and jump in. Have fun. Later you can use all your rules as checks. They'll show you where your weak points are in structure or development, but the checks come after creativity, not before.

Examples

Throughout this chapter we've heard a great deal about the problems involved in writing the first treatments of *The Tragedy of Flight 103: The Inside Story, Yuri Nosenko, KGB*, and *Dead Ahead: The Exxon Valdez Disaster*. To finish off, it may help to see what their partial outlines really looked like, and then compare them to the eventual shooting scripts.

The Tragedy of Flight 103: The Inside Story

THE TRAGEDY OF FLIGHT 103: FIRST TREATMENT.
Writer, Michael Eaton.

1: Planes land at Frankfurt International Airport—a crowded interchange, one of the major crossroads of Europe. People from all over the world stand in line at the arrivals area. Among them MARLAN KHREESAT, a well-dressed businessman from the Middle East, waits at the customs checkpoint with his WIFE hovering behind him. The stone-faced teutonic CUSTOMS OFFICIAL is checking their Jordanian passports and in reply to his questioning Khreesat tells him they have just come from Amman and he is on a working holiday. The customs man says he has no visa to work in Germany and K. explains that he is on holiday to visit friends but that while he is here he intends to renew contacts with German firms which have supplied him in the past—he's an electrician. The line builds up with impatient people behind them but the official slowly keys his name into a computer and consults a list of passport numbers. Eventually he asks how long they intend to stay and is told two or three weeks. The custom official looks again through the passports, finally stamping them and waving them through.———

2: In the airport lounge a man sits waiting for them, reading a newspaper in Arabic: ABDEL GHADANFAR. He waves as they come through, using a form of address which indicates he is a devout Muslim, but no names are used. He takes one of their bags and leads them out to the car park.

As they drive into Frankfurt with passenger flights passing low over their heads, G. tells Khreesat that there have been some interesting developments. New contacts have been made which will aid God's work on earth. K. doesn't want to know. He has a specific task to perform, that's all. He wants to know when they will meet with their friend. K. is told that he is coming down from Neuss tomorrow, inshallah, he will return there with him. His wife will be taken care of—arrangements have been made for her to return next week. Her work is over, she's provided cover for the entry into Germany.——

3: In Neuss, HAFEZ KASSAN DALKOMONI comes out of the Morgenland store, which is run by his brother-in-law ABASSI, and meets with another PALESTINIAN outside. The man shows him a green Ford Taurus with Achen number plates. Dalkomoni looks it over, takes the keys from the man, gets inside and drives off. These actions are interrupted by a device (such as the image freezing into black and white photographs) to show that he is being watched or followed. Over this is the voice of a BFV OFFICER briefing an operational unit. He gives a list of aliases for the man and details of his occupation and age (mid-forties), address (16 Isenstrasse, Neuss), and period of residency in West Germany. He is clearly pleased with himself as he announces that the surveillance photographs have been circulated throughout the security community and Israeli intelligence (the Mossad) have supplied a positive identification. He is Dalkomon—the finance officer for the Popular Front for the Liberation of Palestine—General Command. Part of his background involves serving more than ten years in Israeli prisons.

The treatment looks straightforward, but a number of things are worth noting.

1: *Approach*. In this first draft, Eaton centers his story on the terrorist group who made the bomb. This approach will change as more is found out about Pan Am's security failures.
2: *Background and atmosphere*. These two things are very clearly sketched in. For example, we can almost see and hear the planes taking off and landing when the Arabs exit the airport.
3: *Details*. Although we are dealing with a brief outline, all necessary details are already laid down. A man is not just waiting in a Ford, he is waiting in a green Taurus. Again we are given an exact listing of the aliases of the suspect and his exact address. (Note the importance of accuracy in these investigative-type docudramas.)
4: *Action and development*. While the first sequence is very innocent, the second hints at a mystery. By the third sequence, and just a few minutes into the film, we see that something very fishy indeed is taking place, and begin to place everything in a terrorist framework.
5: *Treatment to script*. What is also important, and can be seen immediately, is how easily the treatment can be turned into a script.

In the end, the script started in a totally different way.

THE TRAGEDY OF FLIGHT 103: SCRIPT.

1: INT. LAVATORY STALL. EUROPEAN AIRPORT

THE LOCKS OF A RATHER BATTERED SUITCASE ARE SNAPPED
OPEN. THE SUITCASE IS OPENED TO REVEAL THE CONTENTS.
HANDS FUMBLE WITH A SMALL RADIO. A DIGITAL CLOCK IS
ATTACHED TO THE RADIO WITH RED TAPE AND THE RADIO IS
WRAPPED IN A PAIR OF PYJAMAS. THE SUITCASE IS CLOSED
AND A JFK LABEL IS ATTACHED TO THE HANDLE.

2: INT. GENTS LAVATORY. DAY

A WELL-DRESSED MAN OF MIDDLE EASTERN APPEARANCE
COMES OUT OF THE CUBICLE WITH A SUITCASE. HE WALKS TO
THE WASHBASIN, LOOKS IN THE MIRROR. TURNS ON THE COLD
TAP. HE IS YOSSI LANGOTSKY.

CUT TO:

3: INT. EUROPEAN AIRPORT CONCOURSE. DAY

LANGOTSKY WALKS ACROSS THE CONCOURSE CARRYING THE
SUITCASE. LANGOTSKY REACHES THE PAN AM CHECK-IN AREA
AND BREAKS INTO A RUN. HE MAKES FOR A CLOSED POSI-
TION WHERE A PORTER IS STANDING BEHIND THE DESK.

> LANGOTSKY
> Excuse me, could you get my case
> onto the New York flight?

> PORTER
> Baggage is closed now.

> LANGOTSKY
> Please, I have to be on that
> flight.

> PORTER
> They're already boarding.

> LANGOTSKY
> Well, I can't take it on as cabin
> luggage.

(THE PORTER SHRUGS; LANGOTSKY TAKES OUT A TEN-DOLLAR
BILL)

>   Listen, there must be some way
>   to help. I have a very important
>   engagement in New York.

HE PASSES THE TEN-DOLLAR BILL UNDER THE COUNTER TO
THE PORTER.

>   PORTER
>   I'll see what I can do.

>   LANGOTSKY
>   Thank you.

THE PORTER TAKES THE SUIT CASE. LANGOTSKY LAUGHS TO
HIMSELF AT THE EASE OF THE OPERATION AND WALKS OFF
FROM THE CHECK-IN DESK.

Subsequently, Langotsky watches the luggage being loaded on the plane and calls the Chairman of Pan Am. When he gets through, he informs the incredulous chairman that he's just put a bomb on the plane. As the scene proceeds, we realize that the bomb is a dummy, and that Langotsky is an Israeli agent employed to test Pan Am's security, which is obviously very bad. What astonishes us is that instead of applauding, Pan Am condemns the test as a stunt. And so we are into the film.

It's a fast opening and a very exciting one. It also tells us immediately what the film is about . . . not just the failure of Pan Am security, but also their refusal to take the subject seriously. The final script is very different from the treatment (partially due to ongoing research changing many perspectives, even as the script was being written) and it is quite fascinating to see how the two stories of Pan Am and the terrorists eventually weave together.

Yuri Nosenko, KGB

Whereas Eaton's treatment for *Tragedy of Flight 103* is very full and detailed, telling you exactly what you are seeing and where you are going, many other writers do a more shorthand version. Brevity plus clarity is the hallmark of Stephen Davis and both these points are easily marked in his study of the Nosenko case.

NOSENKO: TREATMENT.   Writer, Stephen Davis.

United States of America, late 1961. The film's first pretitle image is a closeup of President Kennedy making a speech in the open air. The subject—Cuban communism. The picture is treated to emphasize the image—the words are on the wind. Music establishes an atmosphere of menace——

Roslyn, Virginia. In a closed room a Russian is talking to two men, watched from behind one-way glass by James Angleton, head of CIA Counter Intelligence. Tall, academic, impenetrable, Angleton is almost a stylized version of a spymaster. The defector inside, KGB major Golitsyn, tells a remarkable story of widespread KGB penetration of western security services, masterminded by a newly strengthened Disinformation Directorate——

Langley, Virginia. In the newly completed CIA headquarters, Pete Bagley, a young case officer from the Soviet Russia Division, is taking leave of a deskbound friend prior to returning to the Berne station. That night, at a quiet restaurant outside the city, Angleton joins Bagley's informal supper party. He slips into his chair showing no sign of the bizarre interview he has been witnessing that afternoon, and his face betraying no flicker of the thoughts that must be on his mind——

We are in Geneva. An arms control session is in progress at the Palais des Nations when a member of the Soviet security escort makes covert contact with an American delegate in the men's room, and asks to be put in touch with American intelligence officers——

Pete Bagley answers a phone in his Berne office—a suite marked on the door "EXPORT IMPORT SERVICES INC." He covers the receiver and tells someone over his shoulder, "We have a walk in Geneva." He is on his way at once——

Although the main lines are the same, the beginning of Davis's actual script differs quite considerably from the first treatment. The film still opens with President Kennedy's speech, but the two sequences in Virginia are dropped (one of them appearing much later in the film).

Instead, we cut to Geneva. Pete Bagley has now become Steve Daley, and we hear his voice over shots of an East-West conference.

NOSENKO: SCRIPT.

DALEY:
(V.O.)
This is the story of a long and
complex espionage case. In real

life these things have no neat
conclusions and no happy endings.
This case, however, which over
eighteen years destroyed my
career and my peace of mind,
had at least a clear beginning.

3: INT. MAIN CHAMBER PALAIS DES NATIONS. DAY

THE CONFERENCE IS UNDER WAY.

> DALEY:
> (V.O.)
> Geneva '62. I was a young CIA
> officer stationed in Europe, with a
> bright future ahead of me.

(DALEY IS ALERT AND INTELLIGENT. HE PAYS APPARENT
ATTENTION TO THE PROCEEDINGS, WHICH ARE NOT EXCITING.
AFTER A MOMENT HE MAKES A DISCREET MOVE TO LEAVE
HIS SEAT AND EXIT THE CHAMBER.)

4: INT. CORRIDOR OUTSIDE CHAMBER

(DALEY CLIMBS A STAIRCASE TO THE WASHROOMS.
THE CAMERA SHOWS A TALL MAN ON AN UPPER LEVEL
WATCHING AS DALEY GOES DOWN THE CORRIDOR INTO THE
MEN'S ROOM.)

5: INT. MEN'S ROOM

(INSIDE THE ROOM DALEY IS WASHING HIS HANDS. SOMEONE
ENTERS. DALEY LOOKS UP AND IS SURPRISED TO SEE, IN THE
MIRROR, A STRANGER LOOKING STRAIGHT AT HIM. IT IS THE
TALL RUSSIAN.)

> NOSENKO:
> Mister Daley?

(DALEY TURNS OFF THE TAP AND LOOKS AT NOSENKO IN THE
MIRROR)

> NOSENKO:
> My name is Yuri Nosenko, Major
> Nosenko, KGB. Let us arrange a
> meeting. I have plenty of informa-
> tion for you, for which you will

>   want to pay me. Arrange me safe
>   house. Give me note tomorrow. In
>   case you think this is provoca-
>   tion, here is some I.D.

(HE REACHES IN HIS POCKET AND OFFERS DALEY A DOCU-
MENT, PASSPORT SIZED, MANILA PAPER)

>   You keep this for your superiors.
>   You have it from me as gesture
>   of good faith.

(DALEY, ASTONISHED AND CAREFUL, TAKES THE DOCUMENT)

>   I have names for you. I have
>   plenty. Arrange meeting place for
>   us. We must break now. You go
>   first.

(AFTER A SHORT PAUSE, DALEY STARTS TO MOVE. NOSENKO
HOLDS OUT HIS HAND. HE WANTS TO SHAKE HANDS. DALEY
SHAKES HANDS QUICKLY AND THEN MOVES TOWARDS THE
DOOR.)

Besides the name change, and the dropping of two sequences, there is one other important difference between the treatment and the script. In the former, Nosenko's initial contact is with one of the delegates to the conference. Only later does he meet Daley (Bagley). In the script, it is Daley himself who is accosted in the men's room.

The rationale for the change is easy. Putting Daley in the washroom speeds up the story and involves Daley from the very beginning rather than at a later stage. In this way he also becomes much more responsible for Nosenko's bona fides. He is the one who facilitates the crossover, and it therefore becomes more ironic when he begins to doubt Nosenko's credibility.

Another point that needs some attention is the way a scene which is only briefly sketched in the treatment is fleshed out in the script. Nosenko's covert approach is covered in three sparse lines in the treatment. Yet it's a crucial segment and rightly gets played up in the script.

The last thing worth mentioning is that the script gives us an overview from the start which is absent in the treatment. While the latter moves straight in on the action, the script uses Daley's voice to tell us that the case lasted 18 years and destroyed his career. Why was this addition necessary? Possibly to warn us from the start that the film will be very tortuous, and also to make us watch more closely to see how such a bright young man was destroyed.

Dead Ahead: The Exxon Valdez Disaster

Michael Baker's research for *Exxon Valdez* took months. Below I've set out two extracts from his second treatment, one from the start of the film, one slightly later. Both extracts go into tremendous detail, making the end scripting that much easier.

EXXON VALDEZ:TREATMENT.   Writer, Michael Baker.

1:THURSDAY, MARCH 23, 1989: 8:20 P.M.

Panoramic view of Port Valdez bay ringed by a wall of spectacular snowy mountains that loom spectacularly out of the darkness. Tiny pinpricks of light are moving on the bay road. A
taxi cab. The road runs for a time alongside a huge pipeline
that snakes across the foot of a steep escarpment. The cab
stops at the main gates of a brightly lit installation: the
Alyeska Marine Terminal. Three men get out and are checked
through a security gate. One of the men is bearded: Captain
JOSEPH HAZELWOOD...Rising away from the car (crane shot)
we have a view down the slope to the tanker berth loading
cargo. Its name is clearly visible on the bow: *EXXON VALDEZ*.
Panning off the tanker and across the water we pick out the
lights of Valdez on the other side of the bay.

Probably the most dramatic scene in the film is going to be the crash itself. Baker understands that the viewer will want to know in detail how it happened. He could have put this burdensome task off until the script stage. Instead, he lays everything out very fully in sequence 15 of the treatment. The final script follows the treatment in almost every detail, with very little expansion either in action or dialogue.

TREATMENT (CONTD).

14: THE EXXON VALDEZ PLOUGHS REMORSELESSLY THROUGH
THE DARKNESS.

15: On the bridge, the engine bell logger shows the vessel is
increasing speed up to 13 knots. Helmsman CLAAR is relieved
by KAGAN. Just before leaving CLAAR tells COUSINS (the only
officer present) that the steering is on automatic. COUSINS is
surprised and instructs that the gyro be disengaged.

(A.R.: From here on, the sequence on board continues uninterrupted up to its fateful climax, as follows.)

-The Fathometer trace records a depth of less than 100 fathoms.

-On the starboard bridge wing AB MAUREEN JONES is on the lookout. She sees a red light off the starboard bow flashing every five seconds. She enters the pilot house and warns COUSINS of this. He calmly acknowledges and continues to plot his fix on the navigation chart. Then he stares down at the radar scope looking for ice. AB JONES re-enters to report that the red light is now flashing every 4 seconds. COUSINS again calmly acknowledges, then orders KAGAN to steer right 10 degrees.

-After again checking the radar scope, COUSINS phones down to HAZELWOOD to report that he's started to turn back into the shipping lanes, adding, "I think there's a chance we may get into the edge of this ice." HAZELWOOD says, "Okay" and again asks if COUSINS feels comfortable: "You know what you have to do?" COUSINS assures him he does.

(A.R.: the depth of water decreases. The warnings flash.

Apprehension mounts.)

-The Fathometer shows the vessel in 30 fathoms.

-Perspiring heavily, COUSINS stares at the radar, then phones down to HAZELWOOD: "I think we are in serious trouble, sir. We have some kind of problem with the navigation..." A series of scraping jolts interrupts him and he orders KAGAN to apply hard left rudder. KAGAN hesitates and COUSINS grabs the wheel and frantically spins it hard left. The vessel starts to grind and clang as it runs aground.

-HAZELWOOD races onto the bridge and orders a hard left, then a hard right.

-The Fathometer registers 0.

-Down in the cargo control room First Mate KUNKEL stares in horror at the holding tank gauges. He grabs the phone and tells HAZELWOOD that all center and starboard tanks are rapidly discharging . . .

-On the bridge HAZELWOOD grimly puts down the phone and murmurs, "I guess this is one way to end your career."

One fairly late decision of Baker's was to "envelope" the story, to start off with a pristine view of the Sound at the beginning of the film, and show its pollution at the end. That strategy is *not* seen in the opening of the second treatment shown above, but dominates the start of the script itself, which now takes place in day-time rather than at night.

EXXON VALDEZ. SCRIPT.

1. EXT. OPEN SKY. PRINCE WILLIAM SOUND. ALASKA. DAY

CLOSE SHOT. A large bald eagle glides majestically through the air. Strong. Powerful. Symbol of America.

-Eagle's P.O.V. The breathtaking beauty of the Sound, with its steep forested slopes and its sparkling glaciers running down from a solid range of high, snowy mountains. In the blue-green waters a pod of killer whales heads towards the open ocean. Dense packs of seals crowd outcrops of rock. Sea otters surface and dive. Rookeries of sea birds rise up in ticker tape confusion.

-The eagle soars and wheels against a backdrop of white mountains.

-Its P.O.V. The Alaska oil pipeline, a shiny aluminum serpent snaking its way across the tundra and through the forests.

-The flying eagle is silhouetted against the pink fireball of the setting sun.

9

□ □ □
□ □ □
□ □ □

Dialogue and Commentary

On a recent journey, I read the following in an airline magazine: "Only rarely does Hollywood have anything interesting to say in terms of intelligent dialogue. Lines such as 'Hasta la vista! Baby!' and 'Go ahead, make my day,' now pass as the height of screenwriting."

Well, it's a point of view, but not one I subscribe to. It misses the point. A writer doesn't set out to write the *best* dialogue or *intelligent* dialogue. He or she sets out to write dialogue most *appropriate* to the film.

Most stories today are either action driven or character driven, and there tends to be a different dialogue style for each.

Action films, like *Terminator 2*, *Jurassic Park*, *The Last Action Hero*, and *Cliffhanger* are films told with images and movement. We don't expect much baring of the inner soul of the hero. They are in life-and-death situations. The mere fact that Stallone *can* talk surprises us. To expect him to say something besides "damn" or "It's hellish cold" while sewing up his wounds, or climbing a snow-covered mountain in his sweatshirt, would be over and above the call of duty.

Besides being brief, dialogue in fiction action films tends to be exaggerated, humorous, and unreal...but then so are the characters. We don't want villain John Lithgow in *Cliffhanger* to speak like a Harvard professor. We don't expect him to say

Turner, my man, I think you have made a very serious mistake. You could have stayed on the right side of the law, leading a respectable life. But you agreed to join me in this venture. Unfortunately, I don't think you have any option but to proceed along your chosen path.

What we *do* expect him to say is

You don't get it, Turner, do you? You've passed over now. We're partners in crime. There's no going back.

In these films we expect the dialogue to be brief, unsubtle, and to the point.

I hate you. I love you. But I can't live without you.

But what works for action-driven films doesn't work for character-driven stories. Here we are dealing with characters trying to handle problems of love, divorce, guilt, professional hardships, anxiety, loss, and so on. In these films we are dealing with a different kind of reality. The dialogue is going to be closer to real speech. It's going to reveal more of the people, their thoughts, their background, their hopes, their anxieties, their dreams. The dialogue is also going to be more subtle, more relaxed, more conversational.

This is not to say that the dialogue is not going to be funny, intelligent, and entertaining. Very often it is all these things. So in *Barbarians at the Gate*, Ross Johnson, the CEO of tobacco company RJR Nabisco, can say of a new cigarette, "Tastes like shit and smells like a fart. Looks like we got ourselves a real winner here. It's one Goddamn unique advertising slogan, I'll give you that."

How does all this relate to fact-based dramas? Very simply. Most of the films you'll be scripting will probably be character based and it is useful to see where the guidelines differ from those in action genres. Obviously, it is an oversimplification to talk merely of two kinds of films, especially as the genres merge and blend. However, it is a useful starting point in looking at a tricky subject, because writing dialogue is both the easiest and the hardest thing to do.

In order to write dialogue, you have to have a feel for language and the nuances of speech. It's an art, not a technique. You can know all the rules, pay attention to all the hints and suggestions, and yet still be unable to write good dialogue. And you may know nothing, and yet have that wonderful facility of just getting it right.

Now after that warning, let me add that most of us *can* write fairly decent stuff, and that in a certain way it's easier writing film dialogue than conversations in novels. This is particularly true of fact-based dramas, where the dialogue tends to be very simple and straightforward, and is often based on diaries or reported conversations.

Before getting in deeper, let me suggest three things that will help get you into the right "mind frame."

1: Try and look at the work of some of the writers who are generally acknowledged to be at the forefront of this art. Everybody has his or her own particular list, but I would definitely include among the oldies Herman Mankiewicz, Julius Epstein, Garson Kanin, Paddy Chayefsky, and Billy Wilder. Among modern scriptwriters, my list would include David Mamet, Woody Allen, Nora Ephron, Larry Gelbart, Paul Monash, James Brooks, William Goldman, Babaloo Mandel, Joe Esterhaz, Lawrence Kasdan, and, when he's on, as in *Moonstruck*, John Patrick Shanley. I know most of these are mainstream fiction writers, but it is easier to get hold of feature scripts than TV docudrama scripts, and although the genre is different, there are still enough good examples for you to learn from.

2: Before writing any dialogue, take a few minutes to really think about your characters and get inside their minds. Who are they? What motivates them? What type of people are they? What makes them sad, happy, tense, joyous? Where do they come from? What would be their normal mode of speech and behavior? Yes, I know you will have been thinking about all this for a long time, but now is the time to do a last check, to get to know your characters again before you put words into their mouths.

3: Ask yourself how much dialogue you really need. I know I've suggested that action films can get away with little dialogue, but the same can often be true of character films. Even in character films there are points where atmosphere and action speak louder than words.

For instance, in Jane Campion's wonderful film *The Piano*, there are two key sequences totally carried by action. In the first, Ada's husband spies on his wife and discovers her lying with Baines. A few minutes later he grabs her, pulls her savagely through the woods, and tries to rape her.

The second sequence is instigated when the husband finds a piano key, inscribed with a love declaration from Ada to Baines. This time he mumbles a few words about betrayal, pulls the silent Holly Hunter outside, brandishes his axe, and in one horrific blow cuts off her finger tip. Both scenes are played in virtual silence, and although one knows that Ada is mute, there is the realization later that even had she been able to talk, words would have ruined both scenes.

The Function of Dialogue

Dialogue has three essential uses:

1: To inform
2: To advance the plot
3: To reveal emotions and show the nature of the person talking

Most of the time all three functions overlap, but as a writer it's essential that you understand the merits of each function by itself.

Giving Information

That you use dialogue to give information seems very clear, so what's the catch? Your problem is how to do that without your technique becoming too obvious.

In *Diana: Her True Story*, it is vital that we understand some of the ambivalence that Prince Charles has about marriage. He is not an ordinary person. He cannot just wait around indefinitely. He is heir to the throne, and marriage has consequences for the future of the monarchy and his relationship to the British people.

That's a lot of information and writer Stephen Zito puts it all over in a conversation between Charles and his uncle, Lord Mountbatten.

LORD MOUNTBATTEN
Quite right, but don't imagine
because you have become a sort
of Royal pop idol that the British
people will always support you.
They'll back you *only* so long as
you serve the country. And part
of your duty to the nation is to
marry and produce an heir. The
people need to be assured the
monarchy will continue.

CHARLES
It's true I don't want to get married at this time, but I recognize
my obligation to the State. (A
beat) The trouble is there is no
set role for me. It depends
entirely on what I make of it.
I'm really rather an awkward
problem. I only hope I'm learning
something from you in order to
carry it on some way or other.

LORD MOUNTBATTEN
It's only the monarchy that matters. For you and your wife,
when you have one. So remember
one thing: choose wisely.

CHARLES
You have my word, sir. (with a
smile) I think I'd like to be King.
I'm just not so sure about being a
husband.

Besides information, this piece of dialogue also gives us a few other things. It asserts, through Mountbatten, that only the monarchy matters. This is a vital point for setting up the film's conflict, because later Diana is going to assert that she, as a human being, matters, as well as the monarchy. Charles's last speech also sets the scene for the continuance of his affair with Camilla Bowles.

The style of the dialogue is also quite interesting. It shows Charles as a little bit stiff, formal, awkward. We get information but we also begin to understand his character more deeply. Finally, the scene makes a general point about scriptwriting . . . the frequent need for a good closing line. Here we finish with, "I'd like to be King. I'm just not so sure about being a husband." That line sums up Charles's approach, and we move easily into the next scene.

I've already mentioned *backstory*, and the need for information that precedes the start of the film. This is often given in dialogue between two characters. If the scene is written well, we should be unconscious that we are deliberately being fed information. If the scene is written badly, the information segment will stick out like a sore thumb. *Exxon Valdez* contains examples of both.

In the following scene, we are in Frank Iarossi's house in Houston at night. He is one of the top executives of Exxon and has just been told about the disaster.

IAROSSI is speaking on the phone.

> IAROSSI
> Until we know the scale of the
> problem, Craig, just have every-
> body on alert. I'll get back to you
> as soon as I know more.

He dresses. His wife, in nightgown, helps him.

> IAROSSI
> I don't believe it. Twenty years
> without a major spill and now
> we've got two in one month.

> WIFE
> Is it bad?

> IAROSSI
> I don't know. But that Hawaii
> spill we had three weeks ago was
> 35,000 gallons. That's big, and we
> cleaned up. No problem.

Here the dialogue is simple and is the kind of thing Frank might mention. It's short and we don't pay much attention to how the information about previous spills is thrust upon us. A few minutes later in the film, Dan Lawn, from the department of environmental control, briefs the Governor of Alaska on the situation. This scene is slightly more awkward concerning backstory information.

> GOVERNOR
> Tell me what's going on, Dan.

> DAN
> Well, not a helluva lot, Governor.
> The fact is what we've got here
> is a travesty. Under the contin-
> gency plan Alyeska's response
> barge is supposed to be on site in
> five hours. It took 'em over four-
> teen. They should have seven
> skimmers. They've got three. And
> only two of them are working.
> The plan says the tanker should
> be boomed off to contain further
> leaks. Where's the boom?

> GOVERNOR
> Have they given any explanation?

> DAN
> That's not Alyeska style...that
> plan isn't worth the paper it's
> written on...The pipeline got built
> on the back of promises that the
> oil would only be shipped from
> Valdez if they had a proper oil
> spill plan. Those promises were a
> sham.

There is a lot of information here and it all tends to stick out a bit. The way writer Michael Baker saves the situation is by aiming the dialogue correctly at the Governor. It is information the Governor had to know. Place that conversation between Dan and someone else and it would be twice as obvious.

The second way Baker eases the pain of the backstory is by staging the scene on the bridge wing of the Exxon Valdez itself. That means that the audience is slightly diverted by everything else that is happening on the ship, by chains rattling and other people talking in the background. This give us a useful tip. If you have a lot of backstory or a lot of information break up the dialogue and set it against interesting scenes. In a bar. Against an airport. Traveling to work. In the middle of the action.

Baker's use of Iarossi's wife and the Governor in the above scenes also reveals something else of importance in dialogue writing. In order to put information over via dialogue, whether backstory or current developments of the story, we normally need what I call the "bounce person." Ostensibly the speaker is telling this other person what has happened, or is about to happen, or how he feels, etc. In reality, the author is often just using that other person as a bounce device to convey essential information to the audience.

In the scene on the ship, the Governor is a major player in his own right, but often you will have to bring on some minor character for the main purpose of acting as confidante and bounce prop of your main characters. This is seen very clearly in the script of *Barbarians at the Gate*, where the wives of the central characters, Ross Johnson and banker Henry Kravis exist mainly to hear their partner's troubles and deflect this information to the viewers.

Besides the bounce person, another way to reveal information is through commentary, which we'll discuss later, or via the TV reporter. Most crisis stories sooner or later pull in the media. It is therefore appropriate and handy to get some of your more complex information over via the reporter. This strategy is used a couple of times in *Exxon Valdez* and works quite well:

>   REPORTER
> According to experts this is by
> far the largest oil spill ever
> recorded in U.S. waters. And yet
> apparently there are still well
> over 40 million gallons of crude
> oil on board the tanker...The
> Alyeska Pipeline company is
> required to launch the emergency
> response . . .

As with anything else, you have to be careful of the reporter becoming a cliché figure in these kinds of films. However, where the TV reporter is appropriate, use him or her to get information over that is just too difficult any other way.

Advancing the Plot

Your plot moves forward via physical actions but also via dialogue.

>   POLICE CHIEF
> Get that son of a bitch out of
> there, and see if we can use his
> room to make an entry from the
> side. Is George here? Well, we'll
> just have to go without him.

Not many complications here. The speech is very direct and what some people call "on the nose." There's no subtext to it. No emotional feeling. It's just very strong, very masculine, and a call to action.

Probably a good deal of your dialogue will be written in exactly this way. There is a problem and the character states very specifically how he is going to solve it.

Revealing Emotion and Character

In *Cliffhanger*, our primary interest is to see how Stallone overcomes the villains. We are shown a little bit of who he is, and how he feels, but our primary interest is in his actions. By way of contrast, there are many films, like *Stalin* and *Diana: Her True Story*, where our interest is centered on knowing our hero in depth. Our main question is, who is this in front of us? Who really is this strange monster who governs Russia? How does Diana feel when she is up against the total power of the palace? In these cases, good dialogue is one of the best ways of revealing your characters, their emotions, their feelings, and their inner turmoil.

In *Diana: Her True Story*, we follow the transformation of a rather innocent nineteen-year-old girl into a strong, sophisticated woman. As she goes through crisis after crisis, her language becomes stronger, and her emotions are very powerfully revealed by everything she says.

At the following point in the story, Charles and Diana are on their honeymoon, dancing slowly and kissing each other. Suddenly Diana sees that Charles is wearing cufflinks obviously given to him by his old flame Camilla. They are in the shape of two "Cs" intertwined.

> CHARLES
> Diana. Is something wrong?

> DIANA
> What could be wrong? (baiting him) I do so enjoy talking to you. You know so much about so many things. In fact, I thought you might like to tell me where you got your cufflinks. They're new, aren't they? I don't remember seeing them before.

> CHARLES
> (defensively) They were a gift.

> DIANA
> Really! (a beat) Two "C's" intertwined.

                    CHARLES
          Yes.

                     DIANA
          And you don't find that odd?

                    CHARLES
          Well, I didn't order them.

                     DIANA
          No, Camilla did. And you thought
          you'd wear them on our honey-
          moon.

                    CHARLES
          Diana . . .

                     DIANA
          You bastard!

She walks out on him, as cold as ice.

   Another very interesting dialogue scene revealing the difference in the characters and emotions of Charles and Diana takes place in their bedroom some
months later.

                     DIANA
          I never get a kind word from
          you. A word of praise.

                    CHARLES
          These things are to be earned.

                     DIANA
          I'm trying so hard. All I need is
          a pat on the back now and then.

                    CHARLES
          Doing well is what is expected.

Diana gives him a hard look.

                     DIANA
          Then how about helping me to
          find my way?

CHARLES
You have help. If you need something, just ask Alfred or Christopher. (AR: courtier/advisers)

DIANA
I thought...after we were
married...things would be different.

CHARLES
They are. You are the Princess of
Wales. Royal duty is a wider and
more permanent duty...There are
things that are expected.

DIANA
But what about what the Princess
expects?

They fall silent for a moment.

CHARLES
You're not quite the girl of my
engagement, Diana.

DIANA
Nor are you my Prince, Sir.

In this scene the dialogue reveals Charles as a cold, unfeeling prig. A call for sympathy and feeling, love and understanding and attention, is answered in the frostiest of terms. "Ask Alfred or Christopher." On Diana's side, we see something beyond the yearning and the desire for acceptance. What we are beginning to notice is the way she is maturing and the strengthening of her backbone.

And with the comment, "Nor are you my Prince, sir," we once again have a sharp cut out of the scene.

In *Stalin* too we see character revealed again and again by dialogue. In one of the best scenes, we find Stalin talking to Sergo. Stalin has suggested to Sergo that he return to Georgia and knock a few heads together.

STALIN
All you need are a good pair of
boots. Feel this. (slapping boot)
Go ahead. Feel it.

Sergo reaches down and feels the soft shiny leather

> I could have been making these if
> my father had had his
> way...Wanted me to be a cobbler
> like him. I ran away. Came home,
> he beat the shit out of me. But I
> never made boots for anyone. No,
> I wear them. Any you know the
> best thing about them? (kicks out
> viciously) With boots, kick a man
> in the head and he'll never find
> his teeth. Wear boots, Sergo.

He gives Sergo a playful kick in the ass.

Here we get two things. A bit of backstory about Stalin's origins, and a clear revelation of the man's viciousness and ugly humor. The actual language is very vivid and graphic. "Came home, he beat the shit out of me," and "kick a man in the head and he'll never find his teeth." We don't need to know more. The character of Stalin is set in these few brief words.

The power of dialogue is, of course, dependent not just on the scene but on what comes before. Take the words "I love you. I can't live without you." These are probably the most mundane, over-used phrases in film literature. But put them in a proper context and they can be electrifying, as in Jane Campion's *The Piano*.

Essentially it is a film of few words. The heroine can't even talk and the hero, Baines (Harvey Keitel), uses the shortest of phrases. Most of the scenes between Ada and Baines take place in the half-light, as Ada plays the piano and Baines gently caresses her. Finally, after Ada and Baines have lain together, Baines sits quietly in a chair and tells Ada not to come again.

> BAINES
> I love you, and I don't think
> about anything but you. But this
> is making you a whore and me
> miserable. Take your piano and
> go.

I'm working from memory, so I'm not sure if I've gotten the exact words, but I'm close. The point is, Baines's words come so much from the soul and are so simple and true, that we are moved almost to tears.

The problem with action-driven fiction films is that too often the main characters have little depth and are merely comic-book heroes. For good action docudramas, it is advisable to give more complexity and dimensions to the participants, and dialogue is one of your best means for achieving that end.

One of the best films for studying this point is Cy Endfield's *Zulu*. The film, scripted by Endfield and John Prebble, is based on the Rorke's Drift battle between just over a hundred British troops and over 9,000 attacking Zulu warriors in South Africa in 1879.

The small British forces were led by Lieutenants Charles and Bromfield, respectively played in the film by Stanley Baker and Michael Caine. Before the fighting starts, Charles has to be shown as a plain, no-nonsense engineer and Bromfield established as a dandy and a fop. Much of this is achieved when the two meet for the first time beside the river where Lt. Charles is building a pontoon bridge with two privates. All are deep in the water.

>   LT. BROMFIELD
> Hard work?
>
>   LT. CHARLES
> Bloody awful.
>
>   LT. BROMFIELD
> Still, the river cooled you up a
> bit, eh? Who are you?
>
>   LT. CHARLES
> John Charles, Royal Engineers.
>
>   LT. BROMFIELD
> Bromfield. 24th. That's my post,
> over the hills. Who said you could
> use my men?
>
>   LT. CHARLES
> They were just sitting around on
> their backsides doing nothing.
>
>   LT. BROMFIELD
> I'd rather you asked first, old boy.
>
>   LT. CHARLES
> I was told their officer was out
> hunting.
>
>   LT. BROMFIELD
> Yeah...I'll tell my man to clean
> your kit.

```
            LT. CHARLES
Don't bother.


            LT. BROMFIELD
No bother. I'm not offering to do
it myself. Still, a chap ought to
look smart in front of the men,
don't you think? Well, chin-chin.
Do carry on with your mud pies.
```

There are only a few sentences here of dialogue, but the characters of both men are revealed very quickly. With Charles, the key words are "they were just sitting around on their backsides" and his refusal to have his uniform cleaned. Immediately we sense a bluntness and a straightforward quality. All this contrasts with Bromfield's languid "I'd rather you asked first, old boy," and "a chap ought to look smart in front of the men, don't you think?" When he adds the condescending kicker, "... chin-chin. Do carry on with your mud pies," we know we are in the presence of what looks to be a rather upperclass, spoiled and effete young man.

The effect of the dialogue is also strengthened by the way the scene is shot. Charles is knee deep in water and continually has to look up to Bromfield, who is mounted on a horse, thus adding to the superior-versus-inferior aspect of the sequence. All this helps the film immensely, because later on we see how the men are forced to become partners, and how Bromfield's foppishness is merely a pose covering a great deal of moral and physical courage.

Making It Hang Together

Your objective as a writer is to make the audience feel that the dialogue is natural and spontaneous. Sounds easy, and on the whole it is, providing you can see where the problems lie. What this amounts to is merely observing a few dos and don'ts.

Style

In all of the extracts we've looked at, one thing has stood out. The dialogue has been easy, free, unpretentious, and appropriate for the person. At times it's been a bit formal, but then Prince Charles is formal. At times it's been a bit gross, but then Stalin was gross and boorish. At all times the dialogue has been fairly close to our normal patterns of speech.

I say fairly close, because dialogue, except maybe in a Harold Pinter play, is never just ordinary speech. It's always a bit heightened, a bit sharper, a bit pointed, a little bit more clever or incisive. If it wasn't, it wouldn't work as well.

The style of your dialogue also changes very much according to the genre you are working in. If you are doing a detective drama, or something close to a hard news story, your dialogue will probably be hard and realistic. Write a semi-comedy, like *Barbarians at the Gate*, and your style may become more fanciful and exaggerated. In other words, though realism tends to be the underlying theme of docudrama, it is always tempered by the nature of your subject. Thus what seems absolutely inappropriate for one script may be just right for another. Take for example some of the dialogue in the Australian series *Bodyline*.

The series deals with great cricket battles between England and Australia in the early thirties. The English team seems to be using questionable and dangerous tactics, only just within the rules, and has injured an Australian player. The Australian underdogs are disgusted with their rivals, and are within an ace of quitting the series. The following dialogue then ensues on the train.

>   AUSTRALIAN CAPTAIN
> He's got a cracked skull. There's
> no choice. We must quit.
>
>   FIRST AUSSIE TEAM MEMBER
> There is, Bill. The same choice
> that all the battles have.
>
>   SECOND AUSSIE TEAM MEMBER
> He's right. It's what built this
> country. Going out against all the
> odds and giving it your best. Our
> families came here as convicts. As
> settlers. They didn't shrink from
> the impossible. They went to
> places no one had ever been
> before. Then there were the
> shores of Gallipoli. Somewhere out
> there they taught us about
> courage. About loyalty to your
> mates, and about being Australian.

Well, it's some speech, and all that seems to be missing is a reference to motherhood. It's exaggerated, overwritten, and over the top. In any other drama it would have you rolling on the floor in laughter. Yet here it works beautifully. The style is absolutely appropriate for what is really a devastating war between two nations, thinly disguised as a cricket match. Therefore the references to honor, duty, and the past are emotionally correct and very appropriate for the script.

Brevity

In general, we don't talk in long speeches, and when we're confronted with them, we tend to get bored to death. So where possible, keep your dialogue short. Not choppy, not brusque, but short. Occasionally you will have to go to some length, but beware of the dangers. Dan Lawn's speech to the Governor of Alaska is long. It just about works, but it's so technical another sentence would have killed us.

However, when you have really good dialogue, or a fascinating story, you can get away with anything. In *Death of a Princess*, Antony Thomas has an old princess relate the following to Ryder, the journalist who's seeking the background to the execution.

> THE EMIRA
> Sex. Maybe that's a privilege. To relieve their boredom, these princesses live the most interesting and busy sex lives. Very little romance. Quick liaisons. Sometimes cruel, always dangerous.

> RYDER
> How do they make contact with the men?

> THE EMIRA
> The chauffeur and personal maid. They make the contact and have the secrets. Of course they're bribed, heavily bribed. The irony is it's the woman who chooses the man. There are always ways of finding a man. The sword dances on national days. This is a great opportunity for men to show off. At night, in the desert. The women sitting in their cars, in the dark, watching men, selecting men...There's a road in the desert. Women go there to look men over. Every evening at about five...When they choose a man, if it works, it works. And if it doesn't, they just move on. If they find a man attractive, they just write down his number and tell the chauffeur to make contact.

The speech is long, but what makes it work is that it is absolutely hypnotizing. The facts being revealed go against all our normal concepts of the behavior of Arab women. We are shocked. We want to know more, so we listen, entranced. I should add that the speech also shocked the Saudi Arabians and led to a temporary breach of diplomatic relations between them and the British.

Feeding

You probably didn't notice it, but in the speech above Ryder does the feeding, or the prompting. He asks, "How do they make contact?"and this pushes the Emira to continue. This prompting, this pushing, this assisting, is something we all do all the time without noticing it, and is vital in dialogue writing. What the "prompt" does is provide us with a hook to continue and smooth the transition.

In *Her Final Fury*, there is one scene where Kerry, the D.A., is told that Betty has hired a public relations firm to tell the public her story. Here the feeds and the prompts go back and forth like ping pong.

CARLINA
I put the divorce records you
wanted on your desk.

KERRY
Thanks, John.

CARLINA
Mrs. Broderick's a real piece of
work.

KERRY
Tell me about it.

CARLINA
Seen today's paper?

KERRY
I still haven't had a minute to...

Carlina hands Kerry the paper. She stops, focusing on NEWSPAPER blurb circled in red, titled "Socialite hires PR Wizard from Jail."

KERRY
Get outta here. A public relations
firm? I mean a PR firm...What
is she, a movie star?

> CARLINA
> Maybe we should put in for a
> change of venue.
>
> KERRY
> Where?
>
> CARLINA
> Hollywood.

In this instance, John Carlina feeds Kerry the questions, and then Kerry returns different ones a second later, the one hooking neatly into the other.

The scene also works easily because of the conversational acknowledgments we all use . . . These kinds of backups are going to happen again and again in your scripts. Sometimes the prompt will be a simple "So?" Other times it will be an expression of disbelief: "You're kidding." Sometimes, as above, it will be a simple "thanks." They're not obvious. They're not intrusive, but these prompts keep the conversation going smoothly.

Style, Grammar, and Colloquialisms

People don't talk like stuffed dummies or like the Oxford dictionary. They don't talk like grammar book ads, nor do they sound like the Queen of England. They let their hair down when they talk, and they use slang and colloquialisms. When she sees the newspaper blurb on Betty Broderick, Karen doesn't say, "What a stupid article." She says, "Get outta here."

We normally talk in very simple, unaffected ways, and men and women also talk slightly differently. It's not just a matter of the subjects they talk about, but also the style in which they express themselves.

Swears

On occasion we also swear for emphasis, and what is permitted in scripts has varied over the years. Once the Hollywood production code fined David Selznick $5,000 for having Rhett Butler say, "I don't give a damn," and even that was only allowed after a struggle. And it was only a few years ago that the BBC got heart failure when Kenneth Tynan said "fuck" on one of their programs. Now it's a rare film, at least as far as detective or action films are concerned, that doesn't have swears sprinkled liberally over the script. Even on TV, which is a little more prudish, "Hell," "Bullshit," and "Who gives a crap?" are also occasionally used to add color.

A good example of the kind of looseness we are now used to in TV writing can be seen in the following excerpt from *Her Final Fury*.

```
SC. 108 INT. HOLDING CELL - DAY
```

Betty, scheduled to go into court, sits on one end of a bench in shackles, waiting to go outside and board a bus. She turns to the INMATE next to her.

> BETTY
> Could you shove down? I'm falling off the bench.

> INMATE
> Lose some weight.

> BETTY
> Shove down.

> INMATE
> (pushing) Shove this...

> BETTY
> (to woman deputy) You'll let her get away with that?

> INMATE
> Yep, she is. Ain't no TV around here now. Today you just another sadass, locked up bitch. Like us... You best start behaving your butt in here. Could become home sweet home for permanent. I heard that hung jury had ten against ya. Almost too close for comfort, ain't it?

The inmate's speech is right on. It's tight. Combative. Compact. Confrontational. Slangy. And just right in its dramatic intent of pulling Betty's emotions one notch tighter.

Yet you have to be careful about these things. Too often swearing or loose language is just a substitute for thinking about your script. The only rule is to write what is appropriate for your character. The inmate can say, "I'll bust your fucking ass, you mother fuckin' son of a bitch," but that's not the language you would use for the royal family. To each his own!

Preaching

One difficulty which continually confronts the fact-fiction writer is how to avoid being preachy and didactic. This is the trap that awaits you particularly in historic films and in issue-oriented films.

Hitler dies, and if we are not careful, we have some colonel saying

> COLONEL
> We let him get away too long.
> Humanity must now see that
> scum like this never rule the
> earth again. Finally we have
> reached the light. That light must
> never be extinguished.

We hear this, and we wince in pain. If anything works, it's probably dialogue that goes the other way. That's why the beginning of *Patton* is so refreshing. Patton stands in front of his troops, and instead of exhorting them to a glorious death, says, "The good soldier doesn't die for his country. He makes the enemy die for his country."

Occasionally the situation will demand the over-the-top dialogue, and if the occasion is appropriate you go for it. The earlier excerpt from *Bodyline* was one example, and Paul Monash's *Stalin* gives us a few examples that are even more preachy, but work. So when Stalin returns from exile we are actually waiting for the following:

> LENIN
> Dear comrades, soldiers, sailors,
> workers. I thank you for over-
> throwing the Tsar! But the great
> world war continues. Did you
> overthrow the Tsar to continue
> his bloody war?

> CROWD
> (thundering) No!

> LENIN
> But it does continue! Did you
> overthrow the Tsar so the peas-
> ants would remain landless...so
> the workers and their families
> would continue to starve?

```
                    CROWD
          No!


                    LENIN
          The people demand peace! Now!
          The people demand land! Now!
          Forward to the international social
          revolution, the unfinished revolu-
          tion, the proletarian revolution.
```

It's great stuff. We enjoy the speech in exactly the same way that we enjoy Churchill's pugnacious war speeches like "We shall fight them on the beaches. We shall fight them on the land." These are dialogues totally appropriate to the man, the place, and the time.

In most films there comes a time when you need to sum up the issues. The audience has been following the plot, but you want to emphasize very succinctly what is at stake. There's a danger here of being too obvious or too preachy, but if the dialogue is done well, the scene can be very effective. You get such a scene in *Her Final Fury*. Kerry, the prosecutor, has decided to go for another trial. Her boss asks her if that won't mean another year of hell.

```
                    KERRY
          Of course it will. But if I don't
          take it, it's like she's won. I keep
          thinking of all the time I've been
          trying to protect real battered and
          abused women. I mean the ones
          whose husbands won't leave. The
          women who have no choices. And
          then I think about Betty Broder-
          ick. There's not one shred of evi-
          dence that he ever laid a finger
          on her. She's a fraud. And I can't
          just walk away.
```

This is very good writing. It sums up everything. It sounds natural, and it is excellent drama.

Besides highlighting issues in the middle of a film, you may also want to sum up for the audience at the end. This happens particularly in a film on a crisis situation or on a national threat. A catastrophe has happened . . . Chernobyl, a poison gas leak in India, a horrific crash . . . and it is something that is due to human failure and could have been avoided. That's a very serious point, and quite rightly you want to emphasize it at the conclusion of the script. Yet how you do it needs care.

Michael Baker gets away with it in a speech he gives to environmental officer Dan Lawn at the end of *Exxon Valdez*, but it's a close call.

> DAN
>
> Listen, I'm not against oil. I
> started as an engineer. Helped
> build the pipeline and was proud
> of it. But we all get hooked on
> that black stuff. Oil made the liv-
> ing easy. Now it's choking us to
> death. (Beat) But it needn't have
> happened. The state was warned
> and did nothing about it. Hell,
> this state has earned $30 billion
> off that pipeline. A lot less than
> one per cent of that has ever
> gone to environmental protection.

Making the Dialogue Count

You want the dialogue to be realistic, but you also want to move the plot along. This can present a dilemma. How much talk is necessary? How much becomes irrelevant padding?

In *Exxon Valdez*, Iarossi hears of the oil spill when he's at home in bed. He tells his wife about previous accidents (the backstory) then kisses her goodbye and says, "I'll call you, honey. Don't worry." The dialogue is cut to the minimum. There's no "I'll be away three weeks. Pay the gas bills. Tell the children I'll be thinking of them," or anything like that. The scene has to make two points: (a) there is a crisis and Frank has to move, and (b) it's not the first time. The points are covered swiftly, and we move on.

Sometimes you will take time out for atmosphere, for relationships, for greetings, but you always have to ask yourself, "What points am I making in this dialogue? What is the function of this speech? How does this conversation help things?"

In *Her Final Fury*, we first meet prosecutor Kerry outside her home. Her kids are asking father Steve a few questions.

> GARY
> Dad, are my flip flops stupid?

> STEVE
> Absolutely not.

                    KERRY
        Todd, where is your sweatshirt? I
        laid it out for you.

                    TODD
        I don't need a sweatshirt, Mom.

                    KERRY
        It's supposed to get chilly later.

                    GARY
        (off camera) I can't find my
        shoes.

                    KERRY
        By your closet.

Kerry turns to go back into the house.

                    STEVE
        Guess who just turned herself in
        for fatally shooting her ex-hus-
        band and his new wife?

                    GARY
        (off camera) Where?

                    KERRY
        By the skateboard...(to husband
        Steve) Who?

SC. 43. CORONADO BRIDGE. COMMUTER TRAFFIC

SC. 44. INT. CAR

Kerry drives, listening to the radio.

                    FEMALE NEWSCASTER
        ...the highly publicized divorce
        saga came to a tragic end yester-
        day when both Broderick and his
        new wife were killed...

The function of the first scene is simple. It sets Kerry up as a married woman and a mother. The introduction of the case is more subtle. We know Kerry is interested, but we don't yet know why. The payoff will come later.

The interruptions also help the naturalism of the scene. Husband Steve asks Kerry if she knows who turned herself in over a killing. She can't answer because she is distracted by her kids. When she does ask, "Who?" we get her question answered by the radio announcer. It's a simple but very effective example of dialogue and scene placement.

In *Willing to Kill*, the first of the TV films about the Texas cheerleading mother, we spend a great deal of time in the homes of both Wanda Holloway and Verna Heath. They are shown as the best of friends, and the dialogue rambles on about cooking, kids, recipes, work, and husbands. You are restless for something to happen, but the dull everyday domestic quality of the dialogue is essential. We need this banal setting to show Wanda's relationship with Verna, and to show how extraordinary it is that this very average woman suddenly concocts a murder plot.

Having Fun

In the end you can know all the rules, absorb all the hints, yet your dialogue can fail to breathe. This is usually because you have been working so much with your head, as opposed to intuitive feeling, you've lost the spirit of the thing. Sometimes it's useful to forget everything, take off, and have some fun with the script.

Some years ago David Mamet wrote a short play that was turned into a film called *About Last Night . . .* with James Belushi. At the start of the film, Belushi tells his pal, Rob Lowe, about his experience with "a great broad." The monologue lasts about seven minutes and is hilarious. "She gave me these eyes. What eyes. I got into bed. She stripped. The bed caught fire. I'm waiting. Can I finish before the fire engine comes?" In practical terms, all the scene is doing is telling us Belushi is putting it on, and Lowe is less experienced. Yet to put it that way would be to miss the terrific fun we have hearing the story.

Another scene that can be enjoyed purely for the dialogue appears in Barry Levinson's *Tin Men*. Richard Dreyfuss and his friends are sitting in a diner discussing the TV show Bonanza. Someone asks why the dialogue in the show is always about horses and never about sex and women. That question launches the bunch into a zany discussion about the place of dialogue and realism on TV. The scene doesn't advance the plot very much. It gives you a little atmosphere and tells you a little bit about the group of friends. It could have been dropped from the film without making much difference to the plot, but in the end it is one of the most memorable scenes in the film.

I've taken these examples from fiction films because this "loosening up" isn't seen very much in docudrama. It's there in *Barbarians at the Gate*, and occasionally makes an appearance in *Texas Cheerleading Mom . . .* but otherwise it's a rare quality in fact-fiction films. It's a pity, because when you put logic aside, and take off with your imagination, you can have a great deal of fun.

Dialogue in Docudrama

How does reality restrict your canvas? If this is the general question which confronts you the whole time you write drama-docs, you face one of its most difficult aspects when you come to write dialogue. You are dealing with real people, real lives. What liberties can you take with what they say? How much can you invent? How important is it for you to be accurate with the dialogue? Is it even possible? What is your responsibility to the audience? And what will be the effect of the things you say on people still living?

The questions are endless. There are no easy answers, and in the end everyone has to carve out their own personal position. The attitude you take should be a little bit practical, a little bit philosophical. When I was researching this book, half the writers I talked to said, "Accuracy. That's the only thing that counts." The other half discounted that as impossible. For example, I queried Peter Prince, the author of the Oppenheimer series, about his attitude to docudrama dialogue.

> [In *Oppenheimer*] ninety percent of the time I had to invent the dialogue . . . There were one or two memorable statements to play with, such as "I am become death, the destroyer of worlds," and there were the congressional hearings, but most of the dialogue was made up.
>
> How does one deal with characters based on real live people? The short answer is I never considered the reality of the people behind my characters. This sounds arrogant, but I believe it takes a certain kind of arrogance to write any drama, and certainly to do the thing that is anathema to the academic historians . . . to put words into the mouths of historic figures.
>
> In 1975 I interviewed many survivors of the Oppenheimer era. It was enormously helpful to me, both for what these people told me, and for the impression they gave of themselves. But having extracted what I could from them, I felt I had to shield myself from their independent reality if I was going to work up the nerve to make these people "my" characters.

On a simple level the argument would seem to be are you a dramatist? . . . then all is possible; or are you a journalist? . . . in which case you want to get as close to the truth as you can. But it is never as simple as that. In fact-based fiction, you want drama, and you want the truth. You want to have your cake and eat it, and at times the meal can be quite hard to digest.

Boundaries

If you write about living people, your dialogue and your portrayal of these characters need to take notice of the laws of libel and privacy. This is a hefty subject, and may well affect what you say and how you say it. Rather than talk about it here, I've discussed the whole subject at length in Chapter 13, which deals with many of the legal aspects of writing docudrama.

Audience

To a large extent, the kind of dialogue you write is closely tied to the demands and expectations of the audience. Write a historic drama about Columbus and no one will bother too much about what he says. Write a cozy comedy about George M. Cohan and call it *Yankee Doodle Dandy*, and again few people will question the dialogue. But write about John Kennedy or the Exxon Valdez disaster, and people will expect the dialogue to be much closer to the truth.

Why is that? because in these cases we really want to understand what happened, and how people really behaved. We turn to films like *The Tragedy of Flight 103* or *And the Band Played On* because we want to get very close to the truth, and therefore accurate dialogue is of some importance to us.

Character Accuracy
and Invented Dialogue

Having said all that, could it be that in aiming for accurate dialogue we are attempting mission-impossible? You weren't there when Hitler committed suicide, or when Caesar was assassinated, and even if you were, what you heard would probably be very undramatic. There's a lot of difference between Caesar saying, "This knife in my ribs hurts like murder," and Et tu, Brute?" or between a passerby saying, "Cleopatra's a great-looking girl," and Enobarbus's comment, "Age cannot wither her, nor custom stale her infinite variety."

What one aims for is gripping dialogue which is accurate for the place, the time, the character, and the situation. We really don't know what Charles and Diana said to each other in bed, but his remarking, "You are not the girl of my engagement," and her answering, "Neither are you my Prince," seems well within the realm of possibility. Similarly, we don't know what happened between Stalin and Sergo Ordzhonikidze while Stalin's daughter was being born, but Stalin's comment, "kick a man in the head and he'll never find his teeth," sounds absolutely right for the dictator.

Recorded vs. Non-recorded Meetings

We live in an age of tape recorders, interviews, memoirs, and court transcripts. How do you manage this material in terms of creating dialogue?

You select. You use your judgment. You decide one scene is absolutely dependent on the original material, and another scene can use the materials in a slightly more liberal way. What are your criteria? You do what works best in creating an absorbing drama which is still an accurate interpretation of the events portrayed. This is the way Michael Baker tackles the problem:

> Let's say you have a record of a meeting, completely verbatim. In that case it's a question of selecting what are the best bits. Usually, what you are left

with, after having talked to all sides, or as many sides as possible, is nothing like a verbatim report. What you get is a sense of the spirit of the meeting, and what people's positions were. And on that basis you reconstruct it in as dramatic a form as possible.

And nearly always . . . and this is what amazes me about the difference between dramatic reality and reality . . . because of the inherent need for conflict in drama, nearly always these meetings as scripted are much more "keyed up" and angry than they were in real life. This was certainly true in the Exxon Valdez film. There the original meetings were very low key. The anger came afterwards.

Michael Eaton, the writer of *The Tragedy of Flight 103*, puts the situation this way:

I'm a dramatist and I write the dialogue on the basis of all the source material I have. I take the sources, I take the interviews, I take the journalistic information, I take the public record, and then I put words into people's mouths.

Now sometimes you are writing about a secret meeting, and that can be difficult. So what do you do? You know a meeting took place. A secret meeting between certain people. We know what positions they took at that meeting. So we know what the agenda of the meeting was and what arguments the participants would have used. We also know what actions arose from that meeting, what consequences flew out of it. Therefore we are in a pretty good position to decide which perspective and point of view was in the ascendancy. We know all this, and we go away and write. You might see this as an area or an attitude which is open to an enormous amount of criticism, but I don't see a problem with it really.

But there is a problem which I discussed with Michael later, the question of distortion and misrepresentation of people, their views and their actions. How does he deal with those things?

Throughout the whole process of composition I am in constant contact with lawyers acting on behalf of the TV company making the film. I send them drafts. I send them scenes. And in those scenes I am giving my sources and informing them what lines of dialogue are actually taken as verbatim record, and which ones I'm inventing on the basis of those sources. And the lawyers are informing me of what I can and can't do. And if there is a difference of opinion between the lawyer and the dramatist, I'm afraid it's the lawyer who wins. (AR: There is a further discussion of this subject from the point of view of the TV company in Appendix D.)

When you write reality-based films, you are often asking people to trust you. I'm not talking about the "stars" who have sold you their story for $100,000 and then keep warning you about libel actions. I'm talking about ordinary people who think the story worth telling, and have put their faith in you to tell it accurately. What do you do when you know that telling their story or using their words can endanger them? They've told you that they support Rushdie, but if you identify them, their lives will be in danger. They've told you about their past in the Mafia. They've named names and they keep looking over their shoulders in terror. What do you do in cases like these?

This situation occurs more often than one thinks, and happened to Antony Thomas while researching *Death of a Princess*. Thomas's solution seems a very good way out of the difficulty.

> When I started recontacting my interviewees and said, "I'm thinking of doing a documentary and want you to repeat what you said to me," almost without exception they said, "Are you mad? We are never going to appear in a film making these statements about Arab society and womanhood and Saudi Arabia. It's impossible."
>
> So I moved to a second stage and said, "What if I dramatize this journey?" Then I questioned everyone I had interviewed and asked them whether, if I used their exact words without editorializing them or changing them, they would trust me to create a character who is completely different from themselves, exists in a different context, yet speaks their exact words. The permissions were given and formed the basis for the film. I took the interviews, cut them down slightly, but was careful to maintain what remained word for word, as in the original.

In this case, Thomas's sense of faith to the original text was vital to the integrity of a picture which became mired in controversy. After it was screened, *Death of a Princess* caused a rupture in diplomatic relations between Great Britain and Saudi Arabia. One of the charges brought against Thomas was malicious invention of dialogue, such as the Emira's story of the women who cruise the highways looking for sexual partners. A U.S. oil company even took out an ad in *The New York Times* accusing Thomas of inventing a fairy story. The defense was that the stories and the dialogue were one hundred percent true.

Commentary

In recent years, there has been an increasing use of commentary or narration in dramadocs. It is easy to see why this should have happened. Narration is often one of the simplest and most effective tools for solving a number of your film's difficulties.

Narration can quickly and easily set up the factual background of a film, providing simple or complex information that doesn't arise easily or naturally from the casual conversation of your characters. It can complement the mood of the film, and it can provide focus and emphasis. It doesn't have to judge what is seen, but it should help the viewer understand more fully what is on the screen. In a compact and elegant way, narration can help focus what the film is about and where it's going.

Sometimes the narration comes in the form of the third-person voice which sets the scene for you, and tells you what to expect. So the Canadian film *Democracy on Trial: The Morgentaler Affair* simply begins:

>   NARRATOR
> It is the first of June, 1970.
>
> What is about to happen here will
> be the beginning of the most con-
> troversial legal battle of the
> decade. A battle that will shake
> the Canadian justice system to its
> foundations.
>
> The police, however, know nothing
> of all this. They are here for a
> routine raid on the clinic of an
> abortionist.

As this film about a crusading doctor proceeds, we follow Morgentaler through three complex court battles to keep his abortion clinic open and to fight off jail for himself. Narration sets the scene, and is also used frequently to cut away from the actors and comment on what is happening. The narration is also used to bridge immense time gaps.

>   PRIEST
> Our unwanted children will be
> joined by their unwanted elders.
> Euthanasia will have as many
> headlines in a few years as abor-
> tion is getting now.
>
>   NARRATION
> As the debate heats up, anti-abor-
> tion groups start to apply political
> pressure, rallying thousands of
> supporters in front of the Parlia-
> ment buildings in Ottawa. They
> find a sympathetic listener in Jus-
> tice Minister Lang.

```
                    LANG
        I disagree completely with the
        proposition that it is just the deci-
        sion for the mother . . .

                    NARRATOR
        But despite the anti-abortion cam-
        paign, six months after the raid
        the clinic is still open for busi-
        ness. Several of the nurses are
        also facing criminal charges, but
        no one has any regrets.
```

Here, the narration is clearly identified as narration, but it can come disguised in many forms. In *Exxon Valdez*, as we pointed out, vital information is supplied to us by the TV commentator. The TV show is a nice gimmick, but the reality is that we are using commentary, only slightly dressed up.

Another method for disguising commentary is to have it put over by one of the minor actors in the drama. In the Australian TV series *Bodyline*, the narrator's task is shouldered by the hero's girlfriend. She is the one who tells us what cricket is about, and it is her thankless task to tell us what is happening in the battles of the First World War. *Stalin* has a similar functional figure, played by Svetlana, Stalin's daughter. Thus at the beginning of the film, she is the one who recounts the history of the revolution.

Style and Language

The principles for writing narration are similar to those for writing dialogue.

1: *Write for the ear.* The journalist writes for the eye, but in narration you write for the ear. This means you keep your vocabulary simple and easy to understand.
2: *Grammar and slang.* Most of the time your writing will be relatively standard. You *can* be ungrammatical and you can use slang, but you probably won't, for a good reason. Narration stands in contrast to dialogue, and you'll probably leave the looser language for the latter.
3: *Simple, powerful sentences.* Narration appears to work best using simple, strong sentences with the main verb close to the beginning. Here's what I mean by the simple, strong sentence. "The American troops were young and untried. They came from Texas, Utah, and Oregon. Few had ever been as far east as Chicago. Now they found themselves 5,000 miles away from home, ready to invade mainland Europe. It was June fifth. Few knew it, but D-Day was only hours away."

4: *Atmosphere.* One of the challenges of writing narration is to add an extra dimension to what you see on the screen. The jeeps don't just go around in the night taking men to planes. They go around "in the bitter cold, through the clinging mists, carrying men to the darkness of the waiting planes."

Does narration really fit in with straight drama? I think so, and it's certainly been with us as far back as Shakespeare. After all, isn't Chorus in *Henry V* just our narrator in different garb? So play around with narration and see where it can help, not just to get you out of a tight corner, but also to add something different to your film.

10

□ □ □
□ □ □
□ □ □

Beginning the Script

The Script Format

The moment has come when you are ready to start the script itself. Your first task is to make sure that when you do write, your work follows the basic rules of script presentation and layout.

In his book *Huxley in Hollywood*, author David Dunaway tells the story of novelist Aldous Huxley's arrival in Beverly Hills. He's made a name for himself as a writer in England and wants to get into films, where the money is. His first job, scripting *Madame Curie* for MGM, is a disaster. Dunaway writes:

> The script remains in the MGM vaults: an unpublished 145-page novel. Huxley hadn't yet mastered basic cinematic language . . . The text lacks visual cues. The "treatment" is plotted rather than laid out cinematically.

Had Huxley come down from his rather unworldly perch he would have found out that the basic formal elements of screenwriting are quite simple. There is a standard way of setting out a script, and you can learn the conventions in a few minutes. Many of the rules you will have picked up merely by glancing at the script examples in the earlier sections of this book. You'll have noticed, for instance, that each sequence describes setting, action, who is present, and the dialogue. All this now has to be examined in a little more detail.

Cast Lists

This is not an absolute necessity, but if you are writing a TV show with an immense cast of characters, it's useful to identify them at the beginning of the script. The introductory page to *Exxon Valdez* looks like this.

DEAD AHEAD: THE EXXON VALDEZ DISASTER

CORDOVA (The Fishermen)

Rick Steiner	Marine Biologist
Jack Lamb	Acting President, CDFU
David Grimes	Fisherman/poet/folksinger
Dr. Riki Ott	CDFU pollution specialist

ALYESKA PIPELINE CO.

George Nelson	President, Alyeska P.C.
Chuck O'Donnell	Valdez Terminal Manager
Larry Shier	Valdez Terminal Supervisor

EXXON

Frank Iarossi	President, Exxon Shipping Co.
Craig Rassinier	Exxon oil spill response coordinator
Don Cornett	Exxon PR Chief

STATE OF ALASKA

Dennis Kelso	Commissioner, ADEC
Dan Lawn	ADEC's local man in Valdez

The list then goes on, identifying people from the Coast Guard, from the crew of the tanker, and from the Presidential delegation.

Explanatory Captions

Many fact-based TV dramas use a short caption at the beginning of the film to explain the background of the story, their sources for the script, and (sometimes) how and where they have fictionalized. The caption for Granada TV's *Who Bombed Birmingham* sets things out this way.

> CAPTION
> On the night of 21st November,
> 1974, two Birmingham public
> houses were bombed by the Irish
> Republican Army. 21 people were
> killed and 162 injured.
>
> Six men were convicted. They
> have been in prison since 1974.
> In 1985, three journalists from

the TV current affairs program,
World in Action, began examining
the case. Drawing on court transcripts, taped interviews and contemporary statements, this film is
a reconstruction of a three-year
investigation into the true story
behind the bombings.

The introductory sequence for Michael Eaton's *Shoot to Kill* works in a similar way as a scene setter.

> CAPTION
> During the late 1970's, a policy
> decision was taken at the highest
> level to transfer the task of anti-
> terrorist operations in Northern
> Ireland from the British Army to
> the Royal Ulster Constabulary.
>
> This was known as the "Ulseriza-
> tion" of security forces.
>
> As power gradually shifted to the
> RUC, the role of the Special
> Branch grew dramatically. They
> were charged with coordinating
> undercover operations, and han-
> dling the informer network within
> the Provisional IRA.
>
> To replace the military role of the
> Army, Special Branch assembled a
> top-secret maximum force squad—
> the SPECIAL SUPPORT UNIT . . .
>
> Their watchwords: Firepower,
> Speed, Aggression.

Captions or narration are also occasionally used in the body of the film to indicate uncertainty, and to show the audience what you, as a scriptwriter, are doing.
What happened in the final hours leading to the Lockerbie air disaster is shrouded
in mystery. This is covered in Michael Eaton's script as follows:

137. INT MALTA AIRPORT. DAY

PAN DOWN TO PICK UP SALEEM WALKING TOWARDS T.
PORT ENTRANCE CARRYING THE SUITCASE.

> NARRATION OR CAPTION OVER
> "The precise events of the day
> which was to end with the deaths
> of 270 people remain unclear, and
> the subject of the biggest murder
> investigation in history. But offi-
> cial reports and records, supple-
> mented by our own investigations,
> point to a pattern of security fail-
> ures which marked the day of the
> tragedy."

The Basic Format

For the most part, the layout formats for both film and TV scripts are virtually identical. There are slight variations in the format for tape scripts, but nothing worth bothering about.

1: Scene Setting

The first thing the script has to indicate is location, time of the day, and whether the scene takes place indoors or out. This is done using uppercase and can be underlined or not, as you prefer. The scene is also given a number. What you have looks like this:

3 INT. BETTY'S HOUSE LA JOLLA - NIGHT

or

140 EXT. MALTA AIRPORT - DAY

As you can see, abbreviations are used for "interior" and "exterior."

2: Action and Character Description

Action and character description are set in lowercase and go the full width of the page. When character's names are mentioned, they are referred to in uppercase, as you can see below.

59 EXT. NEW YORK COUNTRYSIDE - DAY

Early dawn on a lonely country road, a day full of promise. A
ribbon of light on the horizon. The sound of birds. JOHN
BIRCH, a handsome man in his late twenties, very middle
class, is leaning against his Cadillac, reading. His chauffeur,
GEORGE, mid-forties, middle-aged, rumpled, has stripped off his
shirt and is changing the car tire. A car with its headlights on
enters the frame.

Here the action is clear, and we have given a minimum description of John
and George. We could have elaborated and indicated that John is a Harvard grad
and snobbish, but that will probably emerge later. In the above we are really setting the scene. Later we may want to describe real action.

JOHN listens in disbelief. He strikes his head as if to hammer
home the message. He is clowning. He draws a hand down
over his face to wipe away the laughter. FRANK moves forward and suddenly punches JOHN in the stomach.

In many British TV scripts, like the example we saw from the start of *Death
of a Princess*, the action is described in uppercase. That's fine, except that the
characters don't stand out quite so clearly.

3: Dialogue
We print the name of the character speaking in uppercase (under-
lining or not according to your preference), and the dialogue in lowercase. The dialogue is also set in from the margins.

                  FRANK
          I thought the big boys had taken
          care of that stool pigeon. You
          mean I'll have to waste another
          bullet on him? Well, maybe I'll
          just use my hands. I haven't had
          any exercise for some time.

                  HARRY
          Just do it quickly and efficiently.
          And don't leave any traces.

                                  CUT TO:

When you put everything together, the page looks like this:

27 INT. SCHOOL HALL - DAY

The platform of a hall in a girl's school. The HEADMISTRESS addresses the girls at their prize giving. She is flanked by THE PRIME MINISTER.

> HEADMISTRESS
> Sir Michael needs little introduc-
> tion. A man who has excelled in
> everything he has done . . .

She looks down at her notes, and is interrupted by DAVE, who bursts onto the platform.

> DAVE
> ...like murdering us poor sods
> here and calling it justice.

CUT TO:

You'll notice that we've ended this and the previous scene with the words CUT TO. This is the standard exit from the scene unless you want to dissolve between scenes, in which case you use DISSOLVE TO:.

4: Camera Directions

Many novice writers fill their scripts full of camera directions and advice to the actors. Don't. That's the task of the director. If you want that job, fine, but for the moment you are just the writer.

But where does your job end? You've envisaged the script in a very definite way and though you acknowledge the director's function, you'd really like him or her to see what you had in mind. Well, you can add to the bare bones of the script, but only cautiously, and only as a hint. While you avoid full camera directions, it's fairly well accepted that the writer may use the following suggestions:

ANGLE ON: This means you want to favor a particular character. Joan is speaking, but you indicate that attention should be paid to Dave.

POINT OF VIEW, or P.O.V.: Here the image on the screen is seen from the point of view of one of the characters. John is having an eye operation. We show John on the table for shot 17, and make shot 18 P.O.V. John. This means we want to see the room through John's eyes, blurred, with the doctors gazing down at him.

CLOSE UP, or C.U.: This is pretty obvious. It's very important that you see Helen's face as she hears about the legacy, or the surgeon's hands as he does the operation, so you put in C.U. Helen, or C.U. hands.

5: Other Script Directions

Besides P.O.V. and everything we've mentioned above, there are two other abbreviations you'll be using quite frequently . . . O.S. and V.O.

O.S. or O.C. stands for OFF SCREEN or OFF CAMERA. We use these abbreviations when we hear a character but don't actually see him on the screen. We had a good example of this in *Her Final Fury* in the scene with prosecutor Kerry and her kids. Kerry is talking to her husband but we also hear the offscreen voice of son Gary yelling for his shoes.

V.O. is simply VOICE OVER. Here we are watching some action, usually no one is talking, and we hear a voice without seeing its origin. For example, we are looking at fighting and we hear, V.O., "Those were hard years. Dad was away. The kids were growing up. There was little money . . . but . . . but we had spirit. Not just us, but everyone on the block."

The final directions that you are likely to use are FLASHBACK, MONTAGE, and DREAM SEQUENCE. You saw examples of FLASHBACK in the Betty Broderick extract, and its uses are fairly obvious. The same is true of MONTAGE and DREAM SEQUENCE. Like flashbacks, these script devices are to be used with caution.

Take the "falling in love" montage, for example. We've all seen it in countless forms. They've spent their first night together; now they . . . ride the motor bike in the surf as the sun goes down, try all the rides at the amusement park, buy everything in all the local stores, take the ferry to Staten Island, and so on. Once that montage worked. Today it has become a cliché.

6: The Master Scene

Most scripts are turned in in what is called the master scene format. This means there is no breakdown of specific shooting directions. That work is done by the director, and what emerges is called the shooting script.

The master scene, which is what we have been talking about all this chapter, occurs, as we've said, in one place, at one time, with one group of characters. It may be composed of one shot, or split into different shots, but this is left for the director to decide, not the writer.

Commencing the Script

Breaking the Ice

You've got your story, and you've done your research. You've also thought about plot, structure, and conflict, and all those things we discussed earlier. You know all about formats, and you may even have written a treatment. Don't be suprised, however, if there is a certain reluctance to start putting words on paper. In spite of all the preparations, there can be a psychological barrier about this final test. Don't worry. Everyone faces it and overcomes it.

This is the point where it is worth relaxing for a moment. You know if you can get the first few pages down, all will be fine. Well, let's think. You know roughly what your first scene is, because you've already set it down in your outline. What was it about? Oh yes, Cambridge University, in the middle of the nineteenth century. Next, ask yourself a few questions. What do you want to establish? A mood of indolence, idleness, luxury, and money. That should be easy. And what else? That linguist Edward Palmer is going to unknown Sinai.

None of this is difficult, but what you have to do is try hard and visualize the scene before you write it. If you've done some research on location, that shouldn't be too hard. Cambridge . . . what does it conjure up? River. Girls. Men in formal teaching gowns. Green lawns. College spires. Picnics. So you give your brain a push and then jump in, and it doesn't matter if it isn't very good, because you are going to go back and revise it later. But you must get started somewhere, so let's dive in.

```
1: EXT. CAMBRIDGE UNIVERSITY 1865 - DAY

It is a bright spring day at Cambridge. A river runs in front
of us and a couple laze in a boat. Behind them couples walk
arm in arm in the college gardens while an old-fashioned
cricket match proceeds in the background. While we hear
shouts of "jolly good" and "well played, sir," the camera moves
into the glass windows of a magnificent college. This is KINGS.
Now we hear another voice emerge over the sounds of the
cricket.

                    JAMISON (V.O.)
          But tell me, sir, this crackpot
          scheme. What will you get out of
          it? . . .

2: INT. KINGS COLLEGE - DAY

                    JAMISON (Cont'd)
          You'll be away a year. Your stu-
          dents will forget you. The academy
          will forget you. Even your patrons,
          the Bible Society, will forget you.
          For what...? A few bits of pottery
          and a heathen's ring.
```

PALMER smiles through all this. He is a handsome man, well over six feet, with an air of cheerful authority.

> PALMER
> Ah, Professor Jamison, where is
> your spirit of adventure? Can't
> you feel the Sinai beckoning?
> Think of yourself. Six in the
> morning, gazing down on the
> sands of time...before you the
> black tents of the nomads, behind
> you maybe the very rock that
> Moses struck. And you're standing
> where no Englishman has been.
> Isn't that better than teaching
> Chaucer to nice Christian gentle-
> men...?

3: EXT. BEDOUIN CAMP - DAY

Three BRITISH OFFICERS are sitting on rocks in the middle of an oasis. Sweat is pouring off all of them, and they continually drink from mess canteens. A fourth OFFICER, BERKELY, rides up on a camel, dismounts, and walks slowly towards the group.

> CAPTAIN
> Any traces...? Anything?

> BERKELY
> Nothing, sir. they tracked him as
> far as Wadi Arrah, and then lost
> him. At this stage he must be
> desperate. No water. No food...

> CAPTAIN
> Wadi Arrah? Damn the bloody fool
> of a man. What does he think he's
> on, a picnic in Regent's Park?

And so you go on, scene by scene till the end of the script. Continually, you'll be asking yourself, does this scene strike the right note? Has it got the element of tension I want? Does it advance the action? Is it funny? Is the placing correct? Is it too short? Is it too long? Does it arise naturally out of the scene before? Does it set up the action to come? You won't know the answers, but it is the questioning that counts.

Outlines v. Scripts

I once saw a greeting card in London. It showed a sparrow looking at a hippopotamus, and the caption read, "Ours is a strange and beautiful relationship." The same can be said of the relationship between your outline and your script.

Your outline is a plan, you hope a very good plan, for something that has yet to be born or created. It is the sketch, the plan, the guide that shows you the possibilities and the problems . . . but it is not the work itself. This means that your script is going to have an independent life, which your treatment can only hint at, and that independence has to be respected.

Let me put this another way. Many beginning writers use the treatment as a safety shield. The danger there is that by slavishly following the treatment guidelines, you may risk losing vibrancy and creativity in the script itself. The script has its own, independent life. As you write, as your characters come alive on the page, they and their dialogue and actions will assume a reality you couldn't even dream about. What you have to do is go with that new reality and forget the treatment. If, later, the script doesn't work, then use the treatment to check some of the technical points, like structure and turning points. Unless you put the treatment aside you will never learn to respect your new-born creation.

Approach

Scriptwriting is a little like long-distance running. The first time out all you want to do is get to the end. Then gradually you start improving your time and having fun. So don't worry about your first script, or your second. Just do them. Jump in. Write. Take some chances. Have a ball. Then reread the scripts, and try acting as your own critic. Ask yourself . . . is this the best, or could I have done better? Is this fine, or could it be improved?

There will be endless revisions, some at your suggestion, some arising from script conferences. You will be asked to rewrite, and then rewrite on top of that. It will happen before production and during production. It will seem as if the process never ends, but then the day comes when the film is finished and you see your name up there on the screen. And that moment is worth everything.

Special Considerations

11

Adaptations

Writing adaptations is tricky, problematic, challenging, and fun. And you must know how to do them, because they are very much in demand. *Malcolm X*, *Citizen Cohn*, and *My Left Foot* were all adapted from biographies and autobiographies; *And the Band Played On* and *Barbarians at the Gate* started their lives as best-sellers; *The Killing Fields*, *Zulu*, and *The French Connection* were taken from articles, while *Eleanor and Franklin* started as a Broadway play.

One can see the attraction for a producer. The story is pre-sold and highly popular and the advertising has already been done. When *Diana: Her True Story* by Andrew Morton was first published in England, it was sold out in hours. It stayed on the best-seller list for weeks and repeated that performance in the U.S. Eventually the screen rights were taken up by Martin Poll Films, and the TV version went on to become one of the highest-rated shows ever, world-wide.

Rights

Before you start work on an adaptation, you must obtain permission to go ahead from the owner of the copyright. There are two ways of doing this:

1: You can make a full purchase of the rights
2: You can take out an *option* on the screen rights

This means you have exclusive permission to purchase the rights within a certain amount of time. You normally purchase the full rights only when and if you are absolutely sure the film can and will be made, or if you are scared some one will get in before you. Otherwise you take an option.

You do this because an option costs much less than the full acquisition of the rights. In effect, you are saying, give me time to think about the whole project, and see whether I really want to go ahead with it, or if I can interest someone in it. Then, if everything works out, I'll come back and purchase the full rights for an agreed fixed sum at a later date.

In some cases you may not have to pay for the rights. This is when the work is in the public domain, or the copyright has expired. As the odds are that most of the books or articles you want to adapt will be fairly recent, this proviso about public domain probably won't affect you very much.

This whole question of rights is fairly complex and I've dealt with it at length in Chapter Thirteen. I merely raise the problem here as a warning . . . don't start adapting anything until you are sure you have a clearance on the rights.

Now, there are some writers who say, "What the hell! Let's take a chance." They then go ahead, start the adaptation, and try to get permission later. Their attitude is, "The adaptation will be so good it will be easier for me to get the permission at a lower price," or, "Once the author sees the adaptation he won't want to refuse me." Well, maybe! I'm not saying it's impossible. It's a bit dangerous and you may finish up with months of work down the drain.

The Task of Adaptation

Adapting something means changing it, altering it, modifying it. For much of the time in screenplay writing, it also means cutting and simplifying. "Big deal," you might say. "Isn't that what they do with *Readers' Digest*? What's so difficult?" The problem is you are working in a totally different medium, film, that achieves its goal in a totally different way from print. You are trying to create a script, from which a film will be made that works through visuals, editing, dialogue, music, and effects. In short, you will be creating a totally new form . . . an *original* screenplay.

There are two approaches to your task. First, you can slavishly follow the original. You say to yourself, "What is in the book or in the play is hallowed, and must be in the film." This means using every incident, character, and piece of dialogue from the original and placing it in the script. I think this is the recipe for disaster.

Or you can say to yourself, "I am creating something totally new. The original work is my jumping-off point. I will be faithful to its spirit and faithful to its feeling. But I'm working in a different medium and that requires different solutions and techniques to bring the work to life."

Occasionally, of course, an audience will require absolute adherence to parts of the original. Selznick couldn't have made *Gone With the Wind* and deprived Scarlett of "I'll never be hungry again," or denied Rhett Butler his "Frankly, my dear, I don't give a damn."

Yet I doubt if this will really trouble you, because most of the books you are using will not be fiction best-sellers, and you will not come across that many memorable phrases. It happens . . . Franklin Delano Roosevelt saying, "We have nothing to fear but fear itself," and Churchill saying, "Never in the field of human conflict was so much owed by so many to so few . . . ," but it's nothing to worry about. In other words, consider yourself free.

Mindset

Before you start work on an adaptation, you have to get in the right frame of mind. You've probably read the book four or five times, and your head is full of details and plots and incidents and so on. That was necessary, but now the time has come to let go. You have to cut the umbilical cord to the original work.

It sounds strange but what you have to do, at least at first, is put a certain distance between yourself and details. Instead, you have to ask yourself how you understood and experienced the book? What were the feelings you were left with? What moved you? What was the underlying spirit and tone of the book? These questions lead you to the heart and soul of the book, and your task is to get your screenplay and the finished film to *evoke* the same feelings and the same reactions.

After getting in the right frame of mind, you have to consider how to achieve your goal. In doing the adaptation, you are going to use all those techniques we've discussed up to now. You are going to construct something which is probably structured in three acts, or seven if it's for television. You are probably going to have a main hero, who has certain goals and faces major obstacles. You are going to have a good beginning and a powerful end. The film is going to go at a sparkling pace . . . and it's also going to look very good.

You are also going to lose masses of the book. Whole chapters, incidents, and characters will disappear. Other sections will be reordered. Characters will be combined and dialogue invented. When that's all done, you are going to consider two last things. You have to remind yourself that the three-and-a-half-hour play, or the 1,000-page book, has to be fitted into a two-hour screenplay. And finally, you may want to ponder the word "Commercial!" You remind yourself that although the book was a *succes d'estime*, it only sold a few thousand copies to a limited audience. In contrast, you are writing a film for a mass audience. That may require you to shape the film in certain ways and think very hard about your presentation of controversies.

Media Differences

Your key problem, as I've already suggested, is that you are adapting a work into a new form. You are going from a medium dominated by words into a medium dominated by images. This has two implications. First, what works in one form doesn't necessarily work in the other, and secondly, different forms use different techniques for expressing the same idea. It's essential therefore to consider some of the differences among books, plays, and films.

1: Books and Biographies

Books work through words and an accumulation of detail. Often there is little action. Pages are spent setting out background, atmosphere, characters, memories, and processes. In *The Hunt for Red October*, page after page was spent on detailing the mechanical workings of the submarines and defense technology. It didn't matter. In books you can skip what is boring, or reread what is complex and difficult to absorb.

Books examine psychology and motivation. They pursue ideas. They wander into the philosophical, they ask questions. They become reflective. They examine inner souls, thoughts, motivations, hesitations. They jump between first person and third person. Often they digress, and frequently the manner of the narration is more important than the story.

I know it is a trifle unfair to lump the characteristics of books together like this, but this way you can easily see the problems. This way you can understand why your work goes beyond modification, and will involve you in creating something totally new.

2: Plays

Plays are dependent on dialogue, which can be straight, elliptical, or even poetic, and on a certain magical relationship between the players and the audience. They can examine the particular, such as a triangle situation in a Noel Coward play, or the human condition, as in the Greek plays.

Generally theater works best examining character relationships and the small, personal, and intimate problems of people. The immediate story may reflect a much larger problem, but it never loses its own particularity. So while Mamet's *Oleanna* provoked a wide debate on the nature of feminism, it always remained grounded in the story of the university professor and his student.

Plays can examine ideas and human struggles but are limited in action and setting. An occasional murder can take place, but not the invasion of the Normandy beaches. Place can change, but only to a limited extent.

Films work in a totally different way. They take advantage of space and the capacity for broad action. They tend to make their points visually rather than through dialogue. They are aided by amazing technical devices, and have all the resources of editing and shot selection at their command.

The greatest change involved in translating plays to films is in *opening up*, making use of film's ability to explore beyond the walls of the stage. Thus while the stage version of *Shadowlands* was mainly confined to college rooms and C.S. Lewis's home, the film version could give us the whole exterior feel of the university with its walks and gardens.

One of the best examples of the screen's ability to open up a play and use its techniques superbly is seen in Kenneth Branagh's *Much Ado About Nothing*. In the original, a messenger says of Don Pedro, "He is very near by this: he was not three leagues off when I left him." A page later he simply says, "Don Pedro is approached," and the Don enters.

How is this simplest of dialogue translated onto film? We see galloping horses, close-up of hooves, men riding in fury, women racing through bedrooms, showers taken in haste, finery buttoned in passion, till two perspiring, eager, wide-eyed groups of men and women confront each other. The sequence creates a wonderful breathless start to the film, and is all suggested by the words "He is near, not three leagues off."

3: Articles

Articles have inspired films, but not nearly as often as books or plays, and it is easy to see why. The most frequent problem with articles, both in newspapers and magazines, is that we have masses of information but no clear filmic story. Often we have a complex situation, an abundance of characters, important, intricate details, but no sense of a clear line which will guide us dramatically through an entertaining story.

While I was researching this book, I collected a number of exclusive articles on two public scandals. One related to the Bank of Credit and Commerce International, and the second touched on a secret sale of weapons parts to Iraq by British companies. My idea was to present these two subjects to you in the section on "finding the film." It just didn't work, because I couldn't myself see a way to make decent films of either subject.

The Bank of Credit and Commerce was an Arabian bank that was involved in some very shaky deals. Its customers had lost millions, and white-collar fraud was alleged at the highest levels. A number of well-known American public figures were also involved, with one of them going to trial.

At first the idea had looked very promising; then I found the subject was simply too complex. There were no heroes, no clear beginning, no clear ending. From the point of view of journalism, each new revelation made fascinating reading, but it was all too dense for a film.

The second series of articles, involving the Matrix Churchill company, suffered in the same way. In the late eighties, the British government under Mrs. Thatcher had publicly banned arms shipments to Iraq. In spite of this, strategic parts were still secretly being sent to the Middle East by a few companies, with the connivance of various officials. This state of affairs blew up in the face of the government, and in 1993, a series of investigatory trials took place.

The facts were fascinating, but again, it was all too much. There were too many characters. The drama was unclear. There was no obvious shape to the film. In short, there was no story as seen in the articles, at least no story that would work well on film, unless one invented a great deal.

In contrast, one has to consider *The Sunday Times* articles about Mordecai Vanunu, the Israeli atom spy. Here the story was clear and defined, with only two or three major characters, a love affair, suspense, and a clear beginning and end. So making a film from the articles was the easiest thing possible.

Method

An adaptation is an original screenplay. The source material is merely your jumping-off point. I keep stressing that because it is so important. Understand that and your work will be much simpler. Now, you know in principle that you are going to be translating from one form to another, and that your principal tasks will be to cut, eradicate, alter, and simplify. But where do you begin?

My own starting point is to consider whether I am aiming for a feature film or a TV movie. I have to make the choice because it has budget implications. If I take Alex Haley's book on Malcom X and do it as a single film for TV, I know the producer will have to work within, say, a four-to seven-million dollar budget. If I do it as a feature, then the producer's budget might stretch to $25 million. With $25 million, I know I can write scenes that would be impossible on the smaller budget.

My next move is to make a breakdown of the book. I do this by taking a lawyer's yellow pad, dividing it into columns, and then listing any scenes, characters, details, and dialogue that interest me. I also make copious notes. I am feeling my own reactions to the material, and trying to envisage where something in the original has possibilities for the film. All the while I'm telling myself, you need drama, a good story, and it must be visual.

I'm also trying to figure out very clearly what the story is really about, what its theme is, and what message, if any, it carries. So if I do a film on Churchill, although I am showing the events of his life, the story is about the triumph of righteousness over evil. In *Diana: Her True Story*, the story shows us the progression of the marriage, but the film is about an individual confronting a calcified monarchy and triumphing, and a young girl finding an inner strength.

Once I've made the breakdown, I begin to consider four problematic areas in detail: story, structure, characters, and cutting and creating.

Story

Very often your original material presents you with too many goodies. You have stories galore, and you don't know which one to choose. This was the main problem in Darryl Zanuck's *The Longest Day*, and also in Joseph Levine's *A Bridge Too Far*.

Both books deal with complex battles of the Second World War, both have hundreds of characters, and both are by the same author, Cornelius Ryan. The second film is about the disastrous battle fought by the British paratroopers for the possession of the Arnhem bridges in Holland in 1944, and was scripted by William Goldman. This is how Goldman writes about it in his autobiography.

Our problem was trying to find a story line. The Ryan book is well over 650 pages of not the largest print. It's filled with fabulous material . . . but which story to tell. There were so damn many . . . There were too many incidents that cried out for inclusion—*five* Victoria crosses were awarded for heroism. Surely I needed those five . . .

None of the main characters died . . . so I began to fiddle with trying to make some small, instantly sympathetic roles—so that I could have someone to kill in the story.

Goddamit, though, which story?

Goldman says that his problem was solved when he lucked into structure. Suddenly he realized that for all its complexity, *Bridge* was a cavalry-to-the-rescue story in which the cavalry fails to arrive.

That was my spine and anything that wouldn't cling to it I couldn't use. All five Victoria crosses fell out of the picture. Super material went by the boards. But it had to.

There it is. You have to make choices. Something has to go. Find your key story and junk what distracts from that. Ask yourself whether it's clearly focused, and whether the conflicts and problems are well shaped and not ambiguous or fuzzy. If you are satisfied on these points, then you can relax slightly.

Sometimes you may have time for a minor story or a sub-plot, but view it very carefully. Is your main story in place, and will it stay in place even if you weave things around it? It will . . . OK, then you can go ahead.

Sometimes your story may not change much from the book, at least in main actions, and yet different emphases can send it off in different directions.

In 1993, HBO finally screened a film version of Randy Shilts's 1987 book *And the Band Played On*. It had been floating around for five years, had interested many film producers, but was thought to present a myriad of problems. At the simplest level it was, as producer Edgar Scherick put it, " . . . a rich but very segmented tapestry, one that didn't appear to me easily rendered to the screen."

Soon after it came out, NBC purchased an option on the book but was never quite sure what the story was about. Although Mr. Shilts's book dealt very widely with the science and politics of AIDS, the subtext deals with the life of gay men and how the practices of some of them affected the spread of AIDS. However, what NBC wanted was a picture about AIDS, but not about gays. That was a different story. When it came time to pick up the option in late 1989, NBC passed, and everything stayed in limbo until HBO revived the project a year later.

Your story may be clear, but you still may not be sure *how* to tell the story. I'm not talking about structure here, but rather through whose eyes we view the proceedings. This is not a new problem and we discussed it at some length in regard to *Exxon Valdez*, where the story was carried by Dan Lawn and Frank Iarossi.

If your protagonist is clear from the original, then fine. If it's not, then you may have to hunt a bit to find the right character. This problem usually arises when your original work tells the stories of dozens of people, but no one seems to have any centrality.

However, at that juncture you've already done some cutting and simplifying. Out of five possible stories and threads you've decided what your story is. Given that, you then hunt for the one or two characters who can carry it in the best way. Or you combine one or two characters, creating a composite who can carry the story line.

Randy Shilts's book *And the Band Played On* has a dazzling variety of characters and presented all the problems mentioned above for scriptwriter Arnold Schulman. But who was going to be the hero? After a discussion with HBO, a decision was made to tell the story from the point of view of Dr. Don Francis, an epidemiologist with the Centers for Disease Control. The decision is not obvious from reading the original, but is the kind of decision you face constantly in adaptations.

Another decision you occasionally have to make is whether or not to keep the voice and viewpoint of the original, or change it. Again, your actions will be determined solely by what makes for a better film. Kazuo Ishiguro's fine novel *The Remains of the Day* is related by its butler hero, Mr. Stevens, who is very prone to reflection and self-questioning. In the film, this first-person voice is rightly abandoned. Instead, we view the man from the outside. We don't need the inner voice because his filmic deeds and interaction with people now reveal the man so clearly.

Structure

Everything you've learned about structure, rhythm, pacing, dramatic rises, emotional easing off, powerful beginnings, and climactic endings applies with equal force to adaptations. As before, you are looking for a logical flow to your story, a dramatic flow, and a flow that will involve the audience and pull in their emotions.

To get a good flow to your film you need a good structure, and to get a good structure you may have to throw overboard a good deal of your original material. As we said, adapting is cutting, amending, simplifying, finding your film story line, and then shaping it and molding it into a powerful and dramatic script.

William Goldman cites several problems he had to face in adapting and scripting *All the President's Men*. As he puts it, "The book had no structure that jumped out at me. And very little dialogue. I also couldn't take great liberties with the material [because everyone was familiar with the story]."

Goldman's crucial decision was to throw away the last half of the book. In his opinion, the main filmic interest in the story ended after a mistake of Woodward and Bernstein regarding the handling of Haldeman. He then asked Woodward to list for him the most important events in the story, in the order in which they happened. All were contained in the first half of the book, so the junking process was justified.

Goldman's script also illustrates one other thing, the difference in the way you start a book and the way you start a film. The book opens with life in Nixon's Washington. And the film . . . ? Right! It starts off with the break-in at the Watergate complex. You don't waste time, you just get straight in there.

Where beginnings can be hard is when you are adapting intricate biographies and complex medical industrial and disaster stories. This is because the writer has had time to play around with background, atmosphere, history, and prehistory before he or she gets into the main story. But you can't do that in film. Instead, you have to move in fast and grab the audience.

This means that in a film about Churchill, you ignore what the book said about the father and the grandfather building their estates, and plunge straight into the hero's career in the army. Similarly, in a film about Henry Ford, you ignore the chapters on the evolution of the steam engine and other mechanical transport, and go straight to young Ford building his first car.

When you adapt a book, beware of your change of audience. The book was possibly a minority taste, bought by only a few people with a prior interest in the subject. Your film, however, aims at a mass audience, and you have to draw them into your subject from the start. That means if they know nothing about the subject, you have to provide context and background immediately, as in the case of *Citizen Cohn*.

HBO's film *Citizen Cohn* is based on the biography of Roy Cohn by Nicholas von Hoffman. Cohn was a lawyer in the *fifties*, and is today probably unknown to many people under the age of forty. This problem of identification and interest was solved by creating two introductory sequences.

The first shows a montage of U.S. news footage from the fifties. The emphasis is on the cold war, the fight against communism, the fear of atomic warfare, the rise of McCarthyism, and the pursuit of Reds. So very briefly we are given the spirit of the times.

The next sequence takes place in a hospital. It's 1986 and a man is dying. A nurse and a doctor hover around the bed.

```
                    NURSE
          Who is this guy?


                  YOUNG DOCTOR
          The White House rang. The Presi-
          dent wanted to know what he
          could do for him.
```

> SENIOR DOCTOR
> Probably wanted to make sure he
> was dead.

> DOCTOR
> Did you know this guy?

> SENIOR DOCTOR
> We knew him all right. Joe
> McCarthy's right-hand man.

> DOCTOR
> My father said he was a great
> patriot...

> SENIOR DOCTOR
> Great patriot...?

> DOCTOR
> The spies. The Rosenbergs. He got
> them executed.

> SENIOR DOCTOR
> Well, twenty dollars says the
> great patriot doesn't make it till
> dawn.

> COHN
> (rising up from the bed) Fuck
> you!

We are now really hooked by the sequence. Who is this man that Presidents feared, who was the right hand of Joe McCarthy, and who got men executed? We want to know more, and suddenly we are into the body of the picture.

Cutting and Creating

The art and craft of adaptation is dominated by two things, the need to cut and the need to invent.

Cutting is the easiest. You weed out irrelevant scenes, chapters, characters, and incidents until you have a malleable story with a clear focus and direction. Creating is the other side of the coin. Here you may need to invent incidents and scenes that may only have been hinted at in the book. Other scenes may exist in the original but need fleshing out. They may also need reordering for better dramatic effect. You may have to amalgamate characters, or create new ones. And you most definitely will have to create dialogue, even though a lot may come from the source.

However, because you are working from real life, and real people will be affected by your script, you must have a clear sense of the parameters of invention. Some of the limitations are legal, some are common sense. As we mentioned before, you are severely constrained by the laws of libel and privacy, and more on that in Chapter Thirteen.

You will have to create dialogue, but if you are careful it shouldn't create problems. If you are lucky, much of the dialogue will appear in your source material or be available from diaries and reports. It will often be stilted, and your task then is to take the essence of the dialogue and turn it into simple conversational English.

Where the dialogue has to be totally invented, you have to ask yourself various questions. Is the new dialogue appropriate to this person in this situation? Does it truly mirror his or her attitude and opinions? Is it something he or she could have said? Is it said in his or her style? And is it likely to give offense? In other words, is the dialogue within the realms of the probable and the possible? If it is, then you have nothing to fear.

Amalgamating characters is also something that you are going to do quite frequently, and it has to be done with great care. If a number of doctors are equally involved in inventing a new drug, and none are in the public eye or well known, you would have a case for fictionalizing or amalgamating them into one. If one of the doctors was more prominent, or claimed to have discovered the drug by himself, then you would probably leave him as he was.

These decisions aren't easy. There are few rules and every case has to be judged on its own merits.

Since the problem of fictionalization is so tricky, and can create immense legal problems, most networks issue guidelines on the subject. For example, they will require information about composite or fictional characters in your script to make sure there is no claim for accidental identification. The guidelines are worth looking at, and I've reprinted a copy of the NBC rules in Appendix D.

Do you feel overwhelmed at this stage? There's no need to be. A Jewish sage was once asked to summarize the Bible while standing on one leg. "Easy," he said. "Treat your neighbors as you would have them treat you." The art of adaptation can be answered in a similarly brief way. "Forget the original and create something new." Pin that over your typewriter and you can't go wrong.

The Process in Practice

In order to show you how the art of adaptation works in practice, I've chosen three books and their film scripts as examples for further analysis.

Empire of the Sun, is a novel based on fact that was turned into a major feature film. My second and third choices, *Diana: Her True Story* and *Barbarians at the Gate*, are non-fiction best-sellers that gave birth to two very successful television productions. All three books and screenplays are very different, and examined together illustrate many of the problems and possibilities of adaptations.

Empire of the Sun

J. G. Ballard's novel *Empire of the Sun* was published in 1984. It tells the story of Jim, a young British boy living in Shanghai in 1941, just as the Japanese are about to take over the city. Based on Ballard's own life, the book starts with Jim's separation from his parents and follows him into imprisonment in a Japanese concentration camp.

The book was very well received in the literary world and Ballard received a great deal of praise. Shortly afterwards, it was made into a film directed by Steven Spielberg and scripted by Tom Stoppard.

It is a tremendously visual book, has wonderful dialogue, contains dozens of characters, and dramatic incidents are piled one upon another. From this it can be seen that Stoppard's task was relatively simple: essentially cutting, amalgamating, and simplifying.

Although Stoppard's script was based on a fictional work, it is well worth looking at, because it shows you the art of adaptation at its best. Below I've tried to give you a few examples of Stoppard's approach, while pointing out some changes from the original.

1: Straight Paralleling from the Book

Early on in the book, Jim loses his parents and is chased by a Chinese boy with a knife. This is repeated more or less exactly in the script, with one difference. In the book the scene trails off with Jim going home to Amherst Avenue. In the film he is "saved" by passing Americans.

2: Displacement of Incidents

A very sharp, significant moment in the film is when Jim returns home and sees his amah and another servant stealing furniture. When he talks to them he is cuffed, and cannot grasp why his amah has changed so quickly from obedient retainer to angry enemy. In the book we are shown the same incident, but everything takes place *at a friend's house*. By changing the incident to involve Jim's own amah, Stoppard makes the scene much more significant for Jim's understanding of the new order of things.

3: Characters

Dozens of characters float through the book, and amongst them Basie, the American, is just one of many who pass through Jim's life. In the film he becomes the second major character after Jim, of major interest to us in his own right.

4: Implied Scenes

At the start of the book we are told that Jim is a chorister, and are then shown him watching *March of Time* with the other choristers. This scene is dropped from the film. Instead, the opening shows us Jim singing in the cathedral. It's a very important scene because in one go it gives us Jim's Britishness, the importance of tradition (which is going to go up in smoke) and the bizarreness of holding on to such things in the middle of the Orient.

5: Amalgamated and Implied Scenes

One of the most powerful sequences in the film is when Jim hunts for pheasants beyond the borders of the camp. He is induced to do this by Basie and the promise of a place in the American's hut. The guards suspect he is there and as they hunt him, the American prisoners take bets on whether Jim will live or die.

It's a great sequence, but it didn't happen that way in the original. In the book, mention of hunting pheasants occurs twice. The first time we simply find Jim out beyond the camp borders looking for the birds. He is almost caught by guards but escapes.

The second time we hear of pheasants is when Jim talks to Basie about something else, and then wonders what the purpose is behind the hunt.

> The whole enterprise of setting traps had nothing to do with catching pheasants. Perhaps one of the Americans was planning to visit Shanghai, and Jim was being used to test the escape route. Alternatively these bored sailors might be playing a game, betting among each other how far Jim could push the traps before being shot by the Japanese sentry in the watch tower.

The filmic blend of the two scenes is excellent. The idea of an escape route is correctly dropped and the emphasis put on the betting. However, the book lacks a rationale. Why would Jim go through such dangers?

This is supplied by a film invention: "to get into the men's quarters." We accept the rationale and also enjoy Jim's triumphant, but invented, entry into the ranks of "the big boys."

6: Ending

In the penultimate chapter of the book, Jim rushes into a camp hospital and is told by a doctor, "Your parents are waiting for you, Jim." It's almost a throw-away. There is no description of the meeting and we go on to a last chapter which details Jim's reflections on the war.

This is fine as a climax for a book, but not for a film. Instead, Stoppard gives us a scene where children wait to be collected by their parents after two or three years' separation. Jim's mother threads her way through the crowd. She sees Jim. They hug, and that's it. It's a simple but effective closure.

Diana: Her True Story

Andrew Morton's book *Diana: Her True Story* came out in 1992, and became an instant best-seller. Later it was made into a TV mini-series by Martin Poll Films, with a script by Stephen Zito.

On the whole, the film follows the book very faithfully, but there is one alteration of emphasis which is very important. Although the book frequently mentions Camilla Parker-Bowles, she is merely one element of anxiety among many. In the film, however, she comes very much to the fore as one of the principal causes for Diana's jealousy and insecurity.

Below I've extracted sections from the book, together with various script sequences, so that you can see in detail the relationship of one to the other. I've also tried to point out the rationale for some of the changes, and have underlined dialogue passages in the script that are taken straight from the book.

1: Beginning
Both book and film start from the same point.

It was a memory engraved upon her soul. . . . She could hear her father loading suitcases into the boot of a car, then Frances, her mother, crunching across the gravel forecourt, the clunk of a car door being shut, and the sound of a car engine revving and fading as her mother drove through the gates of Park House and out of her life. Diana was six years old.

In the film we get the same scene, almost detail for detail. A six-year-old Diana sits at the bottom of the staircase. She hears a car drive away and her father enters.

EARL SPENCER
Don't worry, darling. Everything
will be all right.

DIANA
When will Mummy be coming
back?

EARL SPENCER
She doesn't want to live with us,
Diana. Not any longer.

DIANA
(in tears) She didn't even kiss me
goodbye.

The book then devotes a chapter to Diana's early years. This is all cut out of the film, except for a few nursery and holiday sequences. The atmosphere is taken from the book, but one obvious invented element is added, a small but pertinent question of her grandmother's as they watch the royal family on TV.

                    LADY FERMOY
          Tell me, Diana. What would you
          like to be when you grow up?

                       DIANA
          A ballet dancer or a princess.

                   SARAH SPENCER
          Diana, you're such a ninny!

                    LADY FERMOY
          Sarah! The first Lady Diana
          Spencer almost married the Prince
          of Wales two and a half centuries
          ago.

                       DIANA
          Didn't he love her, Grandma...?

Diana looks at Charles on the TV.

                       DIANA
          He has funny ears.

The scene also introduces us to Lady Fermoy. In the book she is a very incidental character, but in the film her part is enlarged. She becomes Diana's confidante, but is also shown as being very close to the Queen, so that we can get inside the royal view of the relationship.

2: Scene Expansion

In the second chapter, we are told a little bit more about Diana, and are given some information about a number of Charles's girlfriends, one of whom was Diana's elder sister. The book then goes on...

While their romance cooled off, Charles still asked Sarah [Diana's sister] to attend his 30th birthday party at Buckingham Palace in November 1978. Much to Sarah's surprise Diana was also invited. Cinderella was going to the ball.

The book then says that Diana enjoyed herself immensely and moves on to another topic. However, the setting of the party is too good for the scriptwriter to miss and the *expansion* takes up five pages of script. Diana sees the party as something out of a fairy tale. Her sister tells us that Charles is a romantic but never stays in love very long. Lord Mountbatten, Charles's uncle, talks to him about love, and the Queen Mother talks to Diana. It's the first "big scene" in the film and a chance to get to know many of the principal characters.

It also inserts a dramatic point, but one which is absent from the book. According to author Andrew Morton, Charles's escort for the evening was actress Susan George. In the film, there is no mention of the actress; instead Charles dances with Camilla, who will be Diana's rival for years.

```
CAMERA ON CHARLES DANCING WITH CAMILLA

                    CAMILLA
          Well, Fred. See anything here that
          catches your eye?


                    CHARLES
          Yes, I'm holding her in my arms.
```

3: Dialogue Roots

As is clear, most of the dialogue is made up. Even with friends present, it's highly unlikely we would know what Charles whispered to Camilla.

Morton's original book actually contains very little dialogue, and where it does, it usually mentions the source. Where possible Zito, the scriptwriter, incorporates known conversations into the script. *Hints* at conversations also get expanded in the script, though sometimes put into the mouths of different people.

On page 48 of the book we find the following passage:

Unfortunately for Charles, his title brought obligations as well as privileges. His duty was to marry and produce an heir to the throne. It was a subject Earl Mountbatten discussed endlessly with the Queen during afternoon tea at Buckingham Palace, while Prince Philip let it be known that he was growing impatient with his son's irresponsible approach to marriage.

A lot of this passage is transferred to the film, but put directly into the mouth of Lord Mountbatten, Charles's uncle.

```
                    CHARLES
          The problem is, Uncle Dicky, that
          most girls don't see me for what
```

I am. I tend to scare the really
nice ones away.

LORD MOUNTBATTEN
Quite right. But don't imagine that
because you've become a sort of
Royal pop idol that the British
people will always support you.
They'll back you only so long as
you serve the country. <u>And part
of your duty to the nation is to
marry and produce an heir</u>. The
people need to be assured the
monarchy will continue.

On the same page as the first quote from the book we also find this:

The Prince, then nearly 33 . . . had publicly acknowledged the problems of
finding a suitable bride. "Marriage is a much more important business than
falling in love . . . Essentially you must be good friends, and love, I'm sure,
will grow out of that friendship. I have a particular responsibility to ensure
that I make the right decision. The last thing I could possibly entertain is
getting divorced."

On another occasion he declared that marriage was a partnership where
his wife was not simply marrying a man but a way of life . . . Marriage in his
eyes was primarily the discharge of an obligation to his family and the
nation, a task made all the more difficult by the immutable nature of the
contract.

These lines of Charles's and the comments of Morton's finally find their way
into the film script in a courting scene between Charles and Diana in the gardens
of Bolehyde Manor.

CHARLES
When a man in my position marries, the choice must be made
very carefully. It has to be someone special . . . someone who can
fulfil the role. I think you are
lucky if you find the person
attractive in the physical sense as
well as the mental, but marriage
is basically a very strong partnership, Diana, a partnership.

> DIANA
> You've certainly given this matter
> considerable thought.

> CHARLES
> <u>A woman not only marries a</u>
> <u>man; she marries into a way of</u>
> <u>life</u>—a job. She's got to have some
> knowledge of it.

4: Suggested Scenes

Shortly after the book's discussion of Charles's marital needs, there is a short description of a house party in the country. This is the setting for a meeting between Charles and Diana which deepens their intimacy and propels them towards St. Paul's Cathedral and marriage. Lord Mountbatten's murder at the hands of the IRA is merely mentioned in passing in the book, as can be seen from this passage.

Diana was seated next to Charles on a bale of hay and, after the usual pleasantries, the conversation moved on to Earl Mountbatten's death and his funeral in Westminster Abbey. In a conversation which she later recalled to friends Diana told him: "You looked so sad when you walked up the aisle at the funeral. It was the most tragic thing I have ever seen. My heart bled for you when I watched it. I thought, it's wrong. You are lonely. You should be with somebody to look after you."

This casual mention of Mountbatten's death, however, provides the opportunity for Zito to develop three important sequences.

35A EXT. BALMORAL - DAY

Charles is out shooting. He fires both barrels of his shotgun at a bird on the wing. He hits nothing but air and stops in his tracks. He shivers with more than the cold.

As a premonition hits him like a truck, he looks up to see his father coming towards him. One look at Philip's face and Charles knows that something is wrong.

> PRINCE PHILIP
> (Gravely) We've come from Ire-
> land.

> CHARLES
> Uncle Dickie?

> PRINCE PHILIP
> Yes. The IRA.

> CHARLES
> Those bastards!

Father and son stand looking at each other. Even their shared sorrow cannot bridge the distance between them.

> CHARLES
> Thank you.

He turns without a word and walks away. Philip watches for a minute. Then Charles starts to run. He runs wildly, propelled by his grief.

From there, we move to Westminster Abbey to see the funeral itself.

42 INT. WESTMINSTER ABBEY - DAY

Charles movingly delivers a eulogy for his beloved Uncle.

> CHARLES
> The quality of real moral courage,
> of being able to face unpleasant
> tasks that need to be done—and
> yet to be fair and consistent—is a
> rare quality indeed.

CLOSE ON Diana who, with Sarah, Jane and Lady Fermoy, is among the mourners. She can't take her eyes off Charles.

His grief and his dignity move her deeply.

> CHARLES
> But he had it in abundance and
> that is one of the reasons why
> people would have followed him
> into hell. It is also one of the
> reasons why I adored him and
> why so many of us miss him
> dreadfully now.

This scene, which is not in the book, makes two very important contributions to the drama. First, it shows us Diana's growing feeling for Charles. Quite clearly she imagines Charles as having many of the same qualities as Mountbatten, and can clearly also see people following him into hell. Equally important, it shows us a human, vulnerable side of Charles that is missing for most of the film.

In the passage I quoted above from the book, Morton mentions discussion of "the usual pleasantries" and gives a brief quote of Diana's recollection of the funeral. In the film, the few lines are transformed by Zito into a major courting scene, the end of which is set out below.

Charles takes a long look at Diana. She's become an attractive young woman. Sweet and full of life. He's pleased at her good manners and breeding.

                    CHARLES
One feels secure around you, Diana.

                    DIANA
That's kind of you to say, Sir.

                    CHARLES
I think my uncle might have
approved of you.

                    DIANA
Lord Mountbatten must have been
a terrible loss for you.

                    CHARLES
(touched by her sympathy) I
adored him and miss him so
dreadfully now.

(growing quiet) He was more like
a father...He always had time
for me.

                    DIANA
I know exactly what you mean.
My grandmother's the one I
always depend on to set me on
the right path. (full of sympathy)
You looked so sad at the funeral.
I thought, "It's wrong. You are
lonely. You should be with somebody to look after you."

Her words have touched a deep chord. He sees her with new eyes.

                    CHARLES
          (flirting) Well, somebody better
          had.

He gives her a smile that says, "Are you interested in applying
for the job?"

5: Selection and Ordering

At the beginning of Chapter Five of his book, Morton details Diana's increasing depression after marriage, and the failure of Charles to understand or help.

> On that January day in 1982, her first New Year within the royal family, she now threatened to take her own life. Charles accused her of crying wolf and prepared to go riding on the Sandringham estate. She was as good as her word. Standing on top of the wooden staircase she hurled herself to the ground, landing in a heap at the bottom.

A page later, the book continues . . .

> The incident was one of many domestic crises which crowded in upon the royal couple in those tumultuous early days. . . . On one occasion she threw herself against a glass display cabinet at Kensington Palace, while on another she slashed at her wrists with a razor blade; on yet another, during a heated argument with Prince Charles, she picked up a penknife lying on his dressing table and cut her chest and thighs. Although she was bleeding her husband studiously scorned her.

The short note about preparations for riding and falling down stairs obviously offered Stephen Zito terrific dramatic possibilities, which he translates into film as follows:

212 INT. WINDSOR CASTLE - STAIRWAY - DAY

Charles is dressed in his riding habit—black coat, bowler hat,
white breeches, white hunting tie and black butcher boots.
Diana rushes after him.

                    DIANA
          Couldn't you stay home with me?

                    CHARLES
          They won't start the hunt without
          me.

> DIANA
>
> I can't take any more of this,
> Charles. I swear I'm going to do
> something drastic.
>
> CHARLES
>
> Why don't you just come along?
>
> DIANA
>
> Because standing in the mud
> watching you kill innocent animals
> for sport isn't my idea of spend-
> ing time together.

Charles, at a loss, starts to go.

> DIANA
>
> What about me?
>
> CHARLES
>
> What about you? (exploding) All I
> had to do was marry and produce
> an heir. And wait my turn to be
> King.
>
> DIANA
>
> You have a wife.
>
> CHARLES
>
> Yes. So I am reminded.

He turns his back on her. We move with him.

> DIANA
>   (V.O.)
> Charles.

He whirls around to see Diana tumbling down the stairs, crash-
ing hard into the railing. She lies as still as death.

> FADE TO BLACK

The scene is beautifully written in terms of providing a dramatic buildup to
Diana's suicide attempt, and also acts as a climax to the first part of the film. However, the book immediately goes on, as I've indicated, to list other cries for help.

The problem this presents to a writer is whether to use any more incidents, and if so, *which* one, and *when*. The book lumps everything together, but to do so in a film would be to lose dramatic impact. Wisely, Zito holds off the second incident and crisis until a good deal later in the script.

The incident he finally decides to use is the breaking of the display cabinet. This is preceded by two short scenes showing Charles warmly greeting Camilla, who is still a threat to Diana, and Diana angrily watching them from a window.

> DIANA
>
> Damn you!

Charles hears a window slam and turns to Camilla.

> CHARLES
>
> Well, I'm in for it now.

243 HIGHGROVE - BREAKFAST ROOM - DAY

> DIANA
>
> How dare you leave me waiting!

> CHARLES
>
> You might have come over.

> DIANA
>
> (agitated) Did she come to me?
> No. She just waved. (exploding) I
> thought you were done with her!

> CHARLES
>
> I don't intend to give her up alto-
> gether. So you'd better get used to
> it.

Charles starts out of the room.

> DIANA
>
> I'm *not* going to get used to it,
> *Charles*.

Diana, in helpless frustration, smashes her arm against a china cabinet. The glass shatters. A shard cuts Diana. Charles rushes to her and looks down at her bloody arm.

```
                        CHARLES
        Damn you, Diana.
```

The servants have rushed in and stand horrified.

```
                        CHARLES
        The Princess has had another
        accident.
```

The delay in showing the second incident helps the pacing of the story line. When the accident does happen, it provides one more link in the deteriorating domestic situation. Had it been placed closer to the stairs fiasco, it would have lost most of its effect. This didn't matter in the original book, but matters vitally in the script.

Another important point to note is that Zito adds *motivation* for Diana's action by bringing in Camilla. In the book all we know is that Charles and Diana are having a hard time.

Finally, it's worth noting a line from the book which Morton quotes from one of Diana's friends: "His indifference pushed her to the edge whereas he could have romanced her to the end of the world." It's only one sentence but it governs the whole mood of the scene, and gets its filmic expression in "Damn you, Diana."

Barbarians at the Gate

Barbarians at the Gate: The Fall of RJR Nabisco (to give it its full title) was written by Bryan Burrough and John Helyar in 1990. The book is 528 pages long and describes the fight for control of the gigantic food and tobacco company RJR Nabisco in October and November 1988. Soon after its publication *Barbarians* hit the best-seller list, and, along with *Liar's Poker*, paints a damning portrait of greed and lust on Wall Street.

In spite of its fame, *Barbarians* is not a book that immediately strikes you as material for a film. Its subject is the competition to take over a major American company, using a leveraged buyout, or LBO. The main action of the book takes place in boardrooms and in banks. We are introduced to an esoteric financial world and given an immense amount of detail about the way it works. Soon the mind is reeling, trying to grasp the intricacies of junk bonds, asset stripping, stock resets, and "monetization" tax loopholes.

However, a book doesn't become a best-seller by chance. *Barbarians* reveals human lust, desire, and avarice at its worst. It talks of riches beyond the dreams of mere mortals and reveals a world where forty million dollars can be made in an hour, for just waiting around. It appalls us and it fascinates us, and as more than one producer knew, it might just be a great basis for a movie, if the right scriptwriter could be found.

The eventual choice was Larry Gelbart, one of Hollywood's classiest and most successful writers, who among other things did the final script for *Tootsie*. The film itself was made by HBO and was hailed as one of the highlights of the 1993 season. Though production and direction were fine, to my mind most of the film's success was due to Gelbart's brilliant adaptation. Below I've tried to set out some of Gelbart's strategies in bringing such a complex book to the screen.

1: Defining Aim and Direction

The original book is a serious and well-written study of all the intricacies of the takeover world. It looks at the most intimate and arcane details of the *process* of the takeover, and delves deeply into the actions, makeup, and psychology of the principal *players*.

To a large extent, though obviously not completely, the film ignores the details of the *process* and concentrates on the *players*. This is a film about people, greed, and rivalry, and discussions of bonds and percentages stay where they belong, on the financial pages.

The other radical change is that the film is set up as a *comedy* which occasionally borders on farce. The book sometimes hints at this possibility, and in a cool tone shows the absurdity of much of the proceedings, but stays on the right side of seriousness. What Gelbart does is pick up on the suggestions and then vault over the barrier into the laughter section, adjacent to situation comedy.

2: The Conflict

Both the book and the film recognize that they are dealing with a dramatic conflict that structurally evolves very easily. Essentially there are two sides in the takeover battle: the management team, led by Ross Johnson, and their opponents, Kravis, Kohlberg, and Roberts, led by Henry Kravis. The prize is ownership of RJR Nabisco, and whoever wins is likely to make hundreds of millions of dollars in profits.

What the film script does very well is simplify the struggle without losing the spirit of the book. This is done for the most part by reducing the number of major contestants in the takeover. In the book, considerable time is spent in discussing the shenanigans, preparations, and bids of two other rivals for the company, namely Forstmann, Little & Co., and the First Boston Banking Group. In the film they both appear briefly, but vanish after a few scenes, their real significance in the drama hardly mentioned.

Purists may regret this, but I think Gelbart was absolutely right in his choice. With four or five contestants, the race becomes blurred. With only two giants struggling against each other, the issues are clear and emotionally much more compelling.

Gelbart's structural model is the war film, or probably more correctly the baseball film centered around the World Series. We know there's a prize. We know there are two sides battling it out. And given the genre, we know we will be introduced to the contestants, that there will be preparations and training, skull-duggery accidents and unexpected happenings, and eventually the deciding contest, when all is won or lost in a moment.

The point here is that an audience has clear genre expectations and satisfactions. It goes to see westerns, musicals, buddy movies, and war films knowing more or less how things will evolve, and deriving satisfaction from variations on old themes. Making your adaptation fit into a genre type often helps in regard to audience acceptance. Here it helps enormously to see a possibly off-putting financial struggle framed in terms that everyone can understand.

3: The Hero

The book offers us a number of major characters, but no central "hero," which is usually the first requirement for a film. We may not like the hero, though we usually do, but it is essential that the film provides us with one character whose fate absorbs us. Following this elementary rule, Gelbart chooses Ross Johnson, the CEO of Nabisco and leader of the management buyout group, and puts him center stage.

Johnson is a breezy, outgoing character with a beautiful young wife, Laurie, and a penchant for telling dirty jokes. All this we know from the book, as well as his love for corporate luxuries, such as his jet fleet. We also know he is ruthless, money hungry, and has arranged for himself and his close friends to make over fifty million dollars if they win.

Gelbart realizes that these last characteristics, such as the immense greed, while fascinating, can also be off-putting to an audience. He compensates for this by giving Ross some very funny lines, and making him very concerned for the future of the workers and the ultimate good of the company. Thus in one of his most critical speeches, Ross says, "I don't wanna buy this company because my business is buying companies. I need this company to *make* things." It sounds wonderful. It makes us warm to Ross, but it's *not* the man as seen in the book. Gelbart's change is vital in gaining audience sympathy and making the adaptation work.

4: The Cast

There are over sixty major characters in the book. Gelbart wisely reduces this cast to six major characters, and four or five minor ones, with Ross playing the hero, as mentioned, and Henry Kravis his principal opponent.

Gelbart does more than reduce. He also *amplifies* the roles of people hardly mentioned in the book, such as Ross's wife, Laurie, and Kravis's wife, Carolyne. He does this for three reasons. Enlarging the roles of the wives enables him to write a number of domestic scenes, which provide intimacy and contrast with the boardroom scenes. Allied with that, the presence of the wives allows Gelbart to develop a number of very sexy bedroom scenes out of his imagination. Finally, and maybe most important, the attentive wives provide the key "bounce off" figures for providing vital information to the audience, such as how Ross and Henry feel, what they think of their rivals, and how they see their future game plans.

5: Settings

Barbarians is about the world of the super rich portrayed in the Fortune 400, about the search for riches beyond the dreams of any ordinary man or woman. This atmosphere, which the book can only hint at, becomes a major factor in the film. In short, the setting very often becomes as important as the dialogue.

Seventy percent of the action of the book takes place in boardrooms. In the film, Gelbart transforms these conversations to stretch limousines, luxury jets, magnificent tennis centers, opulent ballrooms, and grandiose mansions. In the book we get a passing remark that Kravis has a $5.5-million-dollar Park Avenue apartment, laden with Renoirs. Catching the sentence, Gelbart provides us with a few scenes in Kravis's house that tell us once and for all this film is about money, greed, and Croesus-style wealth.

6: Structure

What Gelbart gives us in his script is a classic seven-act TV structure. In order to do this, he totally eliminates the first 100 pages of the book, which give us the history of Ross and Nabisco, eliminates most of the minor conflicts, and concentrates on the battle between Ross and his bank supporters and Kravis and his henchmen. Stripped to its bare bones, the script looks inevitable in its development, with every scene having a very specific function in furthering the plot.

7: Humor, Invention, and Strategies

The perennial question in doing adaptations is how and where to add to the original in order to bring it to life in a different medium. Gelbart provides many lessons in this sphere.

First, he creates a number of comic and satirical scenes that were never in the book. The funniest is the fancy dress ball in the Plaza Hotel which starts off Act Three. At first all the principals are seen dressing up in the most outlandish costumes, from Marie Antoinette to Billy the Kid. We then proceed through a number of strange encounters on the dance floor, topped by a madcap scene in the men's toilet, where cowboy figures keep popping up all over the place, like over the tops of the stalls, to proposition Ross with buyout offers. This is bedroom farce transferred to a men's urinal.

Another wonderful touch is the creation of Anthony the pizza boy as a running gag. Anthony delivers a pizza to the takeover boardroom, overhears the conversation, and promptly telephones his stock broker to sell IBM and buy Nabisco stock for him. The unexpected quality of the action is very funny. However, this is topped at the end of the film when we see Anthony, the pizza man, wearing an Armani suit and driving by in a Porsche.

Another technique of Gelbart's is to use the television medium to define the time and background of the story, and also to editorialize on the events. Thus we continually see portions of the Bush-Dukakis presidential debates on somebody's screen, and are presented later with news clips of broadcasts by Johnny Carson and Tom Brokaw. These last extracts comment generally on the failure of Premier, on the hazards of smoking, and the vulgarity of the greed and the profits. The TV statements are clearly the sobering last thoughts that remain with you when the comedy is concluded.

8: Major Changes

In an adaptation, you generally try to stay as close to the basic truth and meaning of events as possible. Gelbart follows this axiom, except for his ending. Ross loses his bid, but the reason for the failure of his group is attributed to his greed. As one of the Nabisco directors puts it, "Your greed was over the top. It was simply too naked. There was just no way we could let you have this company."

In reality, this was only a minor factor in the competition. Kravis won because his bid looked more substantial than Ross's, which although higher, was more subject to the problems in the stock market. To have stated things in this way might have been too complex for a TV drama. Since we are following the story of a "hero," Gelbart obviously believed it was more satisfying for the loss to be attributed to human weakness than financial technicalities. I totally agree with this reasoning.

9: Dialogue

Gelbart never misses an opportunity to expand scenes from the book where they give him a chance to create some devastatingly funny and sharp dialogue. Thus the crushing failure of the much vaunted Premier smokeless cigarette is exploited to the full for its comic potential.

In the book, the cigarette is exhibited as an after-dinner surprise for Ross Johnson's guests at his villa. The reaction isn't good. No one likes the taste. The odor is unpleasant. Someone drops a crack that it smells like burning lettuce. Someone else comments, "Boy, this is hard to draw on."

In the script, the scene is transferred from Ross's home to a testing lab, and goes as follows.

23 INT. RJR REYNOLDS CIGARETTE TESTING LAB - LATE AFTER-
NOON

Before a huge cross-section mock up of a Premier cigarette,
Ross and Horrigan listen to the RJR executive, TRAVIS GAINES,
who is in a white lab coat. Behind him is a pie chart indicat-
ing the following figures.

> GAINES
> Of those people we interviewed,
> eighty-six percent approved of the
> idea of a smokeless cigarette.
> Forty-one percent said they'd try
> at least two packs before deciding
> whether to switch brands. Of
> those who had given up ciga-
> rettes, seventy-three percent
> responded favorably to the idea,
> saying they'd seriously consider
> smoking again, if they could be
> positive that the cigarette they
> were smoking was absolutely
> smokeless.

Ross loves those numbers.

> GAINES
> Eight percent of that group sam-
> pled at least one Premier to give
> us their opinion of the product.

> ROSS
> (Expectantly) Bottom line?

> GAINES
> Of all the groups we tested, their
> reaction to Premiers was just
> about uniform.

Silence.

> ROSS
> (pleasantly, anticipatory) Uh-
> huh...?

Gaines, reluctant to go on, looks at Horrigan.

                    HORRIGAN
(sheepishly) They all said they
tasted like shit.

                    ROSS
Like shit?!

He turns to Gaines.

                    GAINES
Shit was the consensus. Yes, sir.

                    ROSS
They all said that? Nobody liked
them?

                    GAINES
Fewer than five percent.

                    ROSS
(To Horrigan) You said you heard
that the results were terrific.

                    HORRIGAN
Nothing wrong with five percent.
I'll take five percent of the smok-
ing market any day of the week.

                    ROSS
Jesus Christ! How much are we
in for up to now?

                    HORRIGAN
Upwards of seven-fifty.

                    ROSS
We've spent seven hundred and
fifty million dollars and we've
come up with a turd with a tip?
God Almighty, Ed. We poured
enough technology into this project
to send a cigarette to the moon,
and all we got out of it is one
that tastes like it took a dump.

                    HORRIGAN
(sheepishly again) We haven't
even talked about the smell.

                    ROSS
What'd they say <u>that</u> was like? A
fart?

                    HORRIGAN
(unhappily, inhales) Yep.

                    ROSS
You're not serious. That's what
they said?

                    1ST SCIENTIST
We've got an awful lot of fart figures, sir.

                    ROSS
Tastes like shit and smells like a
fart. We've got ourselves a real
winner here. It's one God damn
unique advertising slogan, I'll give
you that. Seven hundred and fifty
million dollars!

(A.R.: That's not the end of Ross's troubles, as he finds out a
few moments later.)

                    ROSS
(taking a drag) And what the
hell's wrong with the draw? You
need an extra set of lungs to
take a drag.

                    1ST SCIENTIST
It <u>is</u> a little difficult.

                    ROSS
A <u>little</u> difficult?

                    2ND SCIENTIST
It's what we call the "hernia
effect."

                    ROSS
Oh, is that what we call it? There's
<u>another</u> great billboard. What do we
do? Give away a truss with every
pack? "Warning. This cigarette can
tear your balls off?" . . .

Adaptations are tricky, but interesting, and for exercise you might want to think about a book you would like to adapt and how you would do it. Start off by considering what sections you could lose. Are you happy with the story and shape? Are there sections or incidents you think would work very well visually? Are there scenes or hints of scenes you think you could expand? Are you happy with the characters? Which ones do you want to carry the story? Which ones do you have to abandon? What characters might you combine? Does the hero need a confidante or a buddy? And so you go on, even writing a few scenes with dialogue. Is it hard work? Yes! Is it fascinating? I think so, and if you try it I think you'll agree.

12

Fact Versus Fiction

"A writer's job is to tell the truth. His standard of fidelity to the truth must be so high that his invention out of his experience should produce a truer account than anything factual can be."

ERNEST HEMINGWAY .

Can drama and reality make a happy marriage? Well, as Hamlet might have said, that's the $64,000 question. While docudrama is tremendously popular, it has also drawn the wrath of a number of critics. Thus Jerry Kuehl, one of the most serious opponents of the form, wrote this for the English magazine *Vision*.

> Many docudramas are produced with little regard for historical truth, or psychological plausibility, but with every regard for pecuniary advantage. To see the names of real people with public reputations attached to characters drawn from the stockpile of drama stereotypes . . . is enough to alert the viewer to the fact that he or she is in the presence of a program which intends to exploit but not satisfy an audience's curiosity.

Another vitriolic critic of the genre is Walter Goodman of *The New York Times*, who has stated in no uncertain terms that "The only good docudrama is an unproduced docudrama." Continuing in the same vein, this is what Goodman had to say about *The Final Days*, the TV series about the conclusion of Nixon's Presidency:

> What's wrong? Several things. Real people are treated sometimes flatter-ingly, sometimes cruelly, as though they were made for TV. They exist for our amusement. Real events, which deserve analysis and perhaps action, are presented in a hyped-up watered-down way that short cuts thought.

That's some list! Exploitation . . . ethical failure . . . and lack of seriousness. Then, of course, there is *Newsweek* critic Richard Corliss's review of the three network Amy Fisher movies, where he talks of "Shlockudrama" and "Trash-omon." According to Corliss, what you missed if you hadn't watched was merely six hours of "vidiocy."

Now to say, as Goodman does, even in joking, that the only good docudrama is the unproduced docudrama seems to me the height of nonsense. This is to ignore some of the wonderful contributions to TV, such as *Death of a Princess*, *Barbarians at the Gate*, *Citizen Cohn*, *Friendly Fire*, *Oppenheimer*, and even *Sinatra*, to name only a few.

Yet it is useful for the writer to listen to the critics, so that he or she knows what troubles serious thinkers about docudrama, or about its execution. For example, John O'Connor, another critic with *The New York Times*, was moved to despair while reviewing *Overkill: The Aileen Wuornos Story* and let go with a real general blast against the form:

> Apart from the moral questions of sometimes rewarding criminals with lucrative contracts, the genre has encouraged artistic laziness. Creativity has given way to paint-by-the-numbers reality rip-offs, pieced together from news articles, interviews and court transcripts. The formula has become numbing . . . How much more impressive it would be if this movie had something to offer besides fudged details and standard banalities.

It is difficult to know how many of these problems are due to the writer, and how many are a result of conditions and parameters laid down by the producer. I suspect the latter is the answer, but I'm not always sure.

My own criticism of producers working in docudrama is their frequent failure to take chances, to go for the hard subject, or to push home the real problems. Both CBS and ABC had the chance to adapt *And the Band Played On*. Both failed to take up their options after getting scared over their audiences' reactions to an AIDS drama. In the end it was left to HBO to step in and do a great job.

Sometimes the hard subjects will be tackled but then softened so as to avoid offense. Thus major characterizations are altered and compromising dialogue watered down, not in an effort to get at the truth, but to avoid complaints and protest.

Sometimes the failure of will can be quite amazing. The story that most astonished me was an incident that veteran scriptwriter Ernest Kinoy mentioned to me:

> What you get these days is that networks will start or approve a project and part of that comes from self-delusion. They think, "Wow! Wouldn't it be marvelous," and then they start a whole project on some fascinating or historical issue, then chicken out . . .
>
> For example, Malcolm Stewart, a producer from the coast, called me up and asked me whether I wanted to do the story of Dreyfus. I said, "Sure, why not?" and we went to talk to the NBC executive.
>
> This is modern times, remember. World War Two is over and we know about the Holocaust. So it's clear we don't want to do it the way Hollywood did it in the thirties in a film on Zola. In that film no one mentions that Dreyfus is a Jew. The only time you see it is where the Generals are looking

for a scapegoat and the record shows "Alfred Dreyfus" and at the end it says "Jew." And if you are reading fast you could really miss it. That's as far as the mention of anti-Semitism went in old Hollywood.

With this in mind I said to the executive, "If we do it, we can't do it that way." And he said, "Of course not. We want it tough and hard." So we went away, prepared the treatment, and they OK'd it.

I did the script. It got handed in. Then my producer calls and says you've got to come to a meeting at NBC with one of their executives. The NBC guy was very upset and troubled.

"What's the matter?" I said. "Not dramatic enough?" "No! No! Dramatically it's very exciting, but tell me," he said, "does it have to be so *Jewish*?" And the network dropped it. They never said why they dropped it, but they were concerned it wouldn't play in Peoria.

Truth or Fiction

Writing docudrama is like boxing with one hand tied behind your back, and the rope that binds you is called "truth." You can also view docudrama as a minefield full of both high explosives and . . . rare treasures. To reach the rewards you have to be prepared to live dangerously, and at every step you have to recall the sign over the entrance: "Watch the facts."

So there it is. The key problem for docudrama lies in its relationship to truth and to audience expectation. Can imaginative drama really exist when its hands are shackled by the bonds of accuracy? For you as a writer, the issue then becomes, "How far can you stray from reality, rearrange lives, simplify facts, and assign new motives to key characters?" And that's just for starters.

When a critic can write, "*JFK* is fiction so cunningly disguised that the audience will accept it as fact," we know we are dealing with issues about the form that have to be seriously considered, if not always totally resolved. And whether you call your script a fact-based drama, or a drama suggested by fact, or a movie inspired by real life, sooner or later you are going to ask yourself the essential question . . . how do I balance *truth* and *drama*?

Interestingly enough, not everyone believes they have to be balanced, or that truth and historical veracity are necessarily the most important guidelines in the form. In fact critic Nigel Andrews, who writes for the English newspaper *The Financial Times*, argues very persuasively for exactly the opposite view:

If cinema cannot play fast and loose with history should it bother to play with it at all? . . . Look at the strength freedom with truth gave to some truth-based films: *Bugsy*, *The Long Day Closes*, *Swoon* and *The Best Intentions*. Though none "lied," all pushed, pounded, and poeticised the facts till they turned to art . . . Fidelity, whether to biographical truth or to literary text, is a pedant's virtue.

Along with Andrews, most of the writers I spoke to in preparing this book also argued that truth was just the beginning. They acknowledged its force, but when push came to shove, declared they were dramatists before they were reporters.

The Key Questions

Though the blurring of fact and fiction in drama-docs is a favorite discussion topic of academics, and even led to a Hollywood symposium on the issue, I think there are only three or four real questions at the heart of the issue which should trouble a writer. I've separated them below, but of course they all interact. They concern

1: Accuracy
2: Authorship and attitude
3: Audience

Accuracy

You need to resolve for yourself, from the start, what level of authenticity and accuracy you are offering in regard to dialogue, characters, and events.

I've discussed dialogue elsewhere, but the issue is fairly simple. Where feasible, you try to retain authentic dialogue. Where that's not possible, and that's probably ninety percent of the time, you'll go on to create your own. As regards invented dialogue, not only does it have to be dramatic and compelling, but it should also be in keeping with the character being portrayed. Curiously enough, you'll find that your problems with dialogue have less to do with accuracy than avoiding banality.

Where you use live characters, your aim is accuracy every time. Habits. Personality. Motivation. Traits. Modes of thought. Actions. All these things you want to make as close to the truth as possible.

You will also invent composite characters. Sometimes they will be based on real people; sometimes they will be the friend who accompanies the hero on his journey, as in *Malcom X* and *Hoffa*. On rare occasions, as in *Skokie*, the invented person may even be your protagonist. Intrinsically I see nothing wrong with this as a dramatic device to cut through an overabundance of characters that would only confuse an audience, or to move the plot along.

Where feasible, you stay as close to an accurate portrayal of events and happenings as you can. People want to know how this really happened, the murder, the crash of the Exxon Valdez, the investigation of Oppenheimer, Gandhi's salt march, the forging of Hitler's diaries—and your duty is to give them the information accurately and dramatically.

What people often fail to realize is that there is a difference between truth and accuracy. You can never give the whole truth. You are selecting events and characters to give a version of the truth . . . and *selecting* is the key word. Your aim is accuracy in everything you write about after you have made the selection, and that includes not just facts, but also mood, atmosphere, and feeling.

A lot of criticism levelled at docudrama has to do with not telling the whole story, which as I've just said, is an impossible ideal. Docudrama always offers an interpretation, and no more. But when docudrama *lies* over crucial events or aspects of contemporary people's lives, in films such as *Hoffa* and *Marilyn and Bobby: Her Last Affair*, then no excuse can be given for a practice that drags the whole genre into disrepute.

Marilyn and Bobby, which came out in 1993, depicts a clandestine love affair Bobby Kennedy is said to have had with the actress. Such an affair, however, is vigorously denied by Marilyn's biographer Donald Spoto, who calls the rumor "false and scurrilous." In a newspaper interview, Barry Weitz, one of the film's producers, stated candidly, "We are creating a fiction based on the Kennedys' public lives. We take some privileges." It sounds good except for one problem . . . most of the audience saw the film as fact, not fiction, even though it was marketed as the latter.

Many times writers take real situations and crises, write a drama around the events, and label the outcome "a dramatic presentation having no resemblance to real personalities and events." Does that help things? Does that help you to evade responsibility for accuracy? We're entering tricky waters here. My response is to say be very careful, because the audience will see through the cover and accept your story as *the real* story.

This happened in a Canadian TV series called *The Boys of St. Vincent*, which was broadly based on a scandal at a Newfoundland orphanage run by the Irish Christian Brothers. The original saga was a revolting story of physical and sexual assault by pedophile Brothers and official indifference amounting to virtual complicity. A terrible story, but very interesting material for TV. The series came out with the usual labels of "no resemblance" but no one was fooled. The events on the screen very closely reflected what had occurred in Newfoundland, yet the disclaimers eschewed all responsibility for accuracy. With this disclaimer in hand, the producers intermingled fact and fiction more freely than usual, leaving an audience totally bewildered as to what was what.

"No resemblance" is only one of the labels one comes across where fudging matters of accuracy is concerned. Others include "loosely based on," "inspired by," and "true to the spirit of." Frankly, I never know quite what they mean, except that the writer and producer are usually taking a hell of a lot of liberties with the truth. They want to draw you with the attraction of a real-life story, but at the same time want to have the total freedom of fiction. They want to have their cake and eat it too. I'm just not sure it can be done, but maybe you'll think otherwise when you start writing.

Authorship and Attitude

We want something to be true, but *whose* truth are we talking about? Where do authorship and point of view come into the equation? The answer is right at the start.

Point of view and authorship may be negligible factors in the writing of a simplistic murderess-of-the-week docudrama, but they are vital considerations in the writing of any complex issue or political film. What we have to acknowledge—and yet people seem reluctant to do this—is that truth is often very much in the eyes of the beholder. If that's too strong, we can put it another way. Filmmakers rarely tell "the whole truth." While not lying, they select facts for their films which fit in with their prejudices and their point of view on their subject.

Gandhi was made by a British filmmaker who totally admired his subject. To have expected the film to be a muckraking, warts-and-all portrayal is just nonsense. Similarly, *Malcolm X* was made by an African-American with a tremendous regard for the man and his achievements. To have expected a radically different portrait would have been totally unrealistic.

Now, to be sure there is a question of "When does a portrait turn into propaganda?" but that's a different issue. All I'm saying here is that attitude influences approach, and that truth is a many-splendored thing. A possibly more worrying level of the discussion is that you often get the truth you pay for, or to put it more accurately, the truth the producer pays for.

Both NBC and CBS made films on the Amy Fisher story, but the stories are so diametrically opposed one can only assume that either Amy or Joey is lying. The NBC film is told from Amy's point of view. In it, she becomes a victim in thrall to Joey Buttafuoco, who encouraged her prostitution. For CBS, Joey is a normal, innocent, flirtatious guy being chased by a crazy teenager and the innocent victim of her obsession . . . well, we know films are flexible on facts, but here were two totally irreconcilable views of the truth.

Amy's lawyers panned CBS, calling the portrayal of Joey as a wide-eyed innocent total nonsense, a portrait "that grossly underestimates the public's intelligence." The Buttafuocos and their lawyer stood by their guns, arguing in their turn that the CBS movie was accurate in all respects. For the cynical there is no mystery in the disparity. NBC paid for Amy's story, CBS for Joey's. What's the moral? Sometimes truth comes via the checkbook.

Audience

The easiest way for the scriptwriter to resolve the issue of truth may be to reframe the questions. Instead of asking, "Is my version true?", whatever that may mean, you can simply ask, "What does the *audience* expect? What level of accuracy does it want? Will my blend of fact and fiction confuse people or will they be able to sort out one from the other?" My suspicion is that audience's expectations vary with time, distance from the subject, and the nature of the subject itself.

1: Time

If one looks at film audiences from say, 1920 to 1950, I think one can well argue that their expectation of accuracy was minimal. I think they knew that when Hollywood touched history or biography it was portraying an entertaining romance, rather than the truth. When Sam Goldwyn said, "If you want to send a message, then use Western Union," he could well have added, "and if you want truth, go to the history books, not Hollywood."

Hollywood was in the business of creating myths that sold. And to do that, immense liberties were taken with truth and with facts. Poetic license, if one can call it that, ruled the day. Did it matter if Babe Ruth, Lou Gehrig, and Knute Rockne weren't quite the heroes they were painted? Not really. And so what if a love interest was invented for George M. Cohan? So what if Hollywood covered up Cole Porter's homosexuality? So what if little Al Jolson never ran away from home to sing "Ave Maria" in an orphanage? Who cared? Certainly not the audience, who knew they were being treated to a fairy tale.

Yet sometimes, to Hollywood's chagrin, the subject himself cared about truth. Then life could be difficult, as in the case of *Yankee Doodle Dandy*, about the life of George M. Cohan. Not only was Cohan's domestic life supremely dull, but he refused at first any attempts to "improve" on his story. So the Warner archives are full of the scriptwriters' letters pleading for "creative license" to invent a love interest. They won and the audience was charmed. As the film was released after Cohan died, we don't know *his* final thoughts on the matter. Pity!

Today audience expectations are different. I think they are still willing to a certain extent to go along with the fairy tale, but much less so. Conditioned by TV news and documentaries, and by a higher educational level, they want a greater degree of truth. So while Al Jolson's feet never touch the ground in the Columbia biopic, the producers of *Sinatra* had to show some of the crooner's seamier side, something impossible only a few years ago.

2: Subject Distance

I also believe that the demand for accuracy varies with the time distance from the subject. Historic romances are just that . . . romances, and no more. Columbus peels an orange for his son and looks at the horizon, and we smile, and if he falls in love with Queen Isabella, good for him. But if you take too many liberties in contemporary subject matter, like *The Right Stuff* or *Patton*, you may be in for trouble.

3: The Nature of the Subject

My final guess is that audience expectations of truth and accuracy vary with the nature of the subject itself and its importance to their daily lives. While we probably don't care that much about what happens to a murderess and why she set out on her life of crime, we probably care immensely about what happened in Watergate, about corruption in the White House, about busing, about oil spills, and about the framing of Irish suspects for political murders. The greater our concern for the subject, the greater our need for truth.

Bearing all this in mind, we can understand the concern over *Mississippi Burning* and *JFK*. Both films dealt with searing political issues affecting us to this day, civil rights abuses and a conspiracy or otherwise towards a political assassination. Both films lied, prevaricated, and invented spurious characters and spurious facts. *Mississippi Burning* created an FBI concern with the killing of civil rights workers that was totally at odds with fact, even crediting the discovery of the murdered bodies to the FBI. *JFK*, based on the questionable viewpoint of Jim Garrison, ignored facts, ignored the Warren commission, and invented a highly dubious conspiracy theory.

Do these travesties matter? Yes, because these films have become the basis for the formation of the political attitudes of a new generation, for whom such films, and similar TV shows, are the main means of getting in touch with the past. Nothing illustrates this better than the controversy surrounding Jim Sheridan's film *In the Name of the Father*.

The film is a moving dramatization of the wrongful imprisonment of the Guildford Four. Writing about the film in the English newspaper *The Sunday Times*, historian Robert Kee placed his finger very accurately on the flaws of the film. After accepting the need for a certain amount of artistic license on the part of the producers, he proceeds to list just a few of the movie's key inaccuracies. They include

1: Showing the Guildford Four and the Maguire Seven, which includes Conlon's father, participating in a joint trial. This is untrue.
2: Showing Gerald Conlon and his father in the same cell. Total fiction.
3: Making Gareth Peirce (Emma Thompson) discover the document which confirms Conlon's alibi on the night of the bombing. This in fact was passed to the appeal defense by the prosecution, who had received it from the investigating Avon and Somerset police.
4: Making the alibi the only reason for the quashing of the convictions. The alibi was, in reality, not even mentioned as grounds for the quashing of the convictions. The true grounds were the falsity of certain interview accounts, and the concoction of false custody records by the Surrey police. As the Lord Chief Justice concluded in his appeal court judgment, "If they [the police] were prepared to tell this sort of lie, then the whole of their evidence becomes suspect."

In his final critique of *In the Name of the Father*, Robert Kee points out very succinctly the essential problem of all the mistruths and their overall effect on the film.

> The producers' intention in distorting reality at as many points as they do, while using some real names and real events, must be taken as honorable. They wish to communicate to as wide a public as possible the nature of the monstrous miscarriage of justice done to 11 people after the Guildford pub bombings of 1974. But in doing so, they may have handed something on a plate to the very sort of people long happy to say out of the side of their mouths—wrongly—that no miscarriage of justice took place at all.

One is concerned in a similar way, but for different reasons, with films like *Gandhi* and *Malcolm X*. These films are not so much films as hagiographies, sanitized lives of the saints. Both films oversimplify history, act as propaganda tracts, and have had an enormous effect on unsophisticated audiences. However, we live in a relatively democratic world, so proselytization has to be borne, along with many other things.

I think audience expectations are also dependent on an important factor I mentioned earlier, the nature of the production itself. Where productions are made within the framework of organizations like Granada, the BBC, and HBO, and take their responsibilities from journalism and news, we expect a very high degree of truth and accuracy. Where the productions originate from a drama department, we know the values are different, and our expectations are lower.

Signposting

If the audience has certain expectations of truth and accuracy, I believe it helps to let them know on what basis we've constructed the script.

This is a fairly radical idea, not practiced in Hollywood, but gaining favor in European television, and particularly in the field of journalistic drama-docs. The English filmmaker Leslie Woodhead, who made *Strike* and *The Tragedy of Flight 103*, puts the challenge and the solution this way:

> I am myself convinced that makers of dramatized documentary do have a special obligation to let the audience know what they're up to, what's been called by one American critic: "the right not to be deliberately misled."
>
> In any one program, it's likely that the material being dramatized will be derived from a variety of sources of varying status. It seems to me vital to signpost material to avoid as far as possible a confusion in the audience about levels of credibility.

What Woodhead means by signposting is in fact a fairly simple process. It means telling the audience at the beginning of the film the basis for your filmic material. This usually means a short note saying that the central material comes from a smuggled tape of a crucial meeting, or that this film is based on the diaries of Katrin and Ivan, supplemented by discussions with Tamar and Peter. Invented scenes are specified, as well as suggestions as to their source.

Ignorance and conjecture are also indicated. Thus, close to the end of *The Tragedy of Flight 103*, we are clearly told by the producers of the film that the final details leading to the Pan Am crash are obscure. Having said that, they suggest that events are very likely to have progressed in such and such a way. It's not as neat as just going on without pause, but certainly more fair. Think what such practices would have meant to the Amy Fisher films. We would have known clearly that this was the gospel according to St. Amy, or the score according to Pal Joey. I don't think the enjoyment of the programs would have been any the less, but the audience would have been given a squarer deal.

Historic Nonsense

One of the great unsolved mysteries of the world, alongside the continuing popularity of Kentucky Fried Chicken, is whether *Mutiny on the Bounty* would have been just as popular if it wasn't seen as a true story.

George MacDonald Fraser, in his *Hollywood History of the World*, calls the true story of the Bounty "an epic of the sea to be classed with the Odyssey, and the voyages of the Argo, Columbus and Magellan . . . It is one of the factual dramas that outstrips fiction."

The Bounty sailed to Tahiti in 1787 to collect breadfruit plants to take to the West Indies. Its commander, William Bligh, was a navigator of genius, and according to Fraser, "a humane and considerate commander." The second-in-command, twenty-two-year-old Fletcher Christian, was inexperienced and possibly unstable. Returning from Tahiti, discipline slipped, the men mutinied, and they turned Bligh and the men loyal to him loose in an open boat.

As Fraser rightly says, it was an act of appalling cruelty. The nearest settlement was 3000 miles away, and Bligh had no charts and little food. But in one of the most incredible open boat voyages in sea history, he made it to Timor, and eventually returned to England and court martial.

Hollywood and the film industry eventually made three films of this remarkable episode. In the first, Bligh, played by Charles Laughton, is seen as a sadistic tyrant, while Christian (Clark Gable) is the intrepid Hollywood hero driven to desperation. Their relationship is totally misrepresented throughout the film. Bligh is seen as dishonest and brutal, and the reason for the mutiny is exaggerated nonsense. The film bore no relation to truth, but was superb cinema.

In the 1962 remake, Bligh, played by Trevor Howard, is portrayed as even more sadistic than Laughton, and a commoner. In contrast, Fletcher Christian, played by Marlon Brando at his worst, is seen as an aristocratic fop. Both men were in fact from good but not upper-class families. This second film not only travesties history, but is totally ridiculous in its presentation, a fact maybe accounted for by its many changes of director.

The film was finally made for the third time in 1984 as *The Bounty*, with Anthony Hopkins playing Bligh and Mel Gibson presenting a likeable Christian. For once history was more or less served. Bligh was shown as a human being, the main facts were true, and here and there authentic dialogue was used. Yet the film fell very flat.

Is there a moral in all this? I doubt it. One could argue that film demands really good villains and superhuman heroes, but I'm not sure that Schwarzenegger or Kevin Costner playing Fletcher Christian is the answer. Nor am I convinced that to make a commercially successful film you must totally savage the past. The story of the Bounty was dramatic enough to make a great film without all the fabrications and distortions, and that may be where the disappointment lies.

Yet seen as fiction, MGM's production is wonderful. Laughton's portrayal was magnificent, while Gable gave an excellent matching performance. Who can forget Bligh roaring defiance from his open boat while Christian watches in silence? It's all terrific entertainment, and the film well deserves its Academy Award. But as Fraser says, it's just a pity it established a gross historical falsehood.

True to the Spirit

At one time in Hollywood, biopics fell from the studios faster than leaves in autumn. Although the films were made with the aid and connivance of the studios' research departments, the scholarship had more to do with historic clothes and furniture than with investigating the true nature of biopic's subject. Accuracy was just another selling point, to be tolerated so long as it didn't get in the way of a strong human and dramatic story.

Biography presents a multitude of problems to the filmmaker, not the least being that few lives are dramatic, and even when they are, they can be hell to translate into an interesting dramatic form.

Preston Sturges ran into this problem when writing *The Great Moment*, a film based on the life of Dr. William Morton, the discoverer of ether as an anesthetic. The difficulty was that Dr. Morton's discovery came very early in his life, followed by decades of disillusionment. Quite clearly this was not great material. Sturges writes in his memoirs that he didn't believe in presenting fiction as biography, yet here he had the most interesting event far too early in the first act. There was only one solution, according to Sturges . . . alter the order of things.

> I believe a biographer has two obligations. He must be true to his subject and he must not bore his public. Since he cannot change the chronology of events he can only change the order of their presentation. Dr. Morton's life

as lived was a very bad piece of dramatic construction. He had a few months of excitement ending in triumph and twenty years of boredom and bitterness . . . My job was to show a play about Dr. Morton's life. To have a play you must have a climax, and it's better not to have the climax right at the beginning.

(Preston Sturges, Between Flops.)

The most interesting comment of Sturges's comes in the second sentence. First, there is the commandment to the writer, which is as valid today as when films first started. "Thou shalt not bore thy public." But he also adds what one can take as a second commandment, "Thou shalt be true to thy subject." Now that looks like an easy one, almost as easy as "Don't commit murder or adultery," yet is the commandment which is most frequently broken.

Of course the phrase is terribly elusive . . . be true to the subject. What on earth does it mean? For all his fine talk, Sturges's film was not true to the spirit of Morton's life. And who determines what the true spirit is? Me, you, the voters for the Oscar? I grant there are difficulties, yet would still argue that in most cases the public does have a common viewpoint on what constitutes the essential truth about a person, and the essence of his or her real persona.

How does all this affect you as a writer? It means you have to remember that accuracy is only a beginning. Beyond that, you have to capture the real spirit of a person. If you fail in that, then however technically accurate your film is regarding facts, details, dates, and events, it will be a failure.

The danger usually starts in the democratization and canonization of the subject. The distortion is compounded by a failure to show anything really negative, or complex, or puzzling about the hero. As the blandness increases, the essence is removed from the character and he or she gradually becomes everyman or everywoman. Which makes for wonderful statues and lousy films. And gradually we begin to question why the producers ever bothered to make a movie about this man or that woman, because he or she is so *dull.*

Let's take three examples.

In *The Jacksons: An American Dream* ABC neatly sidesteps all the difficult stuff. The film bends all the awkward details of the Jackson family story and presents Michael and his brothers as sweet, mischievous rascals. Mum is loving and understanding and the real villain of the piece is the father.

It's a passable song-and-dance film. The only problem is that the Michael Jackson we know is totally absent. As Ken Tucker wrote in *Entertainment Weekly,* "It's a Michael who just doesn't come close to the jewelled-gloved, plastic-surgeried, Medusa-haired, monosyllabic, self-proclaimed King of Pop we know and cannot bring ourselves to love."

When he made *Malcolm X,* Spike Lee chose to base his film on Alex Haley's book rather than a more critical biography by Bruce Perry. The latter book gives a very different version of Malcolm's early family life, in which his father and mother are considerably less sanctified. But that's not the problem.

The difficulty with *Malcolm X* is that it dodges all the controversial issues. It soft-pedals his anti-Semitism and his depraved past. And it gives no sense of the real aggressiveness of Malcolm, which might have sent white audiences hurtling from the cinema. Sure, Malcolm recants the hate in his later life, but as one critic rightly said, "The conversion is meaningless—or impactless—in a movie where we scarcely sense those hate arias to begin with."

Terence Rafferty expressed it best in the *New Yorker* when he wrote, "*Malcolm X* is stubbornly impersonal. It has a sort of high-school field-trip quality, an explicitly educational tone. It's revelatory, but dull." There you have it. Malcolm, you was robbed!

The same is true for Chaplin, one of the greatest popular artists of the twentieth century. The slightly bewildered guy with the funny accent who floats through Richard Attenborough's *Chaplin* from 1914 to 1952 bears hardly any resemblance to the genius the world knew, or the sharp businessman and woolly leftist that America knew. This time we can't blame one scriptwriter, because there were four.

Little is shown of the women in Chaplin's private life. Very little time is spent showing how Chaplin filmed his comedies (something Kevin Brownlow did brilliantly in his Thames TV films on Charlie). Instead, we have a film-by-numbers saga about a morose Englishman that is totally impersonal, and totally fails to evoke anything of Chaplin's magnetism or drive.

In both *Malcom X* and *Chaplin*, we occasionally see glimpses of the real person in old newsreels or film clips. And then, as critic Nigel Andrews wrote in *The Economist*, we see what we have been missing. "Danger. Surprise. Attraction. Revulsion. Hilarity. Outrage. All those uneven, vivid, corrugated emotions that are crushed smooth by the genuflecting gestures of the bio-pic."

Yet there is hope. It doesn't have to be this way, as we've seen quite clearly in films like *Bugsy*, *Schindler's List*, *Stalin*, and even *Sinatra*. All of these had faults, and certainly dipped into the barrel of cliches now and then. But they were also dynamic, vivid, and pulsating. And their heroes were real and believable.

In the end, these films fulfilled Sturges's two commandments. They were never boring, and they were true to their subjects. In a strong, dramatic way, the filmmakers had caught the man behind the myth, and that is all one can ask.

13

□ □ □
□ □ □
□ □ □

Rights, Options, and Legalities

Before I became a filmmaker, I worked as a film attorney in London. Every day writers, directors, and producers came to our office in hope and in fear. Their stories were usually the same—they had landed a great movie deal but wanted to make sure it was airtight. They wanted to make sure they would get their money on time, that they wouldn't be sued for what they were doing, that they could go ahead in peace, and that the project didn't have any hidden dangers.

Though they were all creative people, they had the sense to realize that they needed legal advice, not just to protect their rights and percentages, but also to protect themselves against damaging court actions.

In this chapter I've tried to give you a simplified overview of the chief legal problems you are likely to encounter as a writer of docudrama. I hope this will help you see where the problems are. How do you cope with them? There's only one answer that makes sense. You get yourself a good lawyer. Fact-fiction can be dangerous territory and only a competent attorney can provide you with the safety you need on the journey.

Though you'll find legal questions continually dropping on your head, your main concerns are these:

1: Your script rights
2: Your contractual relations with your producer
3: Books and copyrights
4: The rights of your subject in a true-life movie
5: Your relations with the networks

Your Script Rights

You've finished the script. Friends have read it and said it's terrific. You're itching to send it off to a producer or a network, but the first thing you have to do is protect your copyright and try to ensure that the script doesn't get plagiarized. You can do this in any one of three ways:

1: You can take out a formal *copyright*. This is done by registering your script with the U.S. Copyright Office. Forms for this can be obtained from the Registrar of Copyrights at the Library of Congress in Washington, D.C. However, you should note that this procedure is mainly used for copyrighting plays, books, and music, rather than film scripts. For the latter, a more simple procedure is to register your work with the Writers Guild.

2: Any writer, whether a member of the Guild or not, can register his or her story, treatment, or script with the Writers Guild of America, West or East. The registration doesn't ensure your copyright, but it is proof of your authorship, is valid for ten years, and can be renewed. The fees for registration are minimal, and vary slightly, depending on whether or not you are a member of the Guild. On receipt of your script, the Guild will put it on microfilm and store it in safety. If your story is later plagiarized, the Guild's Custodian of Records can be summoned to appear on your behalf.

Details of filing costs and other particulars can be obtained from the Registration Office:

Writers Guild of America, 8955 Beverly Blvd., Los Angeles, California 90048, or 555 West 57th St., New York, N.Y., 10036.

3: The simplest way of all to protect your material, and one which will hold up in court, is to seal it in an envelope and send it to yourself, special delivery, return receipt requested. It's vital that the postmark be clearly seen, as that is your main proof of date of authorship if the question ever comes up. After the envelope gets delivered to you, just file it away in a safe place. Whatever you do, *don't* open it, or the whole effort will have been for nothing.

Contractual Relations with Producers

The four possible markets for your scripts are the independent producer, production companies like Lorimar or David Wolper, the major studios, and the networks. If they like your work, they may option it or buy it outright, or take you on as a writer for hire and get you to work on their own pet projects.

Your task, therefore, is really twofold. First you have to get your work read and accepted. Once that's been accomplished, you have to get yourself the best deal possible.

Submission

Agents

Most writers submit their work through an agent. If a sale is achieved, the agent will take a percentage of your fee as his or her commission. The advantage of a good agent is that he is familiar with the market, knows best where to send your script, and if he believes in it will really push your work. If he has been around a few years, he probably has a good relationship and track record with a large number of producers. This means that if he recommends your work, it stands a fair chance of getting read and being taken seriously.

If your script is accepted for a sale or an option, or if the producer wants generally to hire you as a writer, the agent will help you negotiate terms.

Can you exist without an agent? Yes! Is it advisable? No! Every serious writer that I know works through an agent. Occasionally he or she may make an independent submission to a producer, or pitch an idea without the help of an agent, but usually the agent is there as advisor and facilitator.

The problem is that it is quite hard to get an agent. This means that you may have to submit your script directly to the producer or network, without an intermediary. There are two drawbacks to this.

The first is that because producers are overwhelmed with scripts, and don't know you, the script may finish up in the garbage can, unread. As maybe 20,000 to 30,000 scripts bounce around New York and Hollywood every year, one can, in a way, understand the producers' dilemma. So just getting your script seen can be a major hurdle, and books in their dozens have been written offering both practical and esoteric advice on overcoming this obstacle.

The second point to note is that most producers dislike unsolicited submissions because of fears of a plagiarism suit. They are afraid that if they reject your script and later make a film with a similar theme, you may attack them in court for copying your work. Thus the easiest escape for them is to return your work, unopened. This point doesn't arise when the script is submitted through a recognized agent.

Waivers

The way out of this dilemma is to ask for a release form—a waiver—in advance. This form states that the company has no obligation to you, and that you waive any right to sue it if it produces a similar work.

This demand for a waiver is now standard in most general production and television companies. However, very often one waiver will cover you not just in the present case, but for all future work as well that you submit to the company.

The Address for Submissions

If you have written a feature film, the market for your script is everywhere except the networks, and even there one finds exceptions. Channel Four in England, for example, has for years encouraged and partially financed films like *My Favorite Launderette* and *The Draughtsman's Contract*.

In television, your best bet for the placement of scripts is with good independent producers like Martin Poll, Buzz Berger, Rosemont Productions, or Patchett Entertainment, to name just a few of the top names around.

What one looks for, essentially, is a producer who has already made one or two docudramas, and has good access to the networks. You go to these people because they can move your script in a way that you probably can't. They know the ropes, they have a reputation and a track record, they have the contacts, and they can get the project considered seriously at the broadcast level.

You *can* approach the ABC, CBS, and NBC networks directly, but it is doubtful if you will get a proper hearing. They mainly act as financial sponsors rather than as actual producers, and like their negotiations to be with the production company rather than the freelance writer. The situation is slightly easier with Disney, TBS, and HBO. They too like to work with production companies, but are more accessible than the major networks to individual submissions.

Things are slightly different in England, and possibly slightly looser. There it is more acceptable to approach Channel Four or the drama section of the BBC directly with your idea or script. This ease of access is also true of independent television companies like Yorkshire, Central, or Granada, or production houses like Zenith or Euston Films.

The Deal

If a producer likes your work, he or she will suggest purchasing your script outright, optioning it, or taking you on as a writer for hire. Whatever happens, you've got a tentative *deal*, or a basic agreement. The terms have to be negotiated and can be tricky, and this is where you call in a good agent or attorney.

After your first basic discussions, a *deal memo* is drawn up, outlining the main points of your agreement, and covering fees, rights, royalties, credits, and a dozen other points. The memo then goes to the lawyers of both sides and may be changed if both sides agree. A formal *contract* is then drawn up, based on the memo, but defining every little detail. As most American producers are signatories to an agreement with the Writers Guild (and you probably will be too by this time), the contract will follow the minimum basic agreement terms laid down by the Guild.

If you have sold your script outright, you may be paid *in toto* immediately, or asked to delay receiving part of the payment until shooting commences. This is fine so long as the payment is not dependent on shooting, and a date is fixed for payment if shooting is delayed. If someone suggests part payment, with more to come if and when they commence the film, you are not really talking of an outright sale, but have moved into the area of options.

The Option

We've talked about options before in regard to your purchasing a book or trying to buy the rights to someone's life story. In negotiating with a producer, the roles are reversed. The producer wants an option from you on your film script, so that he can see if he can get a production off the ground. Regarding a television movie, the producer is taking an option to see whether he can get a network or major cable company interested in the project.

The option is exclusive and gives the producer the right to hunt around for a specific length of time, usually six months on a TV project and a year on a film. The actual option money itself can be quite small, say $3,000 or $4,000, but a much larger sum is paid if the script is sold, i.e., the option is taken up.

This final sum is fixed when the option is drawn up, and the initial payment becomes part of it. Thus if the final sum is $50,000 and the option $5,000, only $45,000 will be paid if the script is bought. If the option is renewed for a further six months for another $5,000, this second sum does *not* become part of the final payment. If the option is not taken up at the end of the defined period, all the script rights revert to you.

The Step Deal

If a producer is familiar with your work, or has been introduced to your writing and likes it, he or she may ask you to develop new material or write a script for a project he or she has in hand. The agreement that governs your relationship is called the *step deal*, and usually follows the standard Writers Guild Contract for freelance writers. The description of the agreement as a step deal comes from the fact that the obligations and payments are set out in stages. Only when each stage is complete do you move on to the next one.

If your project is to adapt a book, your first task will be to prepare a treatment. The payment for this is usually 30% of the overall agreed sum. If the treatment is acceptable, you will usually be asked to go on and do the *first draft*, though the producer has the option to assign this to someone else. When you deliver the draft, you will be paid another 40% of the fee. The final option of the producer is to ask you or someone else to do the *final draft*. Once that's turned in, you get the balance of your fee.

As you can see, the step deal is set out to safeguard the producer at every stage. He is the one who has the option to continue or break off the relationship, depending on whether your work is seen as satisfactory to him or the networks. On your side, you are guaranteed payment at fixed stages, whether or not the producer gets to the starting line.

Besides payments, the contract will also specify delivery dates and credits. As most producers are signatories to agreements with the Writers Guild, the contract will also probably ask you to become or remain a member of the Writers Guild. If you are not already a member of the Guild, the existence of your agreement with the producer will enable you to join.

The above sets out the basic lines of agreement, but they will vary slightly according to the situation. Sometimes you will be asked to work up a story or do a revised treatment. At other times you may be asked to do a polish of someone else's material, or do rewrites beyond the second draft. Each of these points has to be incorporated into the contract.

Fees

We've all had the same dream. Our name is Joe Eszterhas, Larry Gelbart, or William Goldman and our latest script, put up for bidding on the open market, has just been bought for three million plus. After savoring that sweet nocturne, we may even have had a second. In this latter fantasy, we become writer Bruce Joel Rubin and we are being paid $100,000 to do script revisions, or we've assumed the guise of Tom Stoppard and are being paid a million a year just to be on call to help Universal.

With luck, scriptwriting can be fun and very well paid. However, of the 6,000 or so writers who belong to the American Writers Guild, only a fraction make the kind of money mentioned above. Most earn a living from television scripts rather than feature movies, and are lucky if their yearly earnings reach $60,000 or $70,000.

Television

The biggest market for drama-doc is television, and the going rate for your script is fixed by agreements among the producers, the networks, and the Writers Guild. The Guild is open to anyone who has had a script accepted by a producer, and in fact you must join once your script has been accepted; otherwise the producer can't go ahead.

The scale of fees is varied and changes almost every year. The highest fee is for a prime-time movie of the week—the Amy Fisher-type show—and earnings from the story and teleplay could be anywhere upwards of $45,000. The Guild fixes basic fees, but what you actually receive depends on your negotiating power. For example, both Paul Monash and Larry Gelbart are top feature writers. When the one wrote *Stalin*, and the other *Barbarians at the Gate*, their fees were reputed to be quite astronomical, and light-years removed from the Guild minimums.

Obviously fame and a track record help in boosting your dollars, but since the fee-negotiating process is an open one I would always argue for using a good agent. With help, even as a beginner, you may be able to raise the selling price of your script or your general work.

In the U.S., a writer can also expect to receive residuals from reruns, and a certain amount from foreign sales of the program. In England, residuals are more limited and depend on whether you are writing for the BBC or an independent station. This too is very much in flux.

Feature Films

Feature films offer the cream, and many writers see television work as the lower rungs of the ladder. However, one has to face certain facts. While the fees can be astronomical, there is also far less work around. Once again, minimum fees are fixed by the Guild, but the actual sums paid may bear no relationship to the Guild scales.

Generally, the fees paid for a feature script are in direct relation to the scale of the budget, with fees of one or two million dollars becoming fairly common for the super productions, like *Jurassic Park*, *Robin Hood: Prince of Thieves*, and *Basic Instinct*. Fees for fact-based films like *Gorillas in the Mist*, *Reversal of Fortune*, *Awakenings*, and *Silkwood* haven't quite hit these heights, but have still been quite substantial.

Will you be able to command a high fee? In the beginning, however good your script, the answer is probably "No." But Hollywood is a strange town. All you need is one hit, or one or two solid successes, and the sky's your limit.

Books and Copyrights

When I discussed book and play adaptations earlier, I mentioned that either you or the producer must obtain permission to go ahead from the owner of the copyright, and that you do this either by a full purchase of the rights or by taking an option. Even if all the negotiations are handled by a lawyer, you must know something about the basic outlines of the process and your objectives in making the deal.

Both the option and the full purchase of the rights have to be set out in a formal contract. The option will contain almost exactly the same clauses as the purchase of rights, except that it sets the purchase in the future, and subject to certain conditions. Below I've set out the main subjects you'll see mentioned in most options and contracts.

Option Fee and Purchase Price

There is no standard fee for purchasing an option. Sometimes you may get an option for nothing. Sometimes it may be as low as $500 or as high as $100,000. Everything depends on who wants the rights, how long they've been around, and your bargaining power.

If a book is a best-seller, like *Diana: Her True Story* or *Barbarians at the Gate*, you will definitely have to pay top dollar for an option, if you can get it at all. In many cases, the book is so popular that the author doesn't want to waste time on the uncertainties of options and will only be interested in an outright sale, which could well reach $300,000 to a million dollars for a best-seller.

Your competition will also be a factor in figuring out the option price and the final purchase price. The more competitors there are for the same book, the stiffer the price. This is one reason producers like to try and get hold of books while they are still in the manuscript or galley proof stage. They want to see its worth while the book is unknown, its value unassessed, and the competition for it minimal. The downside of this action is that the book can fail, but taking an early option to beat the competition may be worth the chance.

The fixing of the final price when you option a play or a book is exactly the same as when a producer options your own script. You fix the price when you take out the option, and that's the price that becomes payable if you take up the option. As mentioned before, your first option payment becomes part of the final payment.

Sometimes you can get depressed reading magazines or newspapers that tell you about astronomical sums being paid for book rights. You say to yourself, "How can I ever compete in such a realm?" Maybe you can't, but if you look around for a bit you'll find there are a tremendous number of books that have been neglected, or were once popular and are now forgotten, that could make great docudramas. In these cases, you may well be able to purchase an option for a relatively low sum. The biography of Sir Richard Burton is a case in point.

Though he is often confused with Burton the actor, Sir Richard *Francis* Burton was altogether a different character. Born in the early nineteenth century, he was soldier, adventurer, Arabist, and one of the greatest linguists of his age. He became one of the first white men to enter the forbidden city of Mecca, and his search for the sources of the Nile with John Hanning Speke forms the basis for William Harrison's novel *Mountains of the Moon*. The Harrison book came out in 1982 and was filmed by Bob Rafelson in 1989.

The producers of *Mountains* probably paid a huge chunk of money for the rights. When they did this one wonders whether they had heard of *Burton: A Biography*, which was written by Byron Farwell and published without fanfare in 1963. My guess is that an option on Farwell's book, which is much more interesting than Harrison's, could have been purchased for a song had one been wise enough at the time.

Sometimes you will option or purchase more than one book on the same subject. This may be costly but serves two purposes. Firstly, it can protect you from plagiarism suits, and secondly, it can protect you from competition when you are on to a hot subject.

Columbia took this route when they made *Out of Africa*. Although they had already purchased the rights to Karen Blixen's original book, they also optioned a biography of her by Judith Thurman in order to keep the competition at bay. I wouldn't be surprised if the producers of *Mountains of the Moon* didn't also option Farwell's book, and another Burton biography by Edward Price, for exactly the same reason.

Sometimes the lawyers of the original author may suggest the insertion of a clause awarding their client not just payment for the book rights, but also a percentage of any net profits you, the scriptwriter, or the producer make on the film. Be very careful of such a clause. It can lead to great complications and should never be inserted without the advice of your lawyer.

What Are You Buying?

When I worked as a film lawyer, my first job was to renegotiate the purchase of the film rights to a book called *The Liquidator*, which was an amusing sendup of the adventures of James Bond. The deal had to be reconsidered because the first lawyer working on the purchase had not secured what our client needed to get a film off the ground. His mistake had been to merely secure the film rights, and that just wasn't enough.

If you take an option on a book for a feature, or purchase it outright, your aim is to secure as many rights as possible. This may seem like greed, but arises from sound commercial reasoning; the rationalization goes like this.

Yes, you want to make a film, but if it is successful, you may want to carry it in many different directions. You may want to make a television series spinoff. You may want to make a radio series. You may want to make further films using the same characters. Following the success of the film, you may want to turn it into a play or a musical. If that sounds far-fetched, just remember that Fritz Lang's *Metropolis*, one of the great German expressionist films of the twenties, unexpectedly reemerged as an eighties musical.

There is almost no end to the rights you can ask for, and fantasy and wishful thinking often creep in. Thus while it makes sense to ask for product marketing rights, i.e., the ability to market tee shirts saying "Jurassic Park," I'm not sure you really need ice-skating show rights, which I've seen in a few contracts.

Many times the owner of the book may be unwilling to give you more than the film or TV rights. The bargaining then becomes interesting, and can go in all sorts of ways. Whatever you do, you must remember your fundamental point. You want to make a film. If you can get anything else besides those rights it's icing on the cake, and that's great, but don't ruin the negotiations because of greed. Appendix C gives you an example of a typical option contract to purchase book rights. In this case, the owner has kept almost everything but the film rights for himself.

Length of the Option

Your option has to be for a long enough period for you to get the project going. This can mean writing a proposal based on the book; writing a treatment or full script; and offering your work to a production company or network for fuller development. All this can take months or years.

If you are a beginner, or a writer without screen credits, or have very little money to lay out, the owner of the rights may want to limit your option to three or six months. This is to see how serious and capable you are of developing the project. The usual period for an option is for a year, with a right to renew it for a further payment. Eyebrows get raised if the option goes on for too long, but I have seen options that have been renewed for five or six years as the would-be screenwriter has plugged away, trying to find a buyer for his or her script.

Whether you go for a short-term or long-term option, it must be exclusive. Without exclusivity, you may find you have done a great deal of work, but someone else has got the film going before you. To avoid such a scenario you have to obtain exclusivity.

Creative Control

Whether you obtain an option or an outright purchase of rights, one thing is essential. You must obtain total creative control of your future script. That means you must have the right to change, dramatize, adapt, and even create fictional elements without being subject to the original author's approval. You want to make a great script, and you must be free to do that without interference.

Often the authors understand this, but sometimes they are reluctant to let go, and it's the latter case you should guard against. You cannot work with the original author looking over your shoulder, advising and criticizing, and having the power to veto what you are doing. You must have absolute control, and that need is recognized in the amount of money you fork over for the rights.

In most cases you are going to keep very close to the spirit of the book and to the main characterization. You liked the book. The public liked the book, and they want to sense a lot of the original on the screen. But to make a book work, the adaptation may have to go in all sorts of directions, and the power to make those changes must be in your hands.

The film *The Mountains of the Moon* presents Burton and Speke as two buddies very much united in their search for the Nile sources. In the end their friendship turns to enmity and rivalry because of the interference of a third party. That works in the film, but that third party is absent from the book, where the disintegration of their friendship is due to many other factors. Without the right of creative change, the screenwriters couldn't have made that alteration. In *And the Band Played On*, a number of characters are combined into one. Without creative control, that too would have been impossible.

Sometimes one allows the author consultation rights. This may happen when the subject is complex or involved and you want the author's advice, or you want to bring him or her into the script discussions. That's all right so long as he or she doesn't have approval, and total script control remains in your hands.

Locating the Rights

Before you can option anything, you have to find out who has the rights, which is usually a fairly simple process.

If you want to trace the rights to a book, you simply write to the publisher or the author's agent. In turn they will tell you who holds the rights, such as the publishing company or the author, or whether they have been assigned to someone else. Sometimes an author may have died and his executors control the rights. Here again, the publisher should be able to tell you whom to contact.

Once or twice when I've tried to contact an author, the publishers have simply given me the address. This is unusual. Most of the time they have forwarded my letters, to preserve the privacy of the author. At other times and for the same reason, they have passed me on to the author's agent.

Occasionally a biographical play comes up, like *Eleanor and Franklin*, and here too there are various approaches. First, you may be able to find out the address of the playwright or his agent from the Writers Guild. If the play is in print it has most likely been published by either Samuel French or the Dramatists Play Service, both of whom are located in New York. Both Samuel French and Dramatists will be able to help you in locating the owner of the rights.

If an exclusive story appears in a magazine, such as the article on drugs and the French Connection which later became the basis for the film, your first move is to contact the magazine. They will either own the rights or put you in touch with the author.

Public Domain

If the material you are hunting for is in the public domain, you won't have to go through the hassle of obtaining rights, as the use of the material is open to everyone. Public domain covers two broad sections of written materials—expired copyright and materials that are part of the public record.

Expired Copyright

As copyright rules vary from country to country, and occasionally from year to year, you have to be very careful what rules apply. In the U.S., current copyright statutes protect a book or an article for the life of the author plus fifty years. Before 1976, copyright protected the author for twenty-eight years, plus a renewal term of a second twenty-eight years, if application was made before the first term expired.

As you can see, the whole subject is fraught with complications, and you really need to get good legal advice rather than assuming the copyright has expired. If you want to check whether a book is in the public domain, you can do so by writing to the U.S. Copyright Office, Library of Congress, Washington, D.C. For a small fee, they will conduct a copyright search and let you know where you stand. The effort to see if something is copyright free is worth it, because the number of books freely available is staggering. Somewhere out there is the one that's just waiting for you.

Public Record Materials

The second area of public domain covers all the materials taken from public records, public agencies, media news stories, and court papers. What this means is that you can use all open official records, and also all openly available information touching someone who is in the public eye.

In general, this has made life quite a bit simpler for writers of drama-doc. Although they were supplemented by various biographies, films like *Stalin, Chaplin, Gandhi, Marilyn: The Untold Story*, and the story of Jackie Kennedy, were all done mainly from public-domain material. The important rider to this is that if the material is in the public domain, one does not have to get the permission of the subject before using it. However, the use of such materials may not necessarily protect you from libel suits or claims for invasion of privacy, but more on that in a moment.

As a writer of fact-based fiction, you may well find that the biggest treasure trove for you in the public domain is the record of court trials. The number of movies of the week that have turned to such materials for inspiration is staggering and includes *Oppenheimer, A Miserable and Lonely Death, Willing to Kill, Fatal Memories, Overkill: The Aileen Wuornos Story*, and *A Woman Scorned: The Betty Broderick Story*, to name but a few.

One thing worth remembering is that generally facts belong to everyone, and as a writer you can use them freely, so long as they are discoverable through the public domain. This means you can use the knowledge discovered from newspapers and TV stories, but can't use facts which are only found in unpublished private letters. What should also be obvious but is worth repeating is that the appearance of a story in a newspaper is no guarantee of its truth.

One of the key decisions in this area concerning available facts comes from the case of Rosemont Enterprises, Inc. v. Random House, Inc. What the court held was that a third party could use copyrighted biographical writing about Howard Hughes in order to promote knowledge. In other words, the court refused to limit the use of historic research to one person. However, the decision, and other cases in the same area, provide limitations, such as the use of facts for educational as opposed to commercial purposes, or the effect on the market value of the original work. So one still has to tread very carefully.

Rights of Your Film Subject

When you want to write a script about someone's life story, and the material exists outside of a book, you have to ask a few basic questions. Is the material known, of public interest and in the public domain, or will you have to purchase the rights to the story? Sometimes even if the material is public, you ask yourself an extra question. Shall I take an option on the rights, just to be safe?

The reason that producers don't always just go ahead and purchase the rights is mainly financial. The purchase of various characters' rights in the Texas cheerleading story came to over $100,000, and the figure is likely to escalate. Not every writer or producer has that kind of money to play around with, so a close examination of material in the public domain becomes the first priority.

Whatever the source of the material for your film, either you or your producer will have to consider several legal and practical issues before you can go ahead. They include

1: Is the story potentially libelous?
2: Will your film lay you open to a suit for invasion of privacy, or one of the other developing torts dealing with personal property rights?
3: Is the story of sufficient public interest and notoriety that you can claim that an accurate depiction of it is allowable as use of known material in the public domain?
4: Is anyone else competing for the same story?
5: Will you be allowed a certain license to write what you want because of the First Amendment, regarding freedom of speech?

A lot of the answers vary with the facts, and with different state jurisdictions and rulings. You will also find it hard to get definitive answers, because this whole legal area is in a state of flux.

Public Personalities

Stories of public figures and entertainers provide the lifeblood of drama-docs. A few years ago the rage was for stories of Ike, Nixon, the Kennedys, President Bush, Elvis, Marilyn, and even Oliver North. Currently, hardly a month goes by without Sinatra, the Jackson family, Roy Cohn, or Tina Turner turning up on the feature or TV screen.

The general rule for public figures and celebrities is that they are considered to have given up much of their right to privacy. This means, broadly speaking, that one can write about them with a greater freedom than in the case of a private person. The one realm where you still have to be as careful with public figures as with private persons is in the area of defamation.

Defamation means writing or screening something false about a person which shows him in a bad light and is damaging to his reputation. Although defamation suits catch the headlines, they are amongst the hardest to prove, as was shown by the cases of General Sharon versus *Time* magazine, and General Westmoreland versus CBS, both of which ended inconclusively. The problem for the public figure who wants to sue is that in the U.S. he has to prove actual malice, knowledge of falsity, and a reckless disregard for facts.

In England, the burden of proof is much easier for the plaintiff. First, one doesn't have to prove actual malice, and second, it is up to the defendant to prove that what he wrote or showed was true. In the States it's the other way around, with the plaintiff having to prove that what was written was false.

The Right of Privacy

The right of privacy is sometimes referred to as the "right to be left alone." If a person thinks his or her privacy has been invaded, he or she may be able to bring a civil action for damages. The tort is a developing one, but at the moment covers four areas:

1: Intrusion on someone's seclusion or solitude
2: Public disclosure of embarrassing private facts
3: Publicity which places a person in a false light in the public eye
4: Appropriation, for the defendant's advantage, of the plaintiff's name or likeness

Translated into ordinary language, this means that if your script is offensive, and you knew parts of it were false or you recklessly disregarded the possibility, you could possibly be sued. The defense may be that the story was accurate, newsworthy, in the public domain, and inoffensive. You can also plead the First Amendment, the right of freedom of speech.

In practice, and following the First Amendment, the courts have tended to move against restricting the freedoms of a writer, at least in docudrama. For example, they've allowed dramatic tricks like "telescoping" to move events along, and permit a great deal of leeway in reconstructing conversations. When debating the merit of a script, they also tend to give more consideration to the public's right to be informed than the individual's right to privacy.

In practice, though the right to privacy is frequently discussed, very few privacy claims have been decided outside of defamation. This means that there are few guidelines as to the extent to which a person's life story can really be used without his or her permission.

The Right of Publicity

Although the right to privacy may be difficult to prove, lawyers have recently been developing another personal right, the right to publicity. What the courts seem to be saying here is that a person's name, reputation, and life story make up an economic asset, a saleable commodity, and a potential commercial property right. Once having recognized that, the corollary is that only the subject in question can control the commercial exploitation of his or her life. This is obviously good for the individual, but complicates the field of docudrama.

Optioning a Life Story

After a number of years writing docudramas and documentaries, I feel that where feasible, you should always try and take an option on a private individual's life story. There are good reasons for this. When you take material from the public domain, you lay yourself open to possible actions for defamation, invasion of privacy, and for stealing publicity rights. As I've argued above, in most situations the plaintiff will find it very hard to prove his case, but that's almost irrelevant.

The reality is that once an action starts, the hassles, the legal proceedings, and the threats of injunctions become more bother than they are worth. If you can avoid all possible lawsuit threats for the expenditure of a few thousand dollars, it seems to me well worth it.

There are a large number of benefits from signing an option agreement with your subject, but the main ones are these:

1: You can obtain a release against defamation, invasion of privacy, or exploitation of the life story rights.
2: You can get the cooperation of the subject, and access to all sorts of private information from him or her that would have been impossible otherwise. You get "the inside story," which of course is the one everyone wants to hear.
3: You are usually given the leeway to fictionalize.
4: If you are lucky, you eliminate the competition for the story.

You may find that in order to tell your story properly, or safeguard against competition, you may have to option more than one person's story. This can mean turning to relatives and friends as well as your main subject. So in the *Texas Mom* story, rights were purchased not just from Wanda Holloway's family, but also from Verna Heath.

The option or purchase contract, which should be drawn up by a really good film lawyer, is very similar to the option contract for a book. Once more, you will be paying attention to purchase price and the duration of the contract, and making sure it is exclusive and irreversible. The contract will also make sure you are protected against legal suits from the subject.

One of the most important sections concerns exactly what rights are granted to you or the producer. Normally, the clause will state that, *inter alia*, you have the right "to depict the subject factually or *fictionally*, and to use the subject's name, likeness, voice, and biography in any and all media, and in all advertising and exploitation." In brief, you are going for complete control of the story and its use.

As in book contracts, you may want to provide for the subject to consult with you on the film. The fee for this should be fixed, and once again, all decisions about the script should be exclusively yours or the producers.

The Demands of the Networks

The main market for docudramas is television. When you or your producer submit a script or an idea to one of the TV networks, it first goes to the programming department, or to the department specializing in your type of story. Thus HBO and Granada both run drama-doc units, which would be the first to vet an idea or consider a script. Once the project has been given the green light, it has to be approved by three departments.

The first of these is the legal department, which will check the option or purchase agreement to see that you've obtained all the necessary rights for making the film. The errors and omissions section then reviews the script to consider matters like defamation and invasion of privacy. Their job is to see that nothing appears or is shown which is likely to lead to a lawsuit. Finally, the script has to be reviewed by the broadcast standards and practices department, which examines the script minutely with regard to truth, fictionalization, and the way people are shown in the film.

All the American networks have codified guidelines for the writing of drama-docs. ABC, for instance, asks that a person's known behavior patterns and attitudes be followed, while CBS warns its producers against materially altering or distorting the public record.

Though the details differ from network to network, they all essentially ask the producer and the writer the same thing. They want you to document the sources for the depiction of people in the script, whether books, articles, interviews, or anything else, and to indicate what is fact and what is fiction. To help you see this in more detail, I've reproduced the NBC guidelines in Appendix D.

Few English TV stations or companies issue official guidelines, yet in practice they follow the same quest for authenticity and legal safeguards. Michael Eaton, the writer of *The Tragedy of Flight 103*, put it this way:

> Throughout the whole process of composition I am in constant contact with lawyers acting on behalf of the TV company making the film. I'm sending them drafts. I'm sending them scenes. And in those scenes I am giving them my sources and informing them what lines of dialogue are taken as verbatim record and which ones I am inventing on the basis of various sources. In return the lawyers are informing me of what I can and can't do. And one of the things that can be quite frustrating to the dramatist is that if there is a difference of opinion between the lawyer and the dramatist, then I'm afraid it is the dramatist who loses the argument all the time.

One of the reasons for the guidelines, and the close English vetting of the scripts, is that it makes insurance of the programs much easier.

All networks, and any producer in his right mind, take out what is called Errors and Omission (E and O) insurance. This insurance covers the station and the network against all the civil liabilities I mentioned earlier, like defamation. This means that if the network is sued, the E and O insurance covers the costs of the litigation. However, when the network applies for the insurance, it has to disclose all the facts about the script. It has to say whether it was done with permission, whether it was done with public domain materials, and what is fact and what is fiction. Because of all the earlier work, the answers to all these questions can then simply be found in the guideline response file, or in the scriptwriter's replies to the company lawyers.

Freedom from Worry

By now, you are probably saying to yourself, "So many problems! Maybe I should become a lawyer instead of a writer." Well, perish the thought. You'll work harder and longer for much less personal satisfaction. I know. I've been there.

Docudrama does involve quite a lot of legalities, but apart from defamation and fictionalization, most of them are things you have to know about in principle rather than deal with in detail. Your attitude should be that of the director to the camera. A good director knows all about lenses, but leaves the framing and lighting to his director of photography. In the same way, you should be knowledgeable about the main legal problems behind writing drama-doc, but leave their day-to-day details to your agent or lawyer. That way you can get on with your main purpose, which is writing the great script.

□ □ □
□ □ □
□ □ □

Afterword

You've finished. The bound script lies on your table in all its pristine glory. The title in the middle of the page says *Triumph at Midnight*. Directly underneath it are the words "a screenplay by Monty R. Maurice." In the lower right-hand corner of the page you've put your address and phone number. You feel proud, but what do you do next?

My own method is to have a drink, put the script aside for a few days, see a good film, relax, and generally knock off for a while. Then, after about a week or ten days, I have a look at it again, and also give it to a few good friends, whose judgement I trust, for comments.

When I read it this time, I am trying to read it as an outsider. I look for flaws, for problems, for inconsistencies. I look at ways to improve dialogue, tighten up the scenes, increase the tension, make the drama really work. I also listen very carefully to my friends' comments. Some I reject, but those that seem reasonable to me I try to incorporate into the script.

All this is supposing I am working on an unsolicited script. What I am trying to do is make the script as good as possible before I send it out, because I know I'll only have one chance with each producer that reads it.

Agents

The best way of getting your script read is to have it submitted to a producer by a good agent. Finding one can be as difficult as getting a good cup of coffee in the Sahara in the middle of a drought.

If you contact the Writers Guild of America, East or West, they will send you a list of agents who are signatories to the Artists-Managers Agreement. This means they are authorized agents, and producers are willing to accept their submissions without fears of later plagiarism suits. The problem is that few agents are willing to read unsolicited material from new writers. The ones who are open to new talent are marked with an asterisk on the Guild's list. Under the Guild's rules, an agency cannot contract with a writer for more than two years at a time; neither can its commission exceed 10%.

However, getting your script read by an agency, and signing a contract with it, are two different things. But at least the Guild's list provides a first-attempt plan. Apart from working from the list, you use whatever friends and contacts you have to get yourself an agent. This can take weeks or months, and is a process full of many letdowns and disappointments. Nevertheless, once you have a decent agent, you'll find that your script is given much greater consideration than if it is submitted out of the blue by yourself as a lone-star writer.

Locale

While there are a few writers who work best far from the madding crowd, this is not really possible for you as a beginning TV or feature scriptwriter. You must be at the heart of the action, which usually means New York or Los Angeles, or London or Manchester. The rationale is simple. You have to be around to talk, to consult, to push, to modify, to badger, to shmooze, to pitch, and to rewrite. And you can't do that from the heart of Tennessee or from the wilds of the Scottish Highlands.

With known and recognized writers it's different. Stephen Davis writes in the depths of Gloucestershire, and Ernest Kinoy turns out his scripts in the hills of Vermont, but these are proven writers, constantly in demand, and they can afford their solitude. For you, as a starting writer, you have to be placed so that you can push, and push hard, at a moment's notice, so that you can extend your chances and grab whatever is available.

This leads to the crux of the matter. In practice, few writers manage to sell their first or even their second script. What such scripts do, however, is offer an entry point. They show an agent or a producer that you can write. Thus, though your original script may not be accepted (though now and then it is), you may be taken on in a script development deal, and asked to work on one or two new projects. Thus your worth, so to speak, is proven on the job.

Breakthroughs

Rejection is probably harder for a writer than for an actor or director. Turned down one day, an actor can audition for a different part the following day. And if a director fails to get chosen for one film, there's always a chance something will come up the following week. In contrast, a writer may have put months of work into a script, so that rejection may mean that a tremendous effort over time has simply gone down the drain.

This is the nature of the game and it happens to everybody. For example, most studios maintain an alphabetical list of writers. Next to each writer's name is a list of his or her scripts that have been made into movies, and also a list of those that haven't. Even for a Hollywood winner like Joe Eszterhas, that second list shows seventeen unproduced screenplays.

If the lists show that there are rejections for even the most visibly successful of writers, they are also beginning to show the names of very new and young scriptwriters like John Singleton, who wrote and directed *Boyz N the Hood*. When Peter Watkins wrote *Culloden* for the BBC, he was in his mid-twenties, and Michael Eaton has never stopped since he turned in *Fellow Traveller* to HBO, and *The Tragedy of Flight 103* to Granada TV.

Today, as I mentioned at the beginning of the book, the demand for docudrama is increasing, and I would almost call it a growth industry. The opportunities for writers are enormous, and though it may be hard at the beginning, if you are any good, the breakthrough will come sooner rather than later. The breakthrough may take six months, it may take a year, but it will come.

Satisfactions

When I started doing the research interviews for this book, besides asking the various writers about their techniques, I also asked them why they wrote, and what gave them the most satisfaction. All of the writers were successful, some earning $200,000 - $300,000 a year from their scripts, and I expected them to put an emphasis on the financial rewards. In fact, few did. Obviously, they like the compensation, but to emphasize that was to miss the point.

Each said that he liked to be his own man. They liked the isolation. They liked to be able to set their own hours, to work when they pleased, to knock off when they pleased. All of them said they responded to pressure, that it got the adrenalin running, that it focused them and whipped up their creative drive.

Not everyone liked research. The ones that did, who were the majority, talked about the ability to travel, to meet people, to see the world, and sometimes to have the license and privilege to open the most secret and guarded of doors.

A few came from a background of concerned documentary filmmaking. These were the ones who told me that what they liked about docudrama was the ability to break free of the limitations of documentary, and yet still aim to change the world.

But one thing they all shared was the sheer pleasure of sitting at the typewriter and knowing that through words they were going to build a world, and a universe, that would inspirationally be theirs alone. Others would people that universe, give it shape, form, color, and reality ... but without their words, there would have been silence. That, above all, was the greatest joy.

A

The Genre: Past and Present

When I first started working on this book, I went back to look at some of the wonderful fact-fiction films of the thirties and forties, like *Disraeli*, *Clive of India*, and *The Jolson Story*. The films were great. Solid, comfortable, and absolutely predictable. And the good guys always won. Today the films of the genre are generally harder, more truthful, more provocative, and occasionally quite disturbing. Yet, when all is said and done, the actual subject matter of the films isn't all that different than the stories being pummelled into shape by Darryl Zanuck and his aides fifty years ago.

Below, I've set out a very abbreviated list of some of the key docudramas, or fact-fiction films and TV productions, from the thirties to the present. This is done in order to help you get some perspective on what's been created in the past, and to see where things are today.

Although you'll probably be familiar with many of the films, or can understand the subject from the title, others will leave you baffled. *Lust for Life*, for example, does little to indicate that it's about Van Gogh, nor does calling something *Moulin Rouge* tell you that you're about to see a film about Toulouse-Lautrec. Things get even worse when you deal with television and suddenly discover that *Stay the Night* isn't an invitation to an erotic weekend but is about a murder. To help you overcome this difficulty, I've used a simple subject guide after the title of the earlier or more unfamiliar films.

Biopics

From 1927 through the early sixties, the Hollywood studios put out over 300 fact-based films. Most of them were biopics, biographical films mostly dealing with the great men of history, sportsmen, or popular entertainers like Al Jolson or the Dolly sisters. Here are a few of them.

The Assassination of Trotsky

The Babe Ruth Story

The Buster Keaton Story

Cast a Giant Shadow (Micky Marcus)

Edison, the Man

Freud

Funny Girl (Fanny Brice)

The Gene Krupa Story

The Glenn Miller Story

The Great Caruso

Isadora (Isadora Duncan)

The Jackie Robinson Story

The Joe Louis Story

The Jolson Story (Al Jolson)

Knute Rockne-All American
 (sports coach)

Lust for Life (Van Gogh)

Madame Curie

The Miracle Worker (blindness)

Mission to Moscow (U.S. diplomat)

Moulin Rouge (Toulouse-Lautrec)

Night and Day (Cole Porter)

The Pride of the Yankees (Lou Gehrig)

Sergeant York (war hero)

Somebody Up There Likes Me
 (Rocky Graziano)

A Song to Remember (Chopin)

The Spirit of St. Louis (Lindbergh)

Star (Gertrude Lawrence)

To Hell and Back (Audie Murphy)

Viva Zapata

Yankee Doodle Dandy (George
 M. Cohan)

Young Mr. Lincoln

General History

Occasionally, the studios took courage and ventured out into wider historical fields. For the most part they avoided any deep analysis of politics, and instead stayed close to their favorite subjects . . . war and heroics. Naturally, both topics got a boost from the Second World War, as can be seen below. Here the British came into their own, revealing a tremendous nostalgia for the days when they stood alone against Hitler's forces. To show this more clearly, I've marked the British films with the sign UK.

The Alamo

Bataan

The Battle of Algiers (France)

The Battle of Britain (UK)

The Battle of the River Plate (UK)

Bernadette of Lourdes (France)

Buffalo Bill

Carve Her Name with Pride (UK)

The Charge of the Light Brigade (UK)

Clive of India

The Colditz Story (UK)

Disraeli

The Desert Fox (Rommel) (UK)

Dunkirk (UK)

The First of the Few (UK)

Inherit the Wind

Khartoum (UK)

Lawrence of Arabia (UK)

The Man Who Never Was (UK)

Midway

Mutiny on the Bounty

PT 109 (John F. Kennedy)

Reach for the Sky (UK)

Scott of the Antarctic (UK)

The Shores of Iwo Jima

Stanley and Livingstone

Target for Tonight
Titanic
Tora! Tora! Tora! (Pearl Harbor)

Yangtze Incident
Z
Zulu (UK)

Films Post-1970

Alive
Amadeus
Awakenings
The Babe
Back Beat
The Ballad of Little Joe
The Best Intentions
Bound for Glory
Birdy
Blaze
The Bounty
Born on the Fourth of July
A Bridge Too Far
Bugsy
Coal Miner's Daughter
Chaplin
Chariots of Fire
Cool Runnings
Cry Freedom
A Cry in the Dark
Dance with a Stranger
The Doors
Eight Men Out
Eighty-Four Charing Cross Road
Escape from Sobibor
Fat Man and Little Boy
1492: The Conquest of Paradise
The French Connection
Gandhi
Goodfellas
Gorillas in the Mist
Henry and June
Hoffa
In the Name of the Father
JFK

The Killing Fields
The Last Emperor
A League of Their Own
Lenny
The Light Horsemen (Australia)
The Long Day Closes
The Longest Day
Lorenzo's Oil
Malcolm X
Matawan
Melvin and Howard
Midnight Express
Mishima
Missing
Mississippi Burning
Mohammed, Messenger of God
Mommie Dearest
Mrs. Soffel
My Left Foot
Nicholas and Alexandra
Not without My Daughter
The Onion Field
Out of Africa
Patton
Patty Hearst
Petain (France)
Prick Up Your Ears
Raging Bull
Reds
Reversal of Fortune
The Right Stuff
Scandal
Schindler's List
Shadowlands
Sid and Nancy

Silkwood

Swoon

The Thin Blue Line

Tucker: The Man and the Dream

The Untouchables

Valentino

Vincent and Theo

What's Love Got to Do with It?

A World Apart

Young Winston

Television: 1970-1990

Amelia Earhart: Her Final Flight

An Englishman Abroad (Guy Burgess)

The Atlanta Child Murders

At Mother's Request (murder)

Berlin Tunnel

Blind Ambition (politics)

The Burning Bed (murder)

Bodyline (cricket)

Cathy Come Home (homeless.
   Pd. 1966)

Charles and Diana: A Royal
   Love Story

Cross of Fire (Ku Klux Klan)

A Cry for Help: The Tracey Thurman
   Story

Culloden (Scottish battle. Pd. 1962)

Death of a Centerfold: The Dorothy
   Stratten Story

The Deliberate Stranger (murder)

Death of a Princess (Arabian
   execution)

Dieppe (World War II)

Disaster at Silo Seven (nuclear
   problems)

Don't Look Back (Leroy "Satchel"
   Paige)

Edward and Mrs. Simpson

Eleanor and Franklin

Everybody's Baby: The Rescue of
   Jessica McClure

The Execution of Private Slovick

Fatal Judgment (murder)

Fatal Vision (murder)

The Final Days (Nixon)

Freud

Friendly Fire (military)

Gideon's Trumpet (law)

Grace Kelly

The Guyana Tragedy: The Story
   of Jim Jones

Hirohito: Behind the Myth

Ike: The War Years

Invasion (Czechoslovakia '68)

The Jesse Owens Story

John and Yoko: A Love Story

The Kennedys of Massachusetts

King (Martin Luther King)

The Last Days of Patton

Letters from a Bomber Pilot

Liberace

Liberace: Behind the Music

Like Normal People

Little Mo

The Longest Night

Love, Lies and Murder (murder)

Mae West

Mandela

Margaret Bourke-White

Marilyn: The Untold Story

A Miserable and Lonely Death
   (Steve Biko)

The Missiles of October (Cuba)

Moses the Lawgiver

Murderers Among Us: The Simon
   Wiesenthal Story

Edward R. Murrow

The Naked Civil Servant (Quentin
   Crisp)

Ninety Days (S. African prison)
No Other Love (human interest)
Nutcracker: Money, Madness, Murder
Out on a Limb (Shirley MacLaine)
Oppenheimer
The Patricia Neal Story
Raid on Entebbe
Rita Hayworth: Love Goddess
Roe vs. Wade (law)
Rosie: The Rosemary Clooney Story
The Royal Romance of Charles
   and Diana
Sadat (Anwar Sadat)
Sakharov
Skokie (anti-Semitism)

Shaka Zulu (South Africa)
Small Sacrifices (murder)
Stay the Night (murder)
Strike (Poland)
Tailspin: Behind the Korean Airliner
   Tragedy
The Terry Fox Story
The Trial of Bernard Goetz
Tumbledown (Falklands War)
Victory at Entebbe
The War Game (Pd. 1965)
Washington: Behind Closed Doors
A Woman Called Golda (Golda Meir)
Yuri Nosenko, KGB HBO
Zulu Dawn

Television: 1990 and After

Afterburn HBO (military)
Against the Wall HBO
Ambush in Waco (David Koresh)
America's Most Wanted
The Amy Fisher Story ABC
Amy Fisher: My Story NBC
And the Band Played On
   HBO (AIDS)
At Mother's Request (murder)
Baby M
Babe Ruth
Baby Snatcher
Barbarians at the Gate HBO
Billionaire Boys Club (murder)
Bomber Harris UK (RAF story)
Bonds of Love (human interest)
The Boys of St. Vincent (church
   scandal)
Casualties of Love: The Long Island
   Lolita Story (CBS)
Charles and Diana: Unhappily
   Ever After?
Chernobyl: The Final Warning
A Child Lost Forever (human interest)

Child of Rage (human interest)
Citizen Cohn HBO (Roy Cohn)
Complex of Fear (rape)
Cruel Doubt (murder)
Danger of Love (Carolyn Warmus)
Dead Ahead: The Exxon Valdez
   Disaster HBO (also known as
   Disaster at Valdez) (UK)
The Deliberate Stranger
Deliver Them from Evil: The Taking
   of Alta View (murder)
Desperate Choices (human interest)
Diana: Her True Story
The Disappearance of Nora (human
   interest)
Doublecrossed (drug running)
Dying to Love You
Elvis
FBI: The Untold Stories
Fatal Memories (murder)
Fergie and Andy: Behind the Palace
   Doors
For the Love of My Child: The
   Annissa Ayala Story

Her Final Fury: Betty Broderick, the Last Chapter

Good Night, Sweet Wife: A Murder in Boston

Highway Casanova (human interest)

Honor Thy Father and Mother: The True Story of the Menendez Murders FOX

Honor Thy Mother (murder)

Hostages UK (Beirut)

I Can Make You Love Me: The Stalking of Laura Black

In a Child's Name (human interest)

Investigation: Inside A Terrorist Bombing HBO (false accusations) (also known as *Who Bombed Birmingham*) (UK)

The Jacksons: An American Dream

Jacqueline Bouvier Kennedy

JFK: Reckless Youth

The Josephine Baker Story HBO

Judgement Day: The John List Story

A Killer Among Friends

Last Wish (human interest)

Leona Helmsley: The Queen of Mean

The Man with Three Wives: Manhunt in the Dakotas (crime)

Marilyn and Bobby: Her Last Affair

Menendez: A Killing in Beverly Hills CBS

Mission of the Shark (war)

A Mother's Right: The Elizabeth Morgan Story

Murder in New Hampshire

A Murderous Affair: The Carolyn Warmus Story

Murder Ordained

My Son Johnny (murder)

Never Forget (history)

Overkill: The Aileen Wuornos Story

The People vs. Jean Harris

Poisoned by Love: The Kern County Murders

Portrait of a Marriage (UK) (Nicholson/West)

The Positively Amazing True Adventures of the Alleged Texas Cheerleading Murdering Mom HBO

Prisoner of Honor HBO (Capt. Dreyfus)

A Question of Attribution (UK) (Anthony Blunt)

Runaway Father

Secret Service

Separate but Equal (Thurgood Marshall)

Shattered Dreams (human interest)

Shoot to Kill UK (N. Ireland)

Simple Justice (law)

Sinatra

Small Sacrifices (family shooting)

Stalin HBO

Sworn to Vengeance (murder)

Tailspin: Behind the Korean Airliner Tragedy (UK)

Take Back My Life (human interest)

Teamster Boss: The Jackie Presser Story HBO

Tonya and Nancy: The Inside Story

The Tragedy of Flight 103: The Inside Story HBO (also known as *Why Lockerbie*) (UK)

When No One Would Listen (human interest)

White Mile HBO (river death)

Willing to Kill: The Texas Cheerleader Story

With Murder in Mind

Without Warning: The James Brady Story HBO

A Woman Named Jackie (Kennedy)

Woman on the Run (murder)

A Woman Scorned: The Betty Broderick Story

The Women of Windsor

B

Case Study: The Cheerleading Mom

One of the best ways of studying the pros and cons of various writing strategies is to compare different films on the same subject.

While preparing this book, I followed the newspaper story of Wanda Holloway, the woman commonly referred to as the Texas Cheerleading Mother. When Wanda's trial was concluded, both ABC and HBO made films about her. ABC, opting for simplicity and directness, called its film *Willing to Kill: The Texas Cheerleader Story*. HBO, however, decided to go to town and came up with *The Positively Amazing True Adventures of the Alleged Texas Cheerleading Murdering Mom*.

Below I've set out a short comparison of both films, to let you see the variety of ways open to you in approaching a story. For brevity, the ABC film is referred to as *WTK* and the HBO film as *Texas Mom*.

1: The Facts

In midsummer 1991, a Texas jury indicted 37-year-old Wanda Holloway for allegedly attempting to hire a hit man to commit murder. His task . . . to kill Verna Heath. According to the police, Wanda believed that Verna's death would so distress her daughter Amber that she would abandon plans to try out for school cheerleader. This would then allow Wanda's 13-year-old daughter Shanna to take over the top spot.

Evidently in Texas it is easy to get a hit man if you know the right person. In Wanda's eyes, according to the police, this was her brother-in-law, Terry. His role was to be that of the go-between, the man who would find the killer.

After hearing Wanda's plans and seeming to go along with them, Terry informed the police of Wanda's request. At the subsequent trial, much of the evidence depended on conversations Terry had taped between himself and Wanda, at the suggestion of the police. Wanda pleaded that her talk of a hit man was a joke, that she never intended to kill Verna, and that Terry was the real party to blame.

Unimpressed, the jury found her guilty, and she was sentenced to prison for 15 years. It was then discovered that the jury had been improperly selected. When the two films were made, Wanda was still out and free.

What was clear was that this was not just another murder, but a case that was totally bizarre and cuckoo. A mother turns to murder because her daughter can't be cheerleader. That was strange stuff, even for Texas, and the media had a ball. Besides national newspaper and television coverage, the story also hit *Time*, *Redbook*, and *People*. What started as a small-town case became a national media celebration, with the participants in turn becoming media celebrities.

So much for the facts.

2: Basic Approach

A: *Willing to Kill*

WTK tells the story in a straightforward, chronological fashion.

In the beginning Wanda is shown as the new girl in town, who is befriended by Verna. A strong friendship develops between them, which is paralleled by the friendship of their two daughters. As they cook and entertain in each other's houses, they reveal their backgrounds and hopes for their children.

All is well until Wanda's daughter Shanna is overlooked in favor of Amber Heath for a place on the school cheerleading team. As Shanna keeps coming off second-best, Wanda notices how everything seems to be rigged in favor of Verna's daughter. One year, Amber is allowed to compete although she comes from a different high school. The following year, Shanna is disqualified for using unauthorized promotion materials, although previously rules were bent in favor of Amber.

Wanda's anger accumulates until the friendship with Verna is totally destroyed. Gradually, she comes to see Verna as her evil archenemy and the main obstacle to her daughter's success. Wanda's gentleness at the beginning of the film has now totally disappeared. Transformed into someone resembling the savage Queen in *Snow White*, Wanda seeks out her brother-in-law and asks him to find a hit man. Shortly afterwards the police arrest her, and she is put on trial. After the guilty verdict, and the subsequent disqualification of a juror, we see Wanda on TV pleading her innocence and begging for the forgiveness of Verna and Amber.

Though the focus is on Wanda, the film is also very much about Verna. She is super-glamorized, and very much the second star lead. We enter into her home life and that of her family and are continually shown things from her point of view.

B: *Texas Mom*

HBO's film differs from ABC's in three fundamental aspects. It has been turned into a comedy, tells two stories instead of one, and uses a very interesting framing device which contributes enormously to the success of the film.

At first *Texas Mom* tells the same story as *WTK*, and in the same chronological way, but with very different emphases. However, after the arrest of Wanda, the film opens up a *second* major story. This deals with the media circus surrounding the affair, the intrusion of television into the lives of Wanda's and Verna's families, and the selling of everyone's rights to the media for the highest sums. This section is extremely funny and is a caustic self-reflexive comment on fact-fiction TV dramas.

Another radical departure from *WTK* is that HBO's film uses a mock television interview to frame the film and to comment on events. As the film opens, newspaper headlines detail for us the sensational arrest and trial of Wanda Holloway. From there we cut to a white-suited Wanda, all dolled up for a TV interview session, along with daughter Shanna. The trial is over, and both Wanda and Shanna are being questioned on what happened and on their attitudes to life, the community, their hopes, and their feelings. These interview sessions pop in and out of the main film about nine or ten times and serve to add a comment and gloss on the evolving story.

The Wanda of this film is very different than the Wanda of *WTK*, who is tall and pretty, but dull. HBO's Wanda is a short, funny, sharp-tongued harpy, who covers the deadliest of intentions with a joke, a smile and a laugh. She's also an iron-willed woman who controls her family with the love and determination of a prison guard.

Given this interpretation, the interviews bounce brilliantly off the main story. While the main film shows us actions and deeds revealing a warped personality, the interviews show us Wanda's bland, self-justifying, and moralizing self. As seen via the interviews, she is a pure God-fearing woman, whose Baptist soul is cleansed by spiritual Ivory Soap.

3: Character Selection

A: Willing to Kill

As mentioned, *WTK* is a two-star vehicle, which concentrates on Verna almost as much as Wanda. In contrast, Verna plays a much more minor role in *Texas Mom*. Another character of importance in *WTK* who appears nowhere in *Texas Mom* is Joyce, the mother of Verna. Her dramatic function is quite simple. Since the film also concentrates on Verna, the writer has to give Verna a confidante, somebody to whom she can open up and tell her side of the story, somebody to whom she can relate her feelings and her thoughts.

This necessary story function is filled by giving us the mother. An alternative solution for the writer might have been to expand the role of Verna's husband, but this wasn't done. This might have been because of the real husband's reluctance to be shown in a major way, or a policy decision that in a film chiefly geared to women, the mother would be a better character to play with.

B: Texas Mom

In both films we find out that Wanda has been married several times, and that her first husband was Tony Harper. In *WTK*, Tony is virtually absent from the script, except for a short scene where he advises his brother Terry to be careful in his dealings with Wanda. By way of contrast, Tony is seen very often in the HBO film, usually in bed with his second wife, or in family meetings dealing with the sale of television rights.

The main character who shifts from second to first place in *Texas Mom* is Tony's brother Terry, the go-between man. In *WTK*, he only appears halfway through the film, when Wanda is seeking a hit man. In *Texas Mom* he is with us from the start, while his turbulent relationship with his own strange and disturbed wife, Marla, provides the film with a dark, funny, and grotesque subplot.

We learn of Terry's life difficulties. We see him at work and we discover his five-point plan for salvation, which includes laying off drink and drugs and straightening out his emotional life. And we see him at home arguing with his wife. He is a complex and fascinating character, who lights the screen every time he appears.

4: Motivation

I've stressed earlier that we have to understand the reasons for our characters' actions, but the "why" of Wanda's actions is almost completely missing from *WTK*. We know she wants her daughter to be a top cheerleader. We know she begins to hate Verna, but none of that strikes us as a strong enough motive to seek someone's murder. Instead, we just have to say, "This woman is crazy," and leave it at that. It is a very happy solution.

Texas Mom offers a slightly better reason for the would-be murder in a scene between Wanda and her second husband, C.D. When C.D. complains that Wanda has spent $320 on a junior high school campaign, Wanda launches into her vision of Shanna's career. Cheerleading is just part of building a portfolio. Cheerleading will help Shanna get a scholarship to college. She'll then get into modeling and the movies and, as Wanda puts it, "bring in a whole lot more on the return than one of your dried-up old oil wells."

Following that speech, we can understand why a cheerleading failure threatens the whole projected career structure. It's not the greatest of motivations, but at least it's something.

There may be a fairly simple reason why both films fail to show what really drives Wanda. Wanda has always denied that she ever wanted to kill Verna. Given that denial, it has been hard for journalists to ask, "Why did you do it?" Lacking a real entry into Wanda's mind, the writer of *Texas Mom* has had to conjecture a reason.

WTK also fails to show us, in any meaningful way, what motivates *Terry's* actions in going to the police. All we see is a quick talk with his brother, who warns him about dealing with Wanda, and a brief mention of his criminal past. The motivation is there, but not in any serious way.

Texas Mom errs on the other side. We know from the beginning of the film that Terry has had encounters with the police, and has been arrested various times. We also know from his five-year plan that he wants to stay out of trouble. Thus the seeds for our understanding of his negative reaction to Wanda's plan are planted very early in the script. Various meetings between Terry and his brother, and Terry and a work friend, also hammer home Terry's fear of entrapment and arrest for something he never did. As Terry sees it, Wanda can easily commit murder and blame it all on him. So the only way out is going straight to the police.

5: Variations in Scene Emphasis

Writing drama-doc is about making choices, and this can be perceived very clearly when we look at the variations in the way the same scene or subject is treated in each film.

A: Terry's Relations with the Police

In *WTK*, Terry tells the police of his fears, talks to Wanda, and then gives the police his secretly recorded tape. And that's that! In *Texas Mom*, the police scenes build into a funny drama in themselves. At first, the police refuse to pay any attention to Terry's story. They then go into an elaborate procedure showing him how to talk to Wanda without being accused of entrapment. Later, two scenes show the police watching Terry phoning Wanda, and congratulating him when he gives them the vital incriminating tape.

B: Wanda's Frustration with School Rules

We know from everything written about the case that Wanda's anger began to build when Cobb Elementary allowed Amber Heath to run for cheerleader although she didn't even belong to the school. We also know that Wanda's later request to the school board to have a new cheerleading post created for Shanna was refused.

In *WTK*, the meeting with the board and their refusal to help Shanna is shown in great detail. The script also uses the exact words used by Wanda in a broadcast interview. This important episode is never seen in *Texas Mom*, but merely referred to in passing.

C: The Arrest

The arrest of Wanda in *WTK* is almost a throwaway. Wanda drives up to her house while the police watch her from across the road. They then get out of their car, tell Wanda she's under arrest for solicitation of murder, handcuff her, and take her away. Wanda is staggered, frightened, and says little as she is taken to headquarters.

Texas Mom starts in the same way, but then broadens out. After asking whether she can call her husband, Wanda stomps into the house with her hips wiggling. Becoming hysterical, she yells into the phone that the cops are taking her to jail. Shanna comes out of her room, gets scared, and talks briefly to her mother. Wanda then asks the police whether she should wear jewelry to the station. The scene finally ends with a punch line from the younger policeman: "God, I miss drug busts."

6: Necessary Scenes

One of the joys of analysis is trying to figure out which scenes are authentic and which are invented. Sometimes it's obvious, and at other times very unclear. One scene which does seem invented for both films is what one might call "the birth of the hit man." This is the scene in which Wanda first gets the idea of killing Verna. It's dramatically necessary because it has to act as a bridge between Wanda's frustration and the search for the killer. Without such a scene, the search for a killer would be too abrupt, and too much of a shock to the viewer.

So both writers have to invent the "necessary" scene, and both versions work fairly well.

In *WTK*, the idea comes up while Wanda is out driving with her husband and a friend. One of them mentions that Verna is a pain, and maybe she could be killed. The conversation, which is treated as a big joke, then goes on to discuss how one would do it. Thus the idea is implanted, and a few days later Wanda meets with Terry.

In *Texas Mom*, the corresponding scene takes place at Wanda's house. Wanda, son Shane, and a friend are watching a talk show on TV. Jokingly, Shane mentions that he'd like to kill the girl who beat him for drum major. They discuss how that could be accomplished. Then, out of the blue, Wanda, also joking, says she'd like to see Verna Heath dead and asks how *that* could be done. The scene then cuts to the studio interview, where Wanda declares that everyone, at least once in his or her life, has jokingly said, "I want to kill someone."

A few minutes later, another scene in *Texas Mom* emphasizes the point that murder really is in Wanda's mind. Wanda drives by the bay and sees a no-swimming sign. It shows a screaming figure sinking into the water. From there we cut to Wanda deep in thought.

"But," the viewer asks, "does this lady really have the guts for murder?" The symbolic answer is given almost immediately. Wanda is lying in bed watching a huge spider crawl up her leg. Without a thought, she squashes it dead, leaving a mess on her leg. If ever there was a scene that defines character by action, it's this.

7: Similar Sequences

The backbone of both films is provided by three essential sequences. They are

1: Wanda's confrontation with the school board. This culminates in Shanna's disqualification from the team because she used forbidden advertising on rulers.
2: The meetings between Wanda and Terry, in which the details and price of the hit are discussed.
3: The trial.

Though the settings sometimes change, for example, the murder discussions take place in a car in one film and at home in the other, the essence of all the scenes remains the same. This is because at least half the dialogue in these scenes is taken from the court transcripts or the secret taping of Wanda. So both films use one of Wanda's most dramatic declarations, "I want her out of here. I want her gone." Clearly the writers have seen the same materials, and being smart, have seized on the same telling incidents and dialogue.

8: Truth

Generally, the writers of both films stay very close to the truth. If the early, cozy friendship of Wanda and Verna in *WTK* seems a little too dramatically convenient, well, that's the way things were. Verna lived only a block away from Wanda and for $25 a month (not mentioned in the film) drove Shanna to school.

Both films show Verna's *own* pushiness in the cheerleading business, though each handles it differently. In *WTK*, Verna's drive for her daughter Amber's success is revealed close to the beginning of the film. In *Texas Mom*, it is mostly left to the final scene, so that the film closes with a shot of Verna doggedly training her daughter on a deserted, windswept football field.

Both pictures of Verna are true. She had been a high school baton-twirling champion herself, while her mother, Joyce Brown, had taught twirling and tap dancing to generations of the local school girls.

In *Texas Mom*, one can almost cite chapter and verse for everything shown connected to the planning and discussions of the murder, and Terry's relationship with the police. The same is true regarding the depiction of the media hullabaloo. The one thing I am unsure of is the truth behind the subplot of Terry's troubles with his wife.

Besides showing what the films share, it is also interesting to note what both avoid. Neither film touches very much on Wanda's early life, or bothers to deal deeply with Wanda's husband. Neither does either film linger very much on Wanda's activities outside the home, except to show her playing the organ in church.

Which is the better film? This is a slightly unfair question, because *Texas Mom* was made with more time and money. It is clearly the more subtle, complex, and interesting film, but both do a good job in staying close to the truth yet providing us with entertaining and compelling drama.

The Option and Purchase Agreement

When we discussed adaptations, I said that the first rule was you don't move until you or the producer have procured the rights to the work you want to adapt. Below I've set out some of the key passages from a fairly standard TV option agreement for a book. I haven't set it out *in toto* because you'd fall asleep before the end, but I have tried to show you how it's arranged, and what the most relevant sections have to say. To help you a little bit further, I've italicized some of the key points.

Things you might especially want to note are:

1: The automatic extension of the option because of certain events, like TV strikes.
2: Paragraph three, which deals with extra compensation for the owner of the rights.
3: The nature of the rights granted. As this is a contract for a TV production, as opposed to a theatrical film, the owner has given away only the TV rights themselves, and nothing else.
4: The nature of the reserved rights. Here the most interesting point is that the owner or author has reserved theatrical motion picture rights.
5: The general question of merchandising rights. Here the rights stay with the owner, but the producer gets 20% out of any related merchandising campaign.
6: The conditions under which rights can revert to the original owner, even though the option has been exercised.

Literary Option and
Purchase Agreement

Dear_____

The following shall constitute the agreement between<_____ Pub-lishing Company ("Owner") and_____ Film Ltd. ("Producer") with respect to the acquisition by the Producer of an exclusive option for television and related allied rights in and to an original book written by_____ ("Auth-or") entitled *Hollywood With the Wraps Off* ("Work"), published by Owner.

1. *Option*: Owner hereby grants Producer an *exclusive* option to acquire the Rights set forth in paragraph 5 to the Work commencing on the date of this agreement and continuing for a period of six (6) months, for which the Producer will pay to Owner on full execution hereof the sum of $1,000, which payment will be applicable against the purchase price set out in paragraph 2. Producer will have the right to extend the option for a further period of six months, commencing upon the expiration of the initial option term, by sending written notice of such extension to Owner prior to the expiration of the initial term, accompanied by payment of such extension of $1,000, which payment shall *not* be applicable against the purchase price set out in paragraph 2. The aforesaid option period shall be automatically extended for the duration of any event of force majeure, including strikes in the television industry.

2. *Purchase Price*: $20,000 for a prime-time network television production; or $10,000 for an HBO, Showtime or non-prime-time network production; or $7,000 for any other form of initial television production.

The applicable purchase price (less applicable option payments previously paid) shall be payable on the Producer's exercise of the option (it being understood that commencement of principal photography shall be deemed exercise of the option, but Producer's engagement in any pre-production and development activities, including the writing of scripts, shall not be deemed an exercise of the option).

3. *Contingent Compensation*:
   a: *Television Sequels*: An amount equal to 50% of the purchase price applicable under paragraph 2 for each television "Sequel."
   b: *Television Series*:
   (i) Prime time network - $2,000 per episode.
   (ii) HBO, Showtime or non-prime time network and all premium channels - $1,250 per episode.
   (iii) All others - $1,000 per episode.
   (iv) 20% of the applicable per-episode royalty for the first five reruns.

    c: *Home Video*: 10% of the Producer's net receipts from the exploitation of home video rights.

4. *Credit*:. . . .

5. *Rights Granted*: This option and purchase agreement is for the *exclusive, perpetual*, and *world-wide television* and related allied rights in the Work (it being understood that *no exclusivity* is being granted with respect to any *character* in the work . . . and the right to use Author's name, likeness and biography on or in connection with the exploitation of the rights granted . . .

6. *Reserved Rights*: Owner reserves the following rights:

    a: All publication rights . . .

    b: Dramatic and Musical stage productions based on the Work with living actors in the immediate presence of an audience . . .

    c: Theatrical motion picture rights to the Work; provided, however, that such rights shall *not* be exercisable by the Owner until the earlier of four years following the initial telecast of the first television production, or six years from the date the option is exercised . . .

    d: All rights to prequels and sequels of the work . . .

7. *Merchandising*: Owner reserves merchandising rights in the Work, including its characters, titles, and all elements thereof. If the Producer exercises the option hereunder and produces a television production, it shall be entitled to receive 20% of the Owner's actual receipts from exercise of merchandising rights that take place, commencing with the date of the initial telecast of Producer's first television production . . .

8. *Reversion of Rights*: In the event that within five years following the Producer's exercise of its option, the initial television program based upon the Work has not been fully produced, all rights granted to Producer pursuant to this agreement shall terminate and revert to the Owner.

The contract concludes with details of warranties and representations, conditions under which the agreement can be assigned, and the owner's responsibility for making any payments to the author.

D

□ □ □
□ □ □
□ □ □

Broadcast Guidelines

As mentioned in Chapter Thirteen, all the U.S. networks have established guidelines for the writing of docudramas, or, as they tend to call them, "fact-based" movies. These guidelines are issued by the Broadcast Standards and Practices Department. Each network has slightly different procedures, and below you can see the notes issued by NBC, along with the company's advice to producers.

NBC Guidelines

(Production Company Name)
(Address)
Re: (Name of the Project)
Dear_____:
I am writing to advise you of the procedures that NBC requires producers and their attorneys to follow with respect to fact-based movies and mini-series. Production Company ("Packager") must do the following in connection with (Name of the Project):

1. Packager must obtain a completely annotated screenplay from the writer, with the annotations showing, line by line, whether particular dialogue is factual and accurate, fictionalized but based on known facts, or wholly author-created. Each notation should be keyed to underlying factual works, such as specific pages of newspaper articles, books, interviews, and the like. The more sensitive the particular scene or statement, the more important it is that there is substantial backup, including multiple sources. Please send one copy of the annotated script to the NBC Program Standards Department and a second copy to the NBC Law Department.

2. NBC expects Packager to be thoroughly familiar with all of the events and occurrences that are reflected in the teleplay so that it can determine if the particular sources upon which the author relies are sound or are contradicted by other sources. If there is a conflict between sources, Packager's attorneys will need to verify that the source chosen by the author is valid and supportable.
3. Because fact-based programs reflect real events, fictionalized material must be used only to advance the plot, not to alter what actually occurred. Therefore, any author-created material must be carefully prepared to avoid placing an individual in a worse light than is completely supported by the facts.
4. The writer must take particular care with composite or fictional characters to ensure that there is no basis for a claim of accidental identification. In particular, the reviewing attorneys should focus on characters who might be identifiable because of some particular position or characteristic or relationship to the plot that the fictional character has.
5. Finally, Packager must see that all necessary and appropriate releases have been obtained.

In NBC's experience, it is often useful to obtain the services of an outside research entity, such as Fact or Fiction. These entities may spot problems of which the reviewing attorneys otherwise would not be aware . . .

Finally, I am enclosing an Annotation Guide for use by the writer of the script for the program. Thank you for your cooperation. We look forward to working with you.

Very truly yours,

NBC Annotation Guide

Annotated scripts should contain for each script element—whether an event, setting, or segment of dialogue—notes in the margin that provide the following information:

1. Whether the element presents or portrays:
   (a) Fact;
   (b) Fiction, but product of inference from fact; or
   (c) Fiction, not based on fact.
2. With regard to characters:
   (a) Whether the character is real, composite (of real individuals), or totally fictional.
   (b) Whether the character's name is real; and
   (c) Whether any corresponding real persons have signed releases.

3. Source material for the element:
   (a) Book;
   (b) Newspaper or magazine article;
   (c) Recorded interview;
   (d) Trial or deposition transcript;
   (e) Any other source.

Note: Source material identification should give the name of the source (e.g., *New York Times* article), page reference and date. To the extent possible, identify multiple sources for each element. Retain copies of all materials, preferably cross-indexed by reference to script page and scene numbers. Coding may be useful to avoid repeated lengthy references.

Descriptive annotation notes are helpful (e.g., setting is hotel suite b/c John Doe usually had business meetings in his hotel suite when visiting L.A.-*New York Times*; April 1, 1981; p. 8).

Marketability

In Chapter Two I touched very briefly on the marketplace for docudrama. In this appendix, I want to expand on one or two points raised in that section. Until now, we've been looking at the problems of writing. However, at the end of the day you want to sell your script and see that it gets made. That means knowing the marketplace, and knowing what the producers want and where to turn.

That means understanding moods, personalities, the instability of fashion, studios, international setups, and country quirks. In short, it means trying to understand a process that is often highly irrational and always aggravating.

Sometimes the successful suffer as much as the novices in this process. Director Richard Attenborough made the rounds for almost twenty years before he found a backer for *Gandhi*. This was because the marketplace seers knew there was absolutely no future for a film about a wizened, half-naked Indian politician who believed in nonviolence and was uninterested in sex. The first time *Chariots of Fire* was hawked around the U.S., it was turned down by every major studio in Hollywood.

So much for the experts.

The marketing of scripts is a massive subject, and there are now almost as many books on it as on the writing process itself. The two books I find most useful in this area are *Script Planning: Positioning and Developing Scripts for TV and Film*, by Tony Zaza, and *Selling a Screenplay*, by Syd Field. Both are very good but say little on three background issues . . . changing fashions, codes and constraints, and film versus the TV market. A pity, because all three deserve attention.

Changing Fashions

The writer has to be aware of how and why fashions change. What was fine for yesterday may be totally wrong for today. Hollywood practice is a good example.

Between 1927 and 1960, over 270 biopics were made in Hollywood by the major studios, with Producer Darryl Zanuck acting as the key arbitrator on taste.

Under his lead, Warner Brothers and others turned out film after film idealizing the famed of history, from Zola and Disraeli to Alexander Graham Bell and Louis Pasteur. And, as mentioned in Appendix A, when they ran out of statesmen and scientists, they turned to entertainers like Gershwin and Cohan, or sportsmen like Lou Gehrig, Knute Rockne, and Babe Ruth.

Today there has been a major shift in biography and in the way lives are translated to the screen. To start with, biography has become the province of TV rather than the feature film. Big-screen features like *Malcolm X* and *Hoffa* are the exceptions, not the rule. Even though *Stalin* cost $18 million, it was made for home viewing rather than the large theater.

Secondly, though the "heroic" bio film is still around, the emphasis, at least on TV, has shifted away from stories of the famous to stories of ordinary people to whom unusual things have happened. In his book *Biopics*, George Custen puts it this way:

> Notoriety has in some sense replaced noteworthiness as the proper frame for biography . . . the perennially famous have been replaced by the momentarily observed.

Codes and Constraints

Not only does the marketability of certain subjects change, but also the way they can be treated. From the thirties through the fifties, for example, Hollywood scripts had to conform to the requirements of the Production Code. This code, originally set up by the producers themselves, imposed a prim morality on everything to do with filmic behavior and language.

Today the code no longer exists, but many of its restraints have entered television. Thus while almost anything is permissible on the big screen, more caution has to be exercised when writing for television. Thus the language, violence, and obscenity of a film such as *Reservoir Dogs* would not be acceptable in the normal television movie of the week. In other words, television says yes to sex and violence, but only within limits.

Film or TV Market

The problem of codes and constraints is really just one element of a larger question. What market should you choose, film or TV? Part of this was touched on earlier, but needs elaboration.

It would be simple if the battle lines were clearly drawn, but they're not. *Barbarians at the Gate* cost $7 million to film and was originally commissioned by Columbia. Eventually the hierarchy at Columbia considered it too problematic to release for a theatrical audience and it was taken over by HBO. Even among networks, there are differences as to what is suitable material for the screen. *And the Band Played On* was considered by NBC, and then dropped because the subject of AIDS was seen as too uncongenial for a family audience. HBO had fewer qualms and went on to make one of the biggest successes of the summer '93 season.

In spite of the confusion, there do seem to be a few tentative guide rules which will help you to see whether your best bet is TV or film.

TV seems best when your story is

1: Local or provincial.
2: Hot news that requires dramatizing while the story is still fresh in the public mind. For example, Jean Harris was convicted of the murder of Dr. Herman Tarnower in February 1981. Her screen biography came out on May 7th, 1981. Betty Broderick was convicted of murder in December 1991, and her story, *A Woman Scorned*, was screened on March 1st, 1992. The Branch Davidian Waco complex was stormed in February 1993, and *Ambush in Waco* was out by May. Such speed and turnaround would have been impossible had these stories been done as features.
   TV also seems first choice when your story
3: Is best done on a low budget.
4: Requires miniseries treatment, like the story of Sinatra or the Jackson family.
5: Is a "woman's movie."

This last proviso may seem strange till one realizes that TV has almost entirely co-opted the woman's movie of the forties, hence the large number of woman-centered docudramas.

Film seems best when your story

1: Is extremely visual
2: Is less tied to headlines
3: Requires large budgets and big stars
4: Is of epic quality, like *Lawrence of Arabia* or *A Bridge Too Far*
5: Has really universal appeal
6: Requires a long production time

Writers Guild of America

As mentioned earlier, the Writers Guild of America is the scriptwriters' union. Its task is to help writers, improve their negotiating situation, and establish minimum pay scales. Conditions for admission to the Guild are reprinted below, together with minimum scale fees as of 1994.

Requirements for Admission to the WGA

"An aggregate of twenty-four (24) units of Credit as set forth on the Schedule of Units of Credit, which units are based upon work completed under contract of employment or upon the sale or licensing of previously unpublished and unproduced literary or dramatic material, is required. Said employment, sale or licensing must be with a company or other entity that is signatory to the applicable WGA Collective Bargaining Agreement . . . The twenty-four units (24) must be accumulated within the preceding three (3) years of application. Upon final qualification for membership, a cashier's check or money order payable to the WGA in the amount of $2,500 is due. Writers residing West of the Mississippi may apply for membership in the WGA, West, Inc. Writers residing East of the Mississippi river should contact the WGA, East, Inc."

Schedule of Units of Credit (Summary)

Two Units For each week of employment within the Guild's jurisdiction on a week-to-week basis.

Three Units Story for a radio or TV program less than thirty minutes.

Four Units Story for a theatrical motion picture short
subject or radio or TV program, or
Breakdown for a non-prime-time serial 30 through 60 minutes.

Six Units Television format for a new serial or series, or
Teleplay or radio play less than 30 minutes.

Eight Units Story for a radio or TV program more than
60 minutes and less than 90, or
Screenplay for a short theatrical film or radio or teleplay 30 through
60 minutes.

Twelve Units Story for a radio or TV program 90 minutes
or longer, or
Story for a feature length theatrical film, or
Radio or teleplay more than 60 and less than 90 minutes.

Twenty-four Units Screenplay for a feature-length
theatrical film; radio or teleplay 90 minutes or longer,
or Bible for any TV serial or prime-time mini-series of
at least four hours.

SAMPLE W.G.A. - MINIMUM FEES DRAMA PROGRAMS (5/2/94 - 5/1/95)

Theatrical Compensation	*Low budget*	*High budget film*
A. *Original Screenplay,*		
including treatment	$38,121	$71,504
Installments:		
Delivery of Treatment	17,274	28,604
Delivery of First Draft	5,012	28,604
Delivery of Final Draft	5,835	14,296
B. *Screenplay,*		
excluding treatment	25,617	52,434
Installments:		
Delivery of First Draft	19,782	38,138
Delivery of Final Draft	5,835	14,296
C. *Additional compensation for*		
story included in screenplay	4,704	9,534
D. *Story or Treatment*	12,509	19,069

E. *Original Treatment*	17,274	28,604
F. *First draft screenplay, with or without option for final draft*		
First Draft	15,012	28,604
Final Draft	10,005	19,069
G. *Rewrite of screenplay*	12,509	19,069
H. *Polish of screenplay*	6,257	9,534

Television Compensation - Network Prime Time

Length of Program: 45 - 60 minutes

Story	$ 8,860
Teleplay	14,610
Story and Teleplay	22, 208

Length of Program: 60 - 90 minutes

Story	11,837
Teleplay	21,049
Story and Teleplay	31,246

Length of Program: 90 - 120 minutes (Episodic)

Story	15,809
Teleplay	27,009
Story and Teleplay	41,109

Length of Program: 90 - 120 minutes (Non-Episodic)

Story	17,254
Teleplay	29,474
Story and Teleplay	44,934

G

□ □ □
□ □ □
□ □ □

W.G.A. Agency List

This appendix gives you an abbreviated list of agents who have subscribed to the W.G.A - Artists' Manager Basic Agreement. As with the minimum fees set out in Appendix F, it is reprinted here with permission of the Writers Guild of America, East.

The Guild writes: "We suggest you first contact the agency and provide a brief description of your professional and academic credentials and of the material you wish to submit. If you wish material returned to you, you must provide a self addressed stamped envelope . . . The Guild cannot assist in seeking the return of your material. It is our policy not to offer recommendations of any agencies. The agents which appear on this list have promised not to charge fees, other than a commission, to any writer."

Agencies with a single asterisk (*) indicate that they will consider new writers. A double asterisk (**) indicates that the agency will only consider writers as a result of references from people known to it.

*A Total Acting Experience, 14621 Titus St., Suite 206, Panorama City, CA 91402 (818) 901-1044

Abrams Artists & Assoc., 9200 Sunset Blvd., #625, LA, CA 90069 (310) 859-0625

Adams, Bret Ltd. (NY), 448 W. 44th St., NY, NY 10036 (212) 765-5630

*Agency Chicago, P.O. Box 11200, Chicago, IL 60611

**Agency for the Performing Arts, 888 7th Ave., NY, NY 10106 (212) 582-1500

*Agency of the Stars, 5464 N. Port Washington Rd., #168, Milwaukee, WI 53217

**The Agency, 10351 Santa Monica Blvd., #211, LA, CA 90025 (213) 551-3000

*Allan, Lee Agency, P.O. Box 18617, Milwaukee, WI 53218 (414) 357-7708

Alton Agency, The, 221 N. Robertson Blvd., #C-1, Beverly Hills, CA 90211 (310) 281-5964

Amsterdam, Marcia Agency, 41 W. 82nd St., #9A, NY, NY 10024 (212) 873-4945

Artists Agency, The, 10000 Santa Monica Blvd., #305, LA, CA 90067 (213) 277-7779

**Artists First, Inc., 450 S. Wetherly Dr., Beverly Hills, CA 90211 (310) 550-8606

Artists Group, The, 1930 Century Pk. W., #403, LA, CA 90067 (213) 552-1100

**Barrett, Helen Literary Agency, 100 Center Grove Rd., Randolph, NJ 07869 (201) 328-2919

Berman, Lois, 21 W. 26th St., NY, NY 10010 (212) 684-1835

*Bk. Management of NY, 152 Madison Ave., #802, NY, NY 10016 (212) 439-5150

Blue Star Agency, P.O. Box 2754, Arlington, VA 22202

*Bon Soir Talent Group, 65 Prospect St., Stamford, CT 06901 (203) 979-0718

**Borinstein, Oreck, Bogart Agency, 8271 Melrose Ave., #110, LA, CA 90046 (213) 658-7500

**The Brandt Co., 12700 Ventura Blvd., #340, Studio City, CA 91604 (818) 506-7747

Breitner, Susan Literary Assocs., 100 Hepburn Rd., Clifton, NJ 07012

Brown, Curtis Ltd., Ten Astor Place, NY, NY 10003 (212) 473 5400

Brustein Company, The, 2644 30th St., Santa Monica, CA 90405 (310) 452-3330

Burnam, The Carolyn Agency, 4258 Springview, San Antonio, TX 78222 (210) 333-5119

California Artists Agency, 3053 Centerville Rosebud Rd., Snellville, GA 30278 (404) 979-8498

Capital Artists, 8383 Wilshire Blvd., #954, Beverly Hills, CA 90211 (213) 658-8118

*Cassandra Agency, 513 Colonial Dr., #6, Orlando, FL 32804

*Castle Rock, The Group, 501 Wilcox St., Castle Rock, CO 80104 (303) 688-1655

**Cavaleri and Assocs., 6605 Hollywood Blvd., #220, Hollywood, CA 90028 (213) 461-2940

**Circle Talent Assocs., 433 N. Camden Dr., #400, Beverly Hills, CA 90210 (310) 285-1585

*Client First Agency, P.O. Box 795, White House, TN 37188 (615) 325-4780

Creative Authors Agency, 12212 Paradise Vill. Pkwy., Pheonix, AZ 85032 (602) 953-0164

Creative Dramatic Voice, P.O. Box 624, Corrales, NM 87048

*Creative Talent Mngmt., 175 E. 11th St., Miller Place, NY 11764

Curtis, Richard Assocs., 171 E. 74th St., NY, NY 10021 (212) 772-7363

*Cyberstorm, P.O. Box 6330, Reno, NV 89513 (702) 322-7241

Diamond Literary Productions, Box 48114, 35 Lakewood Dr., Winnipeg, Manitoba R2J 4A3 Canada

DJM Talent Agency, 5404 N. Nevada Ave., #209, Colorado Springs, CO 80918 (719) 598-5383

*Dr Literary Agency, #1420, 42 S. 15th St., Philadelphia, PA 19102 (215) 722-4568

*Dragon Literary Agency, P.O. Box 16290, Salt Lake City, UT 84116

Dupreee Miller and Assocs., 5518 Dyer St., Dallas, TX 75206 (214) 692-1388

Epstein Wyckoff & Assocs., 280 S. Beverly Dr., Beverly Hills, CA 90212 (310) 278-7222

*Estephan Talent Agency, 6018 Greenmeadow Rd., Lakewood, CA 90713

Favored Artists Agency, 122 S. Robertson Blvd., #202, LA, CA 90048 (310) 247-1040

Film Artists Assocs., 7080 Hollywood Blvd., #704, LA, CA 90028 (213) 463-1010

Freedman, Robert A. Dramatic Agency, 1501 Broadway, #2310, NY, NY 10036 (212) 840-5760

*Gateway Agency, 38 Laura Dr., St. Peters, MO 63376 (314) 272-9508

Geddes Agency, 8457 Melrose Ave., #200, LA, CA 90069 (213) 651-2401

Genesis Agency, 1465 Northside Dr., #120, Atlanta, GA 30318 (404) 350-9212

Gersh Agency, Inc., 130 W. 42nd St, NY, NY 10036 (212) 997-1818

**Gray Goodman Agency, Inc., 211 S. Beverly Dr., #100, Beverly Hills, CA 91212 (310) 276-7070

*Greenberg, Ferne Agency, 612 E. Camino Lujosa, Tucson, AZ 85704 (602) 888-1351

Grossman, Larry and Assocs., 211 S. Beverly Dr., #206, Beverly Hills, CA 90212 (213) 550-8127

*Handy Book Co., P.O. Box 721203, Corpus Christi, TX 78472 (512) 992-4791

Harrison Writers Agency, 315 1st Ave. S., Seattle, WA 98104 (206) 467-7110

**Heathcock Literary Agency, Inc., 1523 Sixth St., #14, Santa Monica, CA 90401 (213) 393-6227

Hegler, Gary L. Literary Agency, P.O. Box 890751, Houston, TX 77289

*Herman, The Richard Talent Agency, 124 Lasky Dr., Beverly Hills, CA 90212 (310) 550-8913

**Hyman, Ellen, 422 E. 81st St., NY, NY 10028 (212) 861-5373

Image Talent Agency, 259 S. Robertson Blvd., Beverly Hills, CA 90211 (310) 277-9134

International Creative Management, 40 W. 57th St., NY, NY 10019

Irwin Management, 2639 N. Francisco, Chicago, IL 60647

Janus Literary Agency, 43 Lakeman's Lane, Ipswich, MA 01938 (508) 356-0909

JNG Entertainment, POB 1142, Gracie Sta., NY, NY 10028 (212) 535-0864

*Joesting Agency, The, P.O. Box 583, Chapel Hill, NC 27514 (919) 929-1475

*Kane, Jerry Talent Agency, 117 S. Tenth St., Haines Cty., FL 33844

Karlan, Patricia Agency, 3575 Cahuenga Blvd., W., #210, LA, CA 90068

**Kern Agency, 270 N. Canon Dr., Penthouse, Beverly Hills, CA 90210 (310) 276-8080

*Kerwin, William Agency, 1605 N. Cahuenga Blvd., #202, Hollywood, CA 90028 (213) 469-5155

King, Archer, Ltd., 10 Columbus Circle, #1492, NY, NY 10019 (212) 765-3103

**Kirstein, Mary Literary Agency, POB 21847, Albuquerque, NM 87154

Kroll, Lucy Agency, 390 West End Avenue, NY, NY 10024 (212) 877-0627

**Lake, Candace Agency, The, 822 S. Robertson Blvd., #200, LA, CA 90035 (310) 289-0600

*Laughton Agency, POB 340, Oakland, NJ 07436 (201) 337-0693

Lazar, Irving Paul, 120 El Camino Dr., #108, Beverly Hills, CA 90212 (213) 275-6153

Lee, Guy & Assocs., 4150 Riverside Dr., Burbank, CA 91505 (818) 848-7475

Literary Artists Management, P.O. Box 1604, Monterey, CA 93940 (408) 394-9354

*Lockwood, Lester, 325 West End Ave., NY, NY 10023 (212) 787-4111

Loo, Bessie, 8235 Santa Monica Blvd., #202, LA, CA 90046 (213) 650-1300

Major Clients Agency, 2121 Ave. of the Stars, #2450, LA, CA 90067, letter of inquiry only.

*Marbea Agency, 1946 NE 149th St., N. Miami Beach, FL 33181

Maris Agency, The, 17620 Sherman Way, #213, Van Nuys, CA 91406 (818) 708-2493

**Matson, Harold Co., 276 Fifth Ave., NY, NY 10001 (212) 679-4490

Meyers, Allan S. Agency, 105 Court St., Brooklyn, NY 11201

*Michael, Christopher Agency, 423 Guyon Ave., Staten Isl., NY 10306 (718) 979-4687

*Milestone Literary Agency, 403 West 48th St., NY, NY 10036 (212) 582-5952

Morris, William Agency, 151 El Camino Dr., Beverly Hills, CA 90212 (212) 274-7451

Morris, William Agency, 1350 Ave. of the Americas, NY, NY 10019 (212) 586-5100

**Morton Agency, 1650 Westwood Blvd., #201, LA, CA 90024 (213) 824-4089

Moss, H. David & Assocs., 8019 Melrose Ave., #3, LA, CA 90046

**Northwest Artists Agency, The, 8392 Montrose, Hayden Lake, ID 83835

*N.Y.C. Artists, Talent Agency, 201 N. Figueroa St., #700, LA, CA 90012 (213) 938-7928

*Original Artists Talent Agency, 818 12th St., #8, Santa Monica, CA 90403 (310) 394-1067

Oscard, Fifi Assocs., 24 W. 40th St., NY, NY 10018 (212) 764-1100

Ostroff, Daniel Agency, The, 9200 Sunset Blvd., #402, LA, CA 90069 (310) 278-2020

*Palmer, Dorothy Agency, 235 W. 56th St., #24K, NY, NY 10019 (212) 765-4280

Pleshette & Green Literary Agency, The, 2700 N. Beachwood Dr., Hollywood, CA 90068 (213) 465-0428

**Preminger, Jim Agency, The, 1650 Westwood Blvd., #201, LA 90024 (213) 475-9491

**Professional Artists Unltd., 513 W. 54th St., NY, NY 10019 (212) 247-8770

Raines & Raines, 71 Park Ave., NY, NY 10016 (212) 684-5160

Regency Literary Agency, 285 Verone Ave., Newark, NJ 07104 (201) 485-2692

**Roberts, Flora Inc., 157 W. 57th St., NY, NY 10019 (212) 355-4165

Rosen Agency, The, 3500 W. Olive Ave., #1400, Burbank, CA 91505 (818) 972-4300

**Rothman Agency, The, 9401 Wilshire Blvd., #830, Beverly Hills, CA 91212 (310) 247-9898

*Saltpeter Agency, The, P.O. Box 147, Wayland, MA 01778 (617) 273-3632

*Satori Entertainment, P.O. Box 923, Lincoln City, OR 97367 (503) 996-6744

**Schechter, Irv Co, The, 9300 Wilshire Blvd., #410, Beverly Hills, CA 90212 (213) 278-8070

Shapira, David & Assocs., 15301 Ventura Blvd., #345, Sherman Oaks, CA 91403 (818) 906-0322

**Shapiro-Lichtman Agency, 8827 Beverly Blvd., LA, CA 90048 (310) 859-8877

Sherrell, Lew Agency, 7060 Hollywood Blvd., #610, Hollywood, CA 90028 (213) 461-9955

Shumaker Talent Agency, The, 6533 Hollywood Blvd, #301, Hollywood, CA 90028 (213) 464-0745

Smith, Gerald K. Assocs., P.O. Box 7430, Burbank, CA 90211 (213) 849-5388

Smith, Susan & Assocs., 121 N. San Vincente Blvd., #400E, Encino, CA 91436 (818) 995-1775

Spotlight Enterprises, 8665 Wilshire Blvd., #208, Beverly Hills, CA 90211 (213) 657-8004

**Steele, Ellen Lively & Assocs., P.O. Box 188, Organ, NM 88052 (505) 382-5863

Stone Manners Agency, 8091 Selma Ave., LA, CA 90046 (213) 654-7575

**Swanson, H.N. Agency, 8523 Sunset Blvd, LA, CA 90069 (213) 652-5385

Talent Bank Talent Agency, 1680 N. Vine, #721, Hollywood, CA 90028 (213) 466-7618

*Talent East, 340A East 58th St, NY, NY 10022 (212) 838-7191

Talent Representatives, Inc., 20 East 53rd St., NY, NY 10022 (212) 752-1835

Targ, Roslyn Literary Agency, 105 W. 13th St., NY, NY 10011 (212) 206-9390

**Tel-Screen Artists International, 2659 Carambola Circle N., Building A, #404, Coconut Creek, FL 33066 (305) 974-2251

**Thal Literary Management, 1680 N. Vine St., #1117, LA, CA 90028 (213) 659-4946

Townsend, Jackie Agency, P.O. Box 560223, Dallas, TX 75356 (214) 637-5700

**United Talent Agency, 9560 Wilshire Blvd., Beverly Hills, CA 90212 (213) 273-6700

Vanguard Assocs., 1888 Century Pk. East, #1900, LA, CA 90067 (310) 284-6880

Wain, Erika Agency, 1418 N. Highland Ave., #102, Hollywood, CA 90028 (213) 460-4224

Waugh, Ann Agency, 4731 Laurel Canyon Blvd., #5, N. Hollywood, CA 91607 (213) 980-0141

Wax, Elliot & Assocs. (213) 273-8217

**Wilson, Shirley & Assocs., 5410 Wilshire Blvd., #227, LA, CA 90036 (213) 857-6977

*Winokur Agency, 5575 W. Umberland St., Pittsburgh, PA 15217 (412) 421-0258

**Witzer, Ted Enterprises, 6310 San Vincente Blvd., LA, CA 90048 (213) 552-9521

Wright, Ann Representatives, 136 E. 56th St., #2C, NY, NY 10022 (212) 832-0110

Index